eopmental Profile

GLENN DOMAN
and
The Staff
of
The Institutes

THE INSTITUTES FOR
THE ACHIEVEMENT OF
HUMAN POTENTIAL
8801 STENTON AVENUE
WYNDMOOR, PA 19038

MOBILITY COMPETENCE	LANGUAGE COMPETENCE	MANUAL COMPETENCE
Using a leg in a skilled role which is consistent with the dominant hemisphere *Sophisticated human expression*	Complete vocabulary and proper sentence structure *Sophisticated human expression*	Using a hand to write which is consistent with the dominant hemisphere *Sophisticated human expression*
Walking and running in complete cross pattern *Primitive human expression*	2000 words of language and short sentences *Primitive human expression*	Bimanual function with one hand in a skilled role *Primitive human expression*
Walking with arms freed from the primary balance role *Early human expression*	10 to 25 words of language and two word couplets *Early human expression*	Cortical opposition bilaterally and simultaneously *Early human expression*
Walking with arms used in a primary balance role most frequently at or above shoulder height *Initial human expression*	Two words of speech used spontaneously and meaningfully *Initial human expression*	Cortical opposition in either hand *Initial human expression*
Creeping on hands and knees, culminating in cross pattern creeping *Meaningful response*	Creation of meaningful sounds *Meaningful response*	Prehensile grasp *Meaningful response*
Crawling in the prone position culminating in cross pattern crawling *Vital response*	Vital crying in response to threats to life *Vital response*	Vital release *Vital response*
Movement of arms and legs without bodily movement *Reflex response*	Birth cry and crying *Reflex response*	Grasp reflex *Reflex response*

How To Teach Your Baby To Be Physically Superb

THE GENTLE REVOLUTION

MORE TITLES IN THE GENTLE REVOLUTION SERIES

HOW TO TEACH YOUR BABY TO READ
Glenn Doman and Janet Doman

HOW TO TEACH YOUR BABY MATH
Glenn Doman and Janet Doman

HOW TO GIVE YOUR BABY ENCYCLOPEDIC KNOWLEDGE
Glenn Doman, Janet Doman, and Susan Aisen

HOW TO MULTIPLY YOUR BABY'S INTELLIGENCE
Glenn Doman and Janet Doman

WHAT TO DO ABOUT YOUR BRAIN-INJURED CHILD
Glenn Doman

HOW SMART IS YOUR BABY?
Glenn Doman and Janet Doman

How To Teach Your Baby To Be Physically Superb

FROM BIRTH TO AGE SIX

THE GENTLE REVOLUTION

Glenn Doman
Douglas Doman
Bruce Hagy

Foreword by Ralph Pelligra, MD

SQUAREONE
PUBLISHERS

Square One Publishers
115 Herricks Road • Garden City Park, NY 11040
(516) 535-2010 • (877) 900-BOOK • www.squareonepublishers.com

Photographs courtesy of Sherman Hines (Toronto, Canada), David Kerper (Wyndmoor, PA), and Alicia Ahumada (Pachuca, Hidalgo, Mexico).

Illustrations, Roz Mansfeld, Mansfeld Association, Philadelphia, PA

Jacket Design, Jacqueline Michelus, Square One Publishers, Garden City Park, NY

Library of Congress Cataloging-in-Publication Data: 87-71174

Doman, Glenn
How to teach your baby to be physically superb
1. Infants   2. Education, Preschool
3. Child development   4. Intelligence levels

I. Title

ISBN:0-7570-0192-0

Printed in Singapore

10   9   8   7   6   5   4   3

CONTENTS

Foreword   ix
Introduction   xiii

SECTION ONE
PHYSICAL INTELLIGENCE — THE BACKGROUND

Chapter 1   *The Brightest People in the World*   1

Chapter 2   *All Children Can Be Physically Superb*   5

Chapter 3   *Parents and Priorities*   11

Chapter 4   *The Evan Thomas Institute and Opportunities*   17

Chapter 5   *Physical Intelligence*   25

Chapter 6   *The Principles of Measuring Physical Intelligence*   35

Chapter 7   *Multiplying Physical Intelligence*   45

SECTION TWO
MULTIPLYING YOUR BABY'S PHYSICAL INTELLIGENCE

Chapter 8   *Newborns, Right-Side Up, Or Upside Down*   49

Chapter 9   *Stage I, The Medulla*   55
Mobility Competence—Movement of Arms and Legs   55
Manual Competence—Developing Grasp Reflex   71
The Balance Program for the Newborn   79

Chapter 10   *Stage II, The Pons*   91
                    Mobility Competence—Crawling   91
                    Manual Competence—Vital Release   103
                    The Balance Program for the Infant   110

Chapter 11   *Stage III, The Midbrain*   113
                    Mobility Competence—Creeping   113
                    Manual Competence—Prehensile Grasp   123
                    The Passive Balance Program   129

Chapter 12   *Stage IV, The Initial Cortex*   141
                    Mobility Competence—Taking the First Steps 141
                    Manual Competence—Cortical Opposition 151
                    The Passive Balance Program   158

Chapter 13   *Stage V, The Early Cortex*   161
                    Mobility Competence—Walking   161
                    Manual Competence—Bilateral
                                 Cortical Opposition   171
                    The Active Balance Program   182

Chapter 14   *Stage VI, The Primitive Cortex*   191
                    Mobility Competence—Walking
                       and Running in Cross-Pattern   191
                    Manual Competence—Bimanual Function   207
                    Fundamental Active Balance Activities 220

Chapter 15   *Stage VII, The Sophisticated Cortex* 227
                    Mobility and Balance Competence—Using a Leg
                                 in a Skilled Role   227
                    Manual Competence—Writing   235

                    Afterword   239
                    Acknowledgments   243
                    Appendix I   247
                    Appendix II   263
                    About the Authors   269

To
all the parents
of the world
throughout history
who have delighted
in standing their babies
atop their own broad shoulders
and saying,
"BEHOLD THE WORLD MY CHILD."

Kids think running is a means of transportation. We adults spend our time chasing them down to convince them this is not true. Fortunately, we rarely succeed.

Andrew, Andrea and David Hines. Photo by Sherman Hines.

FOREWORD

A commonly used aerospace research tool for studying the effects of weightlessness on the human body is to confine normal, healthy adults to complete bed rest. The results of this forced inactivity, or so-called hypodynamic state, are remarkable. Within as little as seventy-two hours, multiple systems in the body begin to show evidence of change and deterioration. There are fluid shifts within the body that lead to hormonal changes and dehydration, the heart and blood vessels begin to lose their tone and strength, and calcium begins to leach out of the bones. The volunteer subjects often complain of headache, backache, constipation, boredom, lethargy and occasionally disorientation. Clearly, forced inactivity is a detrimental and unnatural condition for the healthy, uninjured body.

But what of the corollary condition . . . exaggerated activity? Does it necessarily follow that if forced inactivity is bad for the human body then exaggerated activity or exercise will be of benefit to it? Here again the evidence is quite clear. More than twenty years of research has proven that vigorous physical activity can favorably affect a person's heart, circulation, lungs, body weight, muscle tone, bowel habits, blood pressure, blood sugar, blood fats, stamina, efficiency and general sense of well being.

However, the question must be pursued one step further . . . does it necessarily follow that if programmed activity is good for the adult then it will also benefit the child? The answer is a resounding "YES" . . . all the benefits previously described accrue to the physically active child as well as to the adult. *But of even greater importance are the effects of a properly designed physical program on the child's developing nervous system.*

In this unique book, the authors present an intriguing and scientifically sound concept of brain function and brain physiology. They explain, in clear and flowing style, how a program of physical activity that is integrated into the child's daily life can profoundly influence the processes of brain growth and neurological organization. They show how the cascading effects of these processes stimulate intellectual and social growth as well as physical development.

However, not content with theoretical explanations alone, the authors also provide a precise, step-by-step prescription for accomplishing these goals in the individual child.

Like most professionals doing what they do best, the authors make it all sound so simple. In fact, the great gift that they offer the reader and his or her child is the result of more than forty years of total involvement and intimate association with both the normal and impaired human developmental processes. Their unmatched understanding of mobility and child development stems from an intense search for answers that has taken them to more than 100 different countries and to every continent including Antarctica. They have circled the globe at the equator and lived with the Xingu in Brazil's Mato Grosso and with the very small Bushmen in the Kalahari Desert.

Always searching, they have looked deeply into the past at the movement patterns of Earth's earliest creatures and far into the future at the effects of weightlessness on human mobility and development.

Throughout this book, as in their earlier books, the authors stress these recurrent themes:

The human brain actually grows by use and this growth is virtually complete by six years of age.

Tiny babies would rather learn than do anything else.

Tiny children think that the most precious gift (toy) in the world is the undivided attention of an adult, preferably Mom or Dad.

The greatest teaching team in history is that of parent and child.

Parents can teach a baby absolutely anything which they can present in an honest and factual way.

It is, in a sense, strange that this book on *How To Teach Your Baby To Be Physically Superb* has been so long in coming, since the senior author, Glenn Doman, and the staff of The Institutes first gained worldwide attention by their work in making brain-injured children who were physically paralyzed able to move, then crawl, then creep and finally to walk and run in the same way that newborns first move, then crawl, then creep and finally walk and run.

In the exact same way do the authors teach parents to take unhurt children through these precise same steps from birth to physical excellence.

Perhaps the most important point the authors make so compellingly in this excellent book is that, presently, these vital stages to physical perfection occur by *chance*.

By being presented with the opportunity to do these essential things on *purpose* and in their proper order rather than in a random fashion, children are able to reach a state of physical excellence that will provide them with the opportunity to be virtually anything and everything they wish to be as youths and throughout life.

Not the least of the many valuable points made in this charming and thorough book is the fact that teaching a baby to be physically superb is a process that not only can be mutually joyful and fulfilling for both parent and child, but in fact *must* be so in order to be successful.

When the authors, whom I have known intimately for almost a decade, asked me to write the foreword to this much needed book, I felt honored.

I felt *qualified* to write it for the simple reason that I have with my own eyes seen formerly paralyzed children doing handstands and other gymnastic feats, which the authors do not detail, and little unhurt girls "flying," which the authors do describe.

The authors have molded their unique experiences and perspectives into an innovative field of knowledge which they call, properly, Child Brain Development.

This new discipline has not simply contributed to the field of human development, it has created a new dimension in which it is now possible to understand and *change* the human condition.

Ralph Pelligra, M.D.
Space Medicine

INTRODUCTION

Perhaps it would be wise to start at the end, although the hundred or so people who make up the staff of The Institutes for the Achievement of Human Potential in Philadelphia have devoted all of their lives to starting at the very beginning. Still a reader, it has always seemed to me, has a right to know from the first couple of pages what a book is going to say.

This book will demonstrate that being physically superb is not limited to a few rare children who, by virtue of some special genetic potential, have within them the seeds of physical genius.

This book says that every child born has, by virtue of his splendid gift of the genes of *Homo sapiens*, the inherent *right* to be physically superb.

The right to be physically superb is a birthright.

This book is in praise of the miracle called *human mobility*, which has preoccupied our lives since 1940. Since that time, in days that were more often twenty hours long than eight; and in weeks that were more often seven days long than five; and in months that were more often joyous than despairing; and in years that were divided about equally between awe of the miracle of human mobility and maddening perplexity as to why it sometimes didn't happen at all, we have studied mobility in every way we could find to study it.

We have studied human mobility in the most *practical and hardnosed way* in tens of thousands of newborns, infants, babies, tiny kids, children, adults and old people, from its beginnings, in the form of truncal movements *in utero*, through crawling in infants, creeping in babies, early walking in tiny kids, skilled walking, running and jumping in children, superbly skilled and breathtakingly beautiful athletic prowess in young people, through all its astonishing day-by-day ability to carry us through life, to its ultimate decline and fall in old age.

We have studied mobility in a more *theoretical way* from its earliest origins, perhaps three-and-a-half billion years ago, when the two great kingdoms of living matter took their separate paths to become the growing but physically immobile Kingdom of the Plants and the Kingdom of the Animals, which could move from one place to another at will.

We have studied the beginnings of human mobility in Australopithecus africanus, discovered by our own Professor Dart, whose announcement of that discovery more than sixty years ago stunned the entire world of anthropology. When these ancient creatures rose to walk on their feet and thus freed their hands from the mobility role long enough to pick up a club as a weapon in one hand and a twig as a primitive tool in the other was the way opened for modern man to be born.

Today that ancient club has become the horrendous nuclear weapon and that ancient tool, the twig, has become the computer and all the other sublimely splendid things that man has created.

Since that beginning man has walked upright on the earth with his hands free to use tools—the use of which has made him brighter. With his greater brightness he has been able to invent even more complex tools to use to learn and understand even more about the earth, and thus was modern human intelligence born.

Today man stands as the most brilliant and fearsome of all of the Creator's creatures and the only one of them that has the ability to destroy the planet upon which he lives, or to make it, as a product of his intelligence, a place nearer to the Paradise of which he has always dreamed.

That towering intelligence had its origins in human mobility and in human manual function.

That human mobility and manual function have become more skillful, more beautiful, more complex and more awesome with each succeeding decade.

This is no mere theoretical construction. It is clearly visible in each succeeding presentation of the Olympic Games. In *every* Olympic year, old records of human mobility and manual function are broken and new world records are set.

It is worth noting that most of the present-day gold medal winners are noticeably younger than were the previous winners.

Where will it all end? Today Olympian gymnasts in their teens perform gymnastic feats which were literally not even dreamed of by Olympians of fifty years ago.

It will *not* end.

Inextricably tied to human *mobility* and *manual function* is human *intelligence*.

Indeed, as we shall see, mobility and manual intelligence are two of the six kinds of human intelligence.

What, then, have we learned about human beings in the thousands of people-years that the staff of The Institutes has devoted to understanding and improving human physical performance? We can state it in a single paragraph.

We are totally persuaded that: *Every child born has, at the instant of birth, a higher potential intelligence than Leonardo da Vinci ever used.*

That potential intelligence, inherent at birth, includes, and indeed *begins* with, physical function.

This book will tell all parents who wish to know, how to teach their babies to be physically superb, and why, after almost a half century of dramatically improving human physical ability in children, the authors believe it is a good idea to do so.

There are no chauvinists at The Institutes, either male or female. We love and respect mothers and fathers, baby boys and baby girls. To solve the maddening problems of referring to all human beings as "grown-up male persons" or "tiny female persons," we have referred most often throughout this text to all parents as mothers, and to all children as boys.

Seems fair.

Join your child in his joy.

Marlowe and Rosalind Doman.
Photo by Sherman Hines.

SECTION ONE

**PHYSICAL INTELLIGENCE
THE BACKGROUND**

**BY
GLENN DOMAN**

"Now the brightest people in the world will find the Institutes."

Datin Seri Dr. Siti Hasmah, Glenn Doman and Janet Doman. Photo by David Kerper.

1
"THE BRIGHTEST PEOPLE
IN THE WORLD..."

The Institutes were having one of their charming events, which is to say, we were having an opportunity to watch the tiny kids do their gymnastics.

Also watching with fascination that day was Datin Seri Dr. Siti Hasmah, who is a Malaysian, a mother, a physician and the wife of the Prime Minister of Malaysia, who is himself a physician.

It seemed to me that all of the things she is were written on her face as she watched a three-year-old doing forward rolls and cartwheels with a good deal of baby girl charm, and more than a touch of professionalism.

First, she is a Malaysian woman and that, we have come to believe, means two things, both of which were to be seen on her face. Strength and happiness were there, characteristics she shared with the Foreign Minister's wife, the Ambassador's wife and the other Malaysian women in her official party.

Second, her face is serene in an almost regal way, as is proper to the wife of the Prime Minister of one of the most important nations in Asia.

As she watched the little girl her eyes glowed with the pleasure and joy of a mother. That motherly pride which (in the best of mothers) embraces all of the children of the world continued to show as the children joyfully and proudly demonstrated their physical splendidness in more sophisticated and difficult gymnastic feats. The smile on her face and her motherly pleasure increased as the five-year-olds did *one*-handed cartwheels with ease and a good deal of *éclat*.

Last, I saw on her face the final factor that reflected what she was and what she saw. What I saw was the look of a professional who is surprised and intrigued by a new realization, for Lady Siti Hasmah is also a physician.

Why should so distinguished and important a group of visitors be spending their time watching a three-year-old girl do gymnastics?

More than twenty years ago, one of the geniuses we respect most in the world gave us the best advice we have ever received.

Dr. Jonas Salk, to whom tens of thousands of parents owe their sanity (the ones whose children *would* have had infantile paralysis if it weren't for him), after spending an evening listening to the things we had learned at The Institutes, said, "Now the brightest people in the world will find The Institutes. When they do, tell them once, because the people who *want* to understand will understand the first time you tell them—and those who *don't* want to understand won't understand if you tell them a thousand times. So don't."

Not only was that absolutely sound advice but, in fact, it was highly predictive. Almost from that day, some of the brightest people in the world have found their way to The Institutes, and sure enough—they understood the first time we told them. So have a very small number of the people who didn't want to understand, and sure enough—they didn't.

If it is true that all tiny children can be made physically, intellectually and socially excellent by parents who wish to do so, why would intelligent human beings not come to see for themselves?

There are a number of important people whose prime interest is a world that contains human beings who, because they are physically, intellectually and socially better than they would otherwise have been, are also more humane, more humorous, more kindly and more gentle.

Is it surprising that such important people should want to come from everywhere in the world to see the beautiful, beguiling and splendid children who represent all that they have been seeking?

For more than a quarter of a century, some of the most interesting and interested people in the world have visited The Institutes to stay for a day or a week. Some have stayed for an *unplanned* month or year. Some have come to see with their own eyes and to hear with their own ears what is happening, and have never left—they're now called "staff."

First among the visitors have been the brilliant people from every walk of life who yearn for a better, saner, more humane world, and who are certain that the way to achieve such a world is through the raising of children who are themselves better, saner and more humane.

Those people include a number of the world's geniuses, many of them with Nobel prizes, many of them without.

They include professionals and non-professionals. Among them are Ministers of Education and Secretaries of Welfare from many nations. Among them are South American Ministers for the Development of Human Intelligence and Asian Prime Minister's wives. Among them are Latin Ministers of Foreign Affairs and European legislators. Among them are oriental Presidents of international corporations and far-sighted Italian parents. Among them are Scandinavian officials and NASA scientists. Among them are physicians, anthropologists, engineers, biologists, physiologists, jurists, businessmen, computer scientists, astronauts, educators, psychologists, advanced mathematicians, vice-presidents of the United States, publishers, union officials and a huge number of very bright parents.

They are the cream of the crop.

They are the ones who not only *care* about the world, but are ready to *do* something about improving the world.

They are the ones who see the children of the world as being what tomorrow is made of.

They wish to take back to their homes the knowledge that The Institutes' staff has sometimes worked its way into through many years of the most penetrating search—and which it has sometimes fallen into headlong by the greatest good fortune.

In the vast majority of cases, they have taken it back to a single child or two in a single home somewhere in the world. Sometimes they have taken it back to the children of an entire nation.

It would be a rare day at The Institutes that did not see parents from a half dozen nations, top-flight representatives of one or two nations and, because of what is happening to children at The Institutes and the caliber and position of the people who are there to learn about it, television crews from NBC, BBC, CBC, NHK or other national television corporations, along with newspaper, magazine, radio and other reporters. They are faced with the perplexing question of whether it would make a more attention-grabbing show to report that it was a very good thing that children were becoming physically, intellectually and socially excellent—or, to report that perhaps, for some mysterious reason, it was a very bad thing for children to be physically, intellectually and socially excellent.

In the end, most of the media report that it is a very good thing. A few report that it is somehow a bad thing.

All of the other people who come to The Institutes and stay for a day or more and who meet the kids and the parents of The Evan Thomas Institute decide two things:

1. It is *good* to be physically, intellectually and socially excellent.
2. All kids who are given the chance love to be physically superb.

All kids who are given the chance, *love* to be physically superb!

Marc Mihai Dimancescu, five-and-one-half years old. Photo by Sherman Hines.

2

ALL CHILDREN CAN BE PHYSICALLY SUPERB

*Every child born has, at the instant of birth,
a higher potential intelligence than
Leonardo da Vinci ever used.*

The eighty parents who comprised the seven-day "How To Multiply Your Baby's Intelligence" Course presented by The Better Baby Institute were quietly stunned. They were clearly overwhelmed with two realizations.

The first and most obvious was their reaction to the gymnastics demonstration they had just watched as part of their *How To Teach Your Baby To Be Physically Superb* day.

The children who had just demonstrated ranged from two-week-old Tegan Hagy who with her parents had demonstrated the use of the floor as the world's best piece of gymnastic equipment, to the oldest, five-year-old Marc Mihai Dimancescu.

Marc Mihai had just finished a floor routine he had designed and set to music. It began with three straddle rolls and continued through V-seat, one-leg balance, chaines turns, dive rolls, third ballet position, two cartwheels, fifth ballet position, extended stag position, shoulder roll, V-seat, straddle lift position, pike position, dive roll, Swedish fall, tuck position, forward roll and second position. Marc Mihai finished with a spectacular front somersault that drew an audible gasp from the class of parents as he flew through the air upside down and landed on his feet.

It was literally stunning to watch four-year-olds run three miles nonstop around The Institutes' campus and six-year-olds run three miles in thirty-six minutes. They had watched the two-year-olds brachiate two lengths of the overhead ladder (brachiation is the art of swinging arm over arm from one branch or rung to another) and the ladder used to do it was six feet off the ground and parallel to it. Then, just as a five-year-old finished swinging from one flying trapeze to another, a cry for help came from high up in an old oak tree in the middle of The Institutes' track.

There, twenty feet up in the branches, was four-year-old Brandi Katz (although how she had gotten there was an unsolved mystery). Just as promptly, and almost as mysteriously, Sean Katz, her six-year-old brother, appeared on the scene, running to her rescue, a rope over his shoulder. Sean ran to the tree, from which hung a thick rope which he promptly and easily climbed. He quickly placed a loop of rope under Brandi's arms and, now confident she was safe, Brandi climbed down a rope ladder.

The parent-students were entranced. The beautiful gymnastics routine that Marc Mihai had performed so gracefully and skillfully was only a slight variation on the routines that *all* the five-year-olds did in the first grade of The International School of The Evan Thomas Institute.* The parents had watched spellbound as the tiny children demonstrated with such obvious pleasure the beautiful and skillful things that they did so easily and so grace-fully. The parents had been particularly impressed by the variation that six-year-old Robert Greer had put into his brachiation. When Robert performed his brachiation he had, instead of swinging arm over arm across the ladder, as is the difficult but usual way, reversed the position of every other hand on the rung so that he had not only swung the length of the ladder several times, but actually *circled* as he did so.

This was the fifth day of class for the eighty parents who had come from Europe, Asia, South America and the United States to attend the seven-day course.

They had watched tiny children read in several languages and do advanced math; they had heard the kids play the violin movingly in concert; they had watched them demonstrate their encyclopedic knowledge of art, science, biology, geography, history and a host of other subjects.

Today, they had watched the kids demonstrate in a physically superb way their athletic prowess.

The demonstration had been both splendid and astonishing but it was a second realization which had made it stunning.

What only now fully dawned on them was the fact that these were the *same* kids

who read and spoke two or more languages with such pleasure;
who did advanced math with such glee;
who had encyclopedic knowledge and who were so eager to learn more;
who played the violin well enough to bring tears to the eyes of most of the parents.

As if all that weren't enough, it was now obvious that the *same* little kids were a bunch of jocks as well, doing back hand springs as easily as they played Lully's "Gavotte" on the violin.

It was, as has been said, a stunning revelation.

The Institutes' Director, Janet Doman, who was teaching, was swamped with questions.

"But surely you are not pretending that these children are ordinary children?"

"No, of course not," answered the Director. "Ordinary children can't

---

*An organizational chart listing the various individual Institutes which together com-pose The Institutes for the Achievement of Human Potential can be found at the end of this book. The various programs of The Evan Thomas Institute will be discussed in more detail in Chapter 4.

read at three years of age, read books in two languages without the slightest effort, and do all the other things that all these kids do."

A French mother who was also a pediatrician pressed the point. "Surely you are not telling us that these children who are so extraordinary were ordinary children to begin with?"

A very pretty mother from Milford, N.J. spoke for everyone. She wanted to be absolutely positive. "You are actually telling us that when these children began the program, they were in no way special? Surely, as an example, that boy Robert Greer, the one who circled around while he was brachiating, surely *he* was special when he began the program, wasn't he?"

All the staff members in the auditorium smiled broadly as the Director answered quietly.

"Yes, that's true. You've picked the *only* kid in the group who actually *was* special when he began the program."

Robert Greer is from New Zealand; his parents first brought him to The Institutes when he was four years old. Robert did not come as a student of The Evan Thomas Institute. Robert's family brought him to The Institutes as a brain-injured child.

When Robert Greer had begun as a patient of The Institutes two years earlier, he had indeed *been* special. He had been functionally blind and paralyzed on one side of his body. He had actually graduated from The Institutes' Treatment Program the very week the class had asked the question.

Who are these kids, and how had they gotten to be the way they are?

Are they some elite group of genetically superior superstars born to parents who are Olympic stars, All-American football players or circus performers?

Are they all the children of "Hollywood Mothers" out to make their kids superstars at any price?

Not by any stretch of the imagination.

The majority of them come from homes which are primarily middle class in educational, social and financial terms.

A very few of them come from homes which are very poor in economic terms.

A very, very few of them come from homes that are very rich in economic terms.

They range in age from newborns (who can't do *all* those things quite yet) to two-year-olds (who are *beginning* to do all those things) to three-year-olds (who *can do* all those things) to five-year-olds (who do all those things *very well*), to ten-year-olds (who do all those things *splendidly*).

To summarize the kids, they range in age between birth and ten years of age and have almost nothing in common *except* that they are:

1. Astonishingly competent both physically and intellectually.
2. Thoroughly delightful.
3. Irresistibly beguiling.
4. Students of The Evan Thomas Institute.
5. Kids who have extraordinary parents who have given them extra-ordinary opportunity.

In fact, these were kids who were scheduled, in the normal course of events, to be average and ordinary kids.

But these kids are extraordinary kids in every way, who did *not* grow up by accident but who were instead given the opportunity to achieve their full potential as a glorious and loving gift from parents who had been taught how to do so by the staff of The Institutes.

What is so different about these parents?

Happiest of all was our discovery that since excellence in intelligence was a product of what *happened* to a baby, high mobility was available to every child whose parents wished to give him or her physical excellence.

Nicholas and Barbara Coventry.
Photo by Sherman Hines.

3
PARENTS AND PRIORITIES

"Where children are,
there is the golden age."

"How do you like children?"
"Boiled."

Baron Friedrich von Hardenberg (Novalis)

W.C. Fields

It was one of our lucky days, which means we had found a few minutes to watch the "big" kids (five to ten years old) in The International School of The Evan Thomas Institute, a practice guaranteed to brighten up anybody for at least a week.

It was a gymnastics class. It was, as usual, beautiful to watch and the kids were great. The biggest problem they were facing was trying not to grin as they did their routines.

The *aerial* Michelle had just done topped it off. Michelle is seven years old, and it's very easy to love Michelle. If somebody wanted to *not* love little girls and he wanted to practice on somebody, we'd advise him not to start with Michelle. Come to think of it, *all* the kids in The International School would be awfully hard not to love, and you wouldn't want to practice on *any* of them!

Now, we had never seen Michelle do an aerial before, and didn't know that she could. Indeed, a month earlier, she *couldn't*.

Actually, we had learned only a year or so ago what an aerial was in gymnastic terms.

Since we had managed to get through more than sixty years believing that an aerial was nothing more than the thing on the roof that made the radio and the TV work better, it seems possible that some readers may be equally uninformed as to aerials.

An aerial is beautiful, if somewhat frightening, to behold and seems to us an impossible thing for anyone to do, never mind a seven-year-old girl. An aerial is a *no*-handed cartwheel.

If you can imagine a beautiful but very slim little seven-year-old girl doing an Olympic-style "Present," running a few graceful steps and then throwing herself into the air and turning herself upside down with legs toward the ceiling and blonde hair almost touching the floor, before landing on her feet and assuming the Olympic "Finish" position, you understand why we thought it was beautiful, frightening and impossible.

We remembered Michelle Gauger when she was little more than a baby, when Mrs. Gauger first brought her as a candidate for the On-Campus Program of The Evan Thomas Institute (see Chapter 4). She was, as we remember it, about eighteen months old, a little tiny thing, very cute, very skinny, and very *awkward*. Indeed, we worried a good deal on and off about that awkwardness.

We were reassured, however, by her mother since Mrs. Gauger was quiet, calm and seemed to be quite confident that she could teach her daughter anything. Mrs. Gauger, although we had never discussed with her our concern about Michelle, managed to persuade us that things would work out.

What was a good deal more difficult was that she succeeded in convincing The Evan Thomas Institute staff as well (which was mighty important to Michelle's being accepted, since when application is made to The Early Development Program for admission, it is the *parents* who are examined, rather than the child).

There are two reasons for that.

The first is that The Early Development Program of The Evan Thomas Institute doesn't actually deal with the children at all. Instead, we teach the mother and she teaches her baby. Consequently, it is the mother who is very carefully scrutinized when she and her baby apply.

The second is that we have never met a *child* who is unacceptable for the program. We are persuaded that *every child can be physically superb*, and that Michelle Gauger is a splendid example.

Michelle has come from being a very sweet and lovable but extremely awkward little girl to being a superbly competent seven-year-old. Michelle is an extremely advanced gymnast with the grace and agility which naturally accompany superb physical condition.

When we see a human being in splendid physical condition, we are often inclined to imagine that the beautiful body we are seeing houses nothing more than a "jock" with a head as empty of brains as his body is full of muscles.

Is Michelle (and each of the other little children of The Evan Thomas Institute whom we were watching) a pretty but relatively mindless jock? *All* of the children swim, all of the children dive, all of the children run long distances daily, all of the children do superb gymnastics, all of the children are in splendid physical condition.

Michelle, however, is a long way from being a mindless jock. Michelle reads splendidly and far beyond her age group. (So do all the other kids.)

Michelle does very advanced things with the Macintosh computer. (So do all the other kids.)

Michelle plays the violin beautifully. (So do all the other kids.)

Michelle has the time of her life all day long. (So do all the other kids.)

Michelle thinks that learning about everything is more fun than doing anything else. (So do all the other kids.)

Michelle thinks that knowledge is the best invention since—well—since mobility began. (So do all the other kids.)

If being physically superb makes you a jock, then Michelle and the other kids are certainly jocks—but they are a long, long way from being *mindless* jocks.

Who taught this awkward little girl to do these breathtaking gymnastics, to play the violin, to read Japanese and do all the other remarkable things that Michelle did with such evident pleasure?

Mrs. Gauger did, with an assist from Mr. Gauger.

Neither Mr. nor Mrs. Gauger were gymnasts, spoke Japanese or played the violin when they began the program with Michelle.

So, what kind of people *are* the parents of these extraordinary kids?

All of the parents, the handful of poor ones, the large number of average ones, the tiny number of rich ones, have one thing in common.

All of them think that kids are our most important product.

Because they think kids are our most important product they give their kids the highest priority in family life.

All of them want their kids to begin life where they themselves will leave off. In short, they want their kids to go through life standing on their parents' shoulders.

Not *all* parents wish to give their kids the Number One priority in family life, and that's a decision that all the parents of the world are entitled to make for themselves.

Obviously, adults range from those who can't stand kids to those who would rather be parents than anything else in the world. Between these extremes there are a thousand shades of feeling.

The staff of The Institutes, who have spent virtually every second of their waking hours and every year of their adult lives with parents and children, would *fight* for every adult's right to feel about children exactly as he or she chooses.

By and large, every adult *should* behave about children exactly as he or she feels about them. It works out best for the kids that way.

Someone once asked W. C. Fields how he liked children. His response was brief, clear and to the point. "Boiled," said Mr. Fields. W. C. Fields was a great comedian, and we don't know whether he was serious or not. We also don't remember whether he had any kids or not. If he *was* serious, we hope he *didn't* have any kids.

People who can't stand kids (with a few wild exceptions) shouldn't *have* them. Mostly, they make lousy parents.

People who think that kids are the greatest thing that ever happened (with a few wild exceptions) *should* have kids. Mostly, they make fine parents.

And there are the people who are in between.

Let's look at them all.

First, there are the people who can't stand kids. Our advice to them as a group would be to avoid kids. It works out better for the kids and the adults. We have seen the exception to this in the young man or woman who can't stand kids but who, in the natural course of events, falls into what someone called "the tender trap" and who as a consequence sometime later finds himself or herself looking into a newborn baby's face as a brand-new parent. Dislike and cynicism are replaced by awe and wonder—in a single instant.

Next, there are the people who *love* kids, but who don't have much respect for their potential and who consequently give their children a good deal of affection, many toys and a large number of orders.

Then there are the people who love *and* respect kids but who don't see them as the most important thing in the world. These are fine parents who simply have a set of priorities in which the children come out high, but not first.

The parents who think that kids are the greatest thing yet, however, are the ones who would rather be parents than anything else in the world because they find their family and their kids to be more fun, pleasure, joy and happiness than anything else in the world. These parents have simply decided to give their children a very high priority in their lives, most especially in the all-important years between birth and six years of age.

We call these parents *professional* mothers and fathers. They range from doctors, steelworkers and lawyers to teachers, truck drivers, secretaries and astronauts.

They range from parents who are engineers, businessmen and carpenters to parents who are both doctors *and* astronauts.

The parents this book describes are people of almost every imaginable background. They are people who have an enormous range of interests. It is just that their children are first among their many interests. They have superbly capable and beguiling children.

How did they get that way?

All of the children of The Evan Thomas Institute started out life as all other children do. Since many of them were registered at The Institutes before they were born, it would mean that at birth they were physically and intellectually run-of-the-mill. There is every reason to believe that these children of ordinary parents should run the gamut of newborns from babies who appear to be in robust health and highly competent to babies who are in very poor health and not very competent physiologically.

How did they get to be such extraordinary children in physical, intellectual and social ways by six years of age?

Were they the product of the teaching of the finest coaches of track, gymnastics and swimming, together with the finest professors of art, science and literature the world has to offer, as some young prince or princess might be raised to assume one day the mantle of emperor?

No ma'am!

Were they the product of some super-ambitious set of parents determined to make their child a superstar at any cost to the world, to the child and to themselves?

No sir!

Were they the children of parents who brought them as infants to be exposed constantly to a faculty of Olympians and superstar professors assembled at great cost to form the world's most expensive school for precocious infants?

Not a bit.

The Early Development Program and The International School of The Evan Thomas Institute are entirely free and parents pay not a cent directly or indirectly to be part of them.

How then *did* these children get to be the way they are physically, intellectually and socially?

Obviously the Number One reason is their marvelous parents. The second reason is The Evan Thomas Institute.

Give your children *plenty* of opportunity in a loving and joyous way - then step back and watch them go!

Michelle Gauger and Chip Myers,
*five and six years old. Photo by
Sherman Hines.*

4

THE EVAN THOMAS INSTITUTE AND OPPORTUNITY

*On this earth there is no security—there is
only opportunity.*

Ellen's mother went to the foot of the stairs to call Ellen downstairs. Three-year-old Ellen was wearing those pajamas with feet and shiny soles, and as a consequence she slipped on the top step and down the stairs she fell, head over tin-cups, to land flat on her back at her horrified mother's feet.

Whereupon Ellen jumped to her feet, threw her arms over her head, stood on tiptoes and assumed the Olympic "Finish" position.

Her very tuned-in mother very wisely applauded.

When we first heard that story from the staff, our first thought was, "How very clever of both Ellen and her mother. Ellen snatched victory from defeat."

And so she had. It took us a while to realize that what Ellen had done was a good deal more important than just snatching victory from defeat.

Ellen does not look at learning the way adults do. Neither do the other kids.

It took us a reasonably long time to realize that the children who have the glorious opportunity to learn about all the things there are to learn about in this world, at the hands of parents who take great joy in teaching them, do not look at learning in the same way that the rest of us do.

How *does* Ellen (being a tiny child) look at learning?

Tiny kids would rather learn than eat.

Tiny kids would rather learn than play.

Tiny kids think that all learning *is* play. They do *not* however think that all play is learning as most professionals do. That is because a good deal of what adults regard as proper play for kids is downright silly. Nobody fools kids.

TINY KIDS THINK LEARNING IS A SURVIVAL SKILL.

TINY KIDS WANT TO LEARN EVERYTHING THERE IS TO LEARN, AND THEY WANT TO DO SO RIGHT NOW.

TINY KIDS THINK LEARNING IS THE GREATEST THING THAT EVER HAPPENED.

The *younger* they are, the *more* they believe that learning is a joy.

The *younger* they are, the *easier* it is to learn anything.

The *older* we are, the *less* we believe that learning is a joy.

Indeed, we grownups believe that learning is painful.

In fact, we believe that if it isn't painful it isn't learning.

Not tiny kids.

We adults think learning is divided into subjects, one category each of music, geography, history, biology, math, zoology, and so on.

Indeed, if one of us moves from a discussion of an historical subject to math without warning he is accused of "changing the subject."

Little kids don't see it that way. They hear musical notes in the sounds of refrigerators and in horns in traffic. We see math, and they see solving problems. We see gymnastics as a subject and they see how the human body moves. That is precisely what Ellen saw. Having moved her body skillfully in falling downstairs, it seemed fitting and proper for her to assume the "Finish" position.

It's awesome how right kids are to see the world in such a joyful, sane and whole way.

How had Ellen and all the other kids come to such a sane, creative and holistic view of the world?

The answer is that they were the product of both their parents and the staff of The Institutes.

They were all taught at home by their parents during the first five years of life, on what is called the Early Development Program of The Evan Thomas Institute. The parents had enrolled their children at ages varying from before they were born to as late as four and a half years old. At five years of age the children had graduated from the Early Development Program to The International School of The Evan Thomas Institute, and had begun being taught by the staff of The Institutes as well as by their parents. These children lived at home but actually attended school "on campus."

Not one of the parents of these physically superb kids was a gymnast of any kind. Not one of the parents of these violin-playing children had ever played violin before. Not one of the parents of these American kids who read and speak a good deal of Japanese knew a word of Japanese before beginning the program.

Nonetheless these delightful, highly competent, physically superb and charming children were all taught to be the splendid and highly intelligent children they are by their parents.

How had the parents learned to do so?

They were taught by the staff of The Evan Thomas Institute.

The Evan Thomas Institute is one of the major Institutes of The Institutes for the Achievement of Human Potential, which are all located on the campus in Philadelphia's suburban Chestnut Hill.

Parents come to The Institutes from every continent on earth (except Antarctica) to attend a seven-day course on "How to Multiply Your Baby's Intelligence," presented by The Better Baby Institute. These parents are then certified to register their babies in either the On-Campus or Off-Campus Program.

Tens of thousands, perhaps hundreds of thousands, of parents have taught their babies as a product of having read the books written by the staff. Until the publication of this book at this time, the number of parents who had the detailed knowledge of how to teach their babies to be *physically superb* was limited to the five or six thousand families from around the world who had actually attended The Institutes' seven-day course.

With the publication of *this* book, that information will become available to the millions of parents who have not attended that course, but who have read the previous books by the staff of The Institutes, and who have gently but insistently prodded the staff of The Institutes for the Achievement of Physical Excellence to write this book.

The Institutes' most important material possession is the more than one hundred thousand letters it has received from parents who proudly and pleasurably report exactly what happened when they did with their children the things we had taught them in person or through our books.

Thousands of such letters arrive every year.

In summary, those letters constitute the greatest body of evidence in the history of the world to prove that babies are quite capable of being intellectually and socially excellent, and it is important to remember that the vast majority of the parents who write them have known about the work of The Institutes *only* through the books and other materials written by The Institutes' staff.

With nothing more than these, how have tens of thousands of babies been taught to read, do math, and gain encyclopedic knowledge and in so doing had their intelligence raised remarkably? This was all accomplished by parents who gave their children a very high priority in life.

Five or six thousand of those parents actually spent a week taking The Institutes' "How to Multiply Your Baby's Intelligence" Course. Those parents had the opportunity to watch the tiny children of the E.T.I. actually *do* the extraordinary gymnastic and physical things they do, and thus to go home with the certainty that they could give their children the opportunity to be physically superb. They write from home to report their successes in doing so.

Of the parents who have taken that course, more than a thousand have applied for and been accepted into the *Off-Campus* Program of The Evan Thomas Institute, having earned the right to do so by receiving their certification as Professional Parents in the "How To Multiply Your Baby's Intelligence" Course.

These parents live all over the world and, through the knowledge gained in the intensive seven-day Course at The Institutes and with the help of all of the materials created by The Institutes' staff, are in a particularly splendid position to return home to teach their children to be physically, intellectually and socially splendid under the constant guidance of the staff of the E.T.I.. Very careful records of these children are maintained and the precise results reported by their parents by mail and by phone (and in a few cases by actual visits to The Institutes). Those results are splendid.

Finally, there is the relatively tiny number of children (about forty) who are actually the students of The Evan Thomas Institute *On-Campus Programs*.

This small number of children are all children who live near The Institutes and who are in intimate contact with the staff. These children and their parents are obviously invaluable to the staff because the children take turns demonstrating their abilities to the parent-students from every continent who attend the "How To Multiply Your Baby's Intelligence" Course. Both the children and their parents take great pleasure in acting as teachers and demonstrators for the Course.

It is this On-Campus Program which is without cost of any kind to the parents and children of E.T.I.. Clearly The Evan Thomas Institute On-Campus Program is a demonstration school which is truly unique in the world, and which serves to demonstrate the basic discovery of The Institutes' staff:

> *Every child born has, at the instant of birth, a higher potential intelligence than Leonardo da Vinci ever used.*

It cannot be said too often.

> *Physical intelligence is the first and most basic of the kinds of human intelligence, as we shall see.*

Having spent our entire lives in daily intimate contact with kids of every description, and having found ourselves charmed by the vast majority of them, it is easy to report that the children of The Evan Thomas Institute are, to a man and to a woman—well, to a boy and to a girl—without question the most charming and delightful group of little kids we have ever known.

They are not charming and delightful *despite* the fact that they are stunningly capable physically, intellectually and socially.

They are charming and delightful precisely *because* they are stunningly capable.

The endearing and smashingly capable little kids of the E.T.I. are not the product of wealth, privilege, genetics or their parents' higher education. They are an unadulterated product of parents who gave them unlimited opportunity—and the earlier they got that opportunity, the more easily they learned and the better they learned.

You can teach a two-year-old to ski on snow, and many parents have done so.

You can teach a two-year-old to water ski, and many parents have done so.

You can teach a two-year-old to play golf.

You can teach a two-year-old five languages.

You can teach an Irish two-year-old to read Japanese.

You can teach a two-year-old to play a violin.

You can teach a two-year-old to do absolutely *anything* that you can present to him in an honest and factual way.

The *younger* he is, the easier it is to teach him.

Just give him plenty of opportunity in a loving and joyous way—and step back.

WHAT DO THEY *DO* IN THE E.T.I.?

Susan Aisen, the Director of The Institutes for the Achievement of Intellectual Excellence, writing in *The In-Report* (a quarterly magazine published by The Institutes), had this to say of The Evan Thomas Institute:

All the On-Campus families begin their home program by investing time in two areas—reading and the physical program—to provide their children with a solid intellectual and physical foundation. Once these programs are going smoothly, additional intellectual and physical programs are added one at a time until a full, varied and intense program is achieved.

All the On-Campus Professional Mothers are full-time teachers of their own children and strive for excellence in every area, with great respect for their children's abilities to learn—and with great joy involved in the process.

A physical program that includes crawling, creeping, running, brachiation and swimming will be accomplished and as coordination improves, playing a musical instrument, writing and drawing will be added.

Every child's day of exciting intellectual stimulation and physical opportunity is balanced with a social development program. Even a one-year-old has responsibilities around the house (i.e., putting books away) and a four-year-old has achieved a hundred responsibilities divided among ways to help himself, his brothers and sisters, his mother and father, his environment and even his community.

On-Campus parents with infants attend The Institutes regularly for lectures and appointments with the staff, and learn of additional programs for the development of their tiny ones. Between two and three years of age, tiny kids begin to attend classes at The Institutes one morning each week, with Mom or Dad. The classes are primarily for teaching parents and are designed to give the children the opportunity to use the information they have learned at home daily from their best teachers, their mothers and fathers. The children expand their social abilities even further as they deal with others beyond their own family in a highly organized and responsible way.

During the year, the On-Campus mothers, fathers and tiny kids participate in five "How To Multiply Your Baby's Intelligence" Courses, and help demonstrate how to teach babies to read, to do mathematics, to gain encyclopedic knowledge, to achieve physical excellence and to acquire a first-rate musical ability. The tiny kids choose their favorite books and Bits, their most exciting mathematical problems, design and polish a violin piece with Mom and Dad, and really look forward to the demonstrations. The On-Campus families are a vital part of the Courses' success in teaching the thousands of parents who have come from every corner of the world, over the last eight years, to learn how to teach their own children from birth onward. (This is the Early Development Program of The Evan Thomas Institute.)

Parents and children in the Early Development Program can graduate to The International School and once again must attain a high standard of excellence to do so. Kids entering The International School first grade often read at the third-grade level or above, carry on at least simple conversations in a second language, write musical compositions, play the violin or piano, and have studied many subjects in such areas as history, science and geography. Physically, the aspiring students can brachiate many lengths of the ladder nonstop, run at least three miles nonstop, and swim independently. These students are usually five years of age when they apply. (This is The International School of The Evan Thomas Institute.)

The International School first graders attend classes at The Institutes five mornings weekly and receive instruction in courses such as Greek and Latin word roots, analytical geometry, Japanese language and culture, computer science, natural history, gymnastics and ballet.

The School has hosted many distinguished guest lecturers over the years, such as Buckminster Fuller; Dr. Ralph Pelligra, chief medical officer, NASA Ames Research Center; Richard Norton, technical advisor to The Institutes; David Melton, author; Chatham R. Wheat, financial advisor and insurance expert; and Professor Raymond Dart, the distinguished discoverer of Australopithecus africanus dartii. The students' favorite lecturer is Glenn Doman, whose subject is Child Brain Development. The students are not only provided with expertise by the world's leading authority in this area, but with special time with their greatest friend and admirer.

Visiting instructors such as Donald Barnhouse, mathematician (and minister, scholar and TV commentator) and William Johntz, founder, Project Seed, have respectively enriched the mathematics and the advanced mathematics courses by teaching month-long classes in the school.

The last week in June marks the end of a school semester and graduation. This year, the Early Development tiny kids and International School first, second and third graders participated in a Human Development Field Day. The events were sprint crawling and creeping for two- and three-year-olds, marathon creeping (one mile) and marathon brachiation (1000+ feet nonstop as a team relay) for four- and five-year-olds, marathon crawling (two-and-a-half miles) and marathon brachiation (1000+ feet in thirty minutes as a team relay) for the six- and seven-year-olds.

During the Human Development Field Day, the senior students (fourth graders) coached and cheered their younger fellow students and served as officials of the events. In the evening, the first-grade class graduated in caps and gowns in a formal ceremony as a few of their hundreds of achievements were announced:

* reading novels independently
* writing a computer program
* playing a musical instrument in a concert performance
* reading, writing and speaking in a second language
* successfully solving problems in analytical geometry
* running five miles nonstop
* climbing a rope
* designing and executing a gymnastic floor routine
* successfully coaching a younger student in a subject, class or skill
* performing a major responsibility on a daily basis for the benefit of the class

Following the first-grade graduation ceremonies, the senior class hosted the younger students and their families at a reception in their honor.

The following morning at dawn, the senior students arose and entered a community triathlon (a quarter-mile swim, five-mile bike ride, and two-and-a-half mile run done consecutively without stopping). Our eight- and nine-year-olds were challenged by the *twelve and under* category—our girls finished first and fourth; our boys, first, second and fourth.

The senior class also enjoyed a full week of natural history and camping in Bucks County, Pennsylvania, at the Pioneer Institute, culminating in the third annual Voyage of the Raft (RA III) Expedition.

The RA III is a handsome pontoon raft constructed by the students in the second grade. The raft supports a dozen people comfortably and safely. This year the kids themselves navigated this large raft for part of the trip down the Delaware River.

Families and students have come from North America, South America, Europe and Asia to participate in the program of The International School. The school continues to be enriched by the various languages and cultures that have been represented over the years.

We look forward to continuing this tradition, and to welcoming new members from our Off-Campus Program in the challenging new years to come.

> Susan Aisen
> Director,
> The Institute for the
> Achievement of
> Intellectual Excellence
>
> reprinted from
> *The In-Report**

---

* Articles such as these with regard to the On-Campus Program are always sure to draw hundreds of letters from parents all over the world proposing that they move to Philadelphia virtually immediately, in order to enroll their children at the first possible opportunity. Unfortunately, because this is a very small demonstration program, this is neither a very practical or effective solution for them, so we have created the *Off*-Campus Program, of which we speak so often and are so very proud, to help them provide programs such as these for their children in their own homes and their own hometowns. Parents and children who have participated successfully and enthusiastically at this level can then be invited to join the On-Campus Program, if openings occur. A more extensive description of the Off-Campus Program appears on page 266 of the Appendix.

The right to be physically superb is a birthright.

Fumio Tsukada, nine years old.
Photo by Sherman Hines.

5
PHYSICAL INTELLIGENCE

*There is nothing that God hath established
in a constant course of nature, and which
therefore is done every day, but would
seem a miracle, and exercise our
admiration, if it were done but once.*

John Donne, 1627

We people are surrounded by miracles that we see daily and at which we marvel not at all.

It isn't that we don't want to see miracles, it's just that we often don't know when we see one, especially if it's a miracle we see all day, every day.

The human body *is* such a miracle and even more of a miracle is the brain that runs it. This book will sing the praises of those miracles and tell how, by *understanding* these everyday miracles, we can use them to give our kids the opportunity to be physically superb instead of thwarting those miracles through the simple process of not recognizing that they are miracles.

Want some examples?

If you happen to be pregnant at this moment and happen to *know* that you are, try looking at your watch for one minute. Do you know what happened during those sixty seconds? At the end of the sixty seconds, your baby had *a quarter of a million more brain cells than he had when you began counting, sixty seconds earlier.*

Try another?

Like to know what the *capacity* of his little brain will be when he is born?

It will be *ten times* the capacity of the United States National Archives.

What does this mean in intellectual terms? Well, that's another miracle. If you happen to live in Chicago, then when your baby is born, English will be a foreign language to him, no more and no less foreign than French, Italian, German, Spanish or Urdu, just as French is foreign to a child born in Paris today. Then the miracle happens. By three years of age, and without ever laying eyes on a teacher, he will have a totally functional working knowledge of his language. *All the computers in the world hooked together could not carry on a freewheeling conversation in English at the level of any average three-year-old English-speaking tot.*

What does that mean in physical terms? That's another miracle. The U.S. Army and other major armies of the world have spent billions of dollars trying to make a machine that could walk upright and thus travel over all kinds of terrain. Not only have they all failed to invent a two-legged machine that will walk upright, but they have not even been successful in making a *four-legged* machine that will do so efficiently. To this day, the most mobile piece of equipment in any army is called *infantry*. Infantry traverses deserts, crawls through caves, crosses rivers, moves through jungles and climbs mountains.

Interesting that the word *infantry* comes from the word *infant*.

Very appropriate.

The *real* problem in making such a walking machine is not the staggering problem of imitating human arms and legs, although that is a daunting problem indeed. *The real problem is inventing the control mechanism that will direct the walking machine.* That mechanism in the superbly mobile human being is called the human brain.

The relationship between mobility and intelligence is an intimate one and at no time is it as important as it is in babies and tiny children.

In human beings, the urge to move is second only to the urge to breathe. It is at the very root of all other human abilities.

The ability to move, the age at which we are permitted to move, and the manner in which we move play a major role in separating primitive societies from civilized societies—and separating individuals within a civilized society from one another, as we shall see.

If mobility plays such a basic role in our lives and in our culture, why have we not paid more attention to it? This is not a situation in which there are any villains. We simply haven't known.

How, then, have the staff of The Institutes come to these conclusions?

In the days that immediately preceded and followed World War II, the early staff members of what are today called The Institutes for the Achievement of Human Potential had not the foggiest notion of how to make babies physically, intellectually or socially superb.

Indeed, if anybody had proposed such things to us, we would have considered him to be mad. In fact, what we *had* decided to do was considered mad enough in its time.

We were then responsible for the treatment, such as it was, of brain-injured children who ranged in severity from children who were paralyzed, blind, deaf, and speechless and who had been diagnosed as idiots, to children who had minor problems in movement, vision, hearing, speech and learning. They ranged in diffuseness of the brain injury from children who had all of those problems to kids whose injury was so focal as to have only one of those problems.

We had made up our minds that we were going to do something about them. Indeed, we had made up our minds individually and collectively that we were going to set up an objective of making such kids totally well, like other children—or that we were going to spend the rest of our lives trying.

Before World War II few people, if any, had seriously tried to do anything about brain-injured children. They were, in most cases, hidden away in attics or back rooms of nursing homes and dealt with in attitudes that had not changed substantially from the time of Christ and his disciples.

"Master, who did sin, this man, or his parents, that he should be born blind?" (John 9:2).

Indeed, such an attitude persisted well into the twentieth century, and if any man had made any serious attempt to change that attitude, he might well have met with the same disapproval as did Christ when He successfully made the blind man see.

By the years directly preceding World War II, that view had been successfully changed by a handful of pioneers led by Dr. Temple Fay, dean of modern neurosurgery, to the view that brain injury was a physical injury to the brain and not an inherent punishment for earlier sins.

By World War II, the enlightened view was that, while brain injury was a hopeless disease, its victims could sometimes be made into useful or semi-useful cripples. That, we concluded, was not good enough.

While it was clearly better to make useless cripples into useful cripples, it would also clearly be *infinitely* better to make them into non-cripples, or at least so we reasoned, believed and determined.

It was a wild and heretical determination in the late 1940s.

Where should we begin?

If we were going to make brain-injured children well, we would first have to know what well, or normal, or average children were like.

Nobody knew.

It sounds incredible, we know, but the truth was—nobody knew.

Arnold Gesell, Louise Bates Ames and Frances Ilg, and their group at Yale, had made the first serious study of normal children to determine what they did or did not do at various ages. This study became an early classic, and we used those findings as one of the bases for our own study which continues to this day (although taken in directions we would not have dreamed in those days so many thousands of ignorances ago).

What Gesell, Ames and Ilg had done was great as far as it went. The trouble was it didn't go far enough to do us any good except to save us from having to repeat it ourselves.

What they had done was, so to speak, to tell us *everything* that a child did in those all-important years between birth and five years of age.

On the other hand, if we were to make brain-injured children normal, we would have to know a much more important thing.

Of all the thousands of things a well child did in the process of growing up from birth to six, *which things mattered?* In short, of all the multitude of things the baby did, *which things were causes and which things merely results?* Of all the multitudinous things, *which things if removed from his life would prevent him from developing normally?*

Take, as an example, the function of normal walking. If we took a baby at birth and considered all the various physical acts that he did between the time at birth when he moved his arms and legs to the time at six years when he walked, ran and jumped in a beautiful and rhythmic cross-pattern, and examined these functions of moving, wiggling, rolling over, sitting, crawling, somersaulting, creeping, climbing stairs, skipping, hopping, climbing trees, running—which of those things, if taken out of his life, would prevent him from walking? Suppose we never permitted him to sit up. Would this prevent him from walking normally? Suppose he were encouraged to sit up for long periods of time. Would doing so make him walk sooner or walk better, or would it give him a spinal curvature?

We did not know.

Neither, we feel obliged to point out, did anyone else.

We had literally thousands of such questions and no one knew the answers. There is an old saying about what you ought to do if you want something done. We decided to take that advice and do it ourselves.

We did not at the time know that what we were *really* studying was *normal* abilities, *subnormal* abilities and *supernormal* abilities and what *caused* those three states of being.

We did not then realize what they were, nor were we to know for another ten years. It took us another ten years to realize that those abilities at their lowest, average and highest levels are what the world *means* when it talks about "intelligence."

For the first ten years that we studied kids, we studied them wherever and whenever we could find them. We studied ten-year-olds, fifteen-year-olds, four-year-olds, eighteen-month-olds, eighteen-week-olds, eighteen-day-olds, eighteen-hour-olds and we studied babies being born.

We talked to and we studied young women who hoped to have babies, we talked to and studied young women who had just discovered they were pregnant, we talked to and studied young women in their first trimester of pregnancy, second trimester and third trimester, we talked to young women in the labor room who were about to have their first babies and those women who were about to have their eleventh.

We studied babies being born; we studied them ten minutes later. We studied them as they matured.

We studied kids in their cribs, kids in their beds, kids in their playpens, kids in their bathinettes and in their bathtubs. We studied them in their kindergartens and in their classrooms.

We studied them wherever and whenever we could find them. We studied our own kids, each other's kids, our relatives' kids, our friends' kids, our neighbors' kids, our hurt kids and our hurt kids' kids.

We studied American kids and Mexican kids; Canadian kids and French kids; German kids and Italian kids; Luxembourgian kids and Belgian kids; Brazilian kids and Argentinian kids; Venezuelan kids and Japanese kids; Australian kids and Thai kids; Chinese kids and Israeli kids; Iranian kids and Moroccan kids; Egyptian kids and English kids—in short, we observed, talked with, studied, lived with or recorded kids in more than one hundred countries.

We still do.

We studied very sophisticated kids, farm kids, city kids, inner-city kids, desert kids, forest kids, jungle kids, island kids, rich kids, poor kids, middle-class kids, factory kids and so on and so on and so on and so on. Ad infinitum.

We still do.

What have we learned?

We have learned the answers to the vast majority of the questions we had asked.

Perhaps the most important thing we have learned is the intimate relationship between mobility and intelligence.

We have seen the difference between the way things are for human beings—and the way they might be—*and the distance between* are *and* might be *is huge.*

We have come to believe that the way things *could* be is, in point of fact, the way things *should* be, and were intended by nature to be.

By the end of the 1950s we had learned the functions that *mattered* in man. By the beginning of the 1960s we had learned how to measure them although we still had not the foggiest notion that what we knew we were measuring (man's unique abilities) were actually the true measurement of a child's intelligence.

We had found that there were precisely six things that characterized man and made him different from all the other creatures. These six functions were unique to man and all of them were functions of man's uniquely human cerebral cortex or, as it is sometimes called, the neocortex.

Of all the creatures man, and man alone, has been endowed with the unique cerebral cortex—the highest development of the ancient brain and man, and man alone, enjoys the six functions which are the unique functions of his unique cortex.

Three of these functions are motor in nature and are entirely dependent upon the other three, which are sensory in nature.

Man's three unique motor functions are:

1. *To walk, run and jump* in an upright position and in a true cross-pattern with opposite limbs moving together (right arm, left leg—left arm, right leg).
2. *To speak,* in a contrived, invented, symbolic, vocal language at which we have arrived by agreement and convention (English, French, Japanese, or Spanish, for example).
3. *To write,* in a contrived, invented, symbolic, visual language at which we have arrived by agreement and convention (English, French, Japanese, or Spanish, for example).

These three motor skills belong to man, and man alone, and are not shared by the lower creatures. These unique physical abilities are unique to man because they are each a product of man's unique cortex.

These three motor skills are based upon man's three unique sensory skills.

Man's three unique sensory abilities are:

1. *To see,* in such a way as to read that contrived, invented, symbolic, visual language at which we have arrived by agreement and convention.
2. *To hear,* in such a way as to understand that contrived, invented, symbolic, vocal language at which we have arrived by agreement and convention.
3. *To feel,* in such a way as to be able to identify an object by feel alone and without the confirmation of seeing, smelling or tasting it.

These three sensory skills belong to man, and man alone, and are not shared by the lower creatures. These unique sensory abilities are unique to man because they are each a product of man's unique cortex.

Six functions.

It doesn't seem as if these are enough to make the staggering difference between man and the other creatures, these six simple functions—but they are.

Suffice it for now to say that after years of work with thousands of children all over a large part of the earth's surface, we discovered that by measuring those six functions of the human cortex we could measure what is the essence of humanity.

It is these six things that measure not only humanity but the degrees of humanness.

It is in reality those six things which are the neurologist's test of normality. The patient is tested in relation to:

1. Competence in Mobility (walking).
2. Competence in Language (talking).
3. Competence in Manual Ability (writing).
4. Visual Competence (reading and visual understanding).
5. Auditory Competence (hearing and understanding).
6. Tactile Competence (feeling and understanding).

It is competence in these six things that measures success in school.

We came to realize that if you showed us a child who did these things exactly *with* his peers, we would show you a child in school with his peers.

If, however, you showed us a child who did these things *below* his peers, we would show you a child struggling to get into or to stay in school with his peers and to the exact degree that he was below his peers would he stay in school, stay in school at the bottom of his class, or fail to stay in school at all.

If you showed us a child who was totally incapable of doing any one of these six things at all, we would show you a child who was in a "special" school. Indeed, that is precisely who the special schools are for.

1. The child who was completely unable to move by six years of age would be found in the crippled children's school.
2. The child who was completely unable to talk by six years of age would be found in the school for dumb (in the sense of being speechless) children.
3. The child who was unable to use his hands would also be found in the school for crippled children.
4. The child who was totally unable to see would be found in the school for the blind.
5. The child who was totally unable to hear would be found in the school for the deaf.
6. The world has very few human beings who are totally unable to feel in the full sense. Those who are, we find to be totally paralyzed. It is not possible to work or even move without feeling.

If any of the six kinds of children listed above were found in a "normal" school, they were there at the school's forbearance and tolerance.

Most important of all, we found that if a child did these six things at a *higher* level than his peers, then that child was considered to be superior to the exact degree that he did any one of those six things better than his peers.

Finally we found that these six things are life's test of inferiority, averageness or superiority.

In short, we found that superiority in *all* of these things almost invariably resulted in high position in life.

We found that almost invariably if an individual had a high level of *most* of these functions and yet failed in life, the failure was due to a very low level of one or more of these functions.

We found that almost invariably if an individual had a *low* level of most of these six functions and succeeded in life, the success was due to a very high level of one of these six functions.

It had taken ten years on the part of the whole team and uncounted thousands of hours of work, but we at last knew what to measure. It still left us with a very large question.

If these were the correct six things to measure, how precisely did we go about actually measuring them?

Since the average child did not acquire these abilities until six years of age (the age at which the growth of the human brain is virtually complete in a practical sense) it would not permit us to measure a child below six years of age unless he was the rare child who had acquired these skills at a younger age. When we found such children, they were considered superior to the exact degree that they were less than six years old at the time they acquired the skill.

We discovered that a child who could perform these functions at five years of age was almost invariably considered very superior, a child who could do so at four years was a high-level genius, and a child who could do them at three years of age would be considered to have an I.Q. of 200.

Was there a way to trace these functions back to birth and thus make it possible to measure a child at any age?

We shall spare the reader the thousands of questions which had to be answered, the hundreds of blind alleys into which we charged with great enthusiasm only to bang our noses into blank walls, the scores of avenues which *almost* took us where we wanted to go.

We shall not detail the footpaths, roads, dog teams, horses, camels, donkeys, jeeps, trucks, cars, taxis, occasional limousines, buses, trains, single-motored planes, rafts, seaplanes, canoes, helicopters, outriggers, DC-3s, rowboats, "Super Connies," catamarans, DC-4s, barges, 707s, hovercraft, DC-8s, boats, 727s, steamships, 737s, superliners, 747s, or supersonic Concordes which we have walked, ridden or flown in order to visit the individual, family, tribe, community, city, country, state, kingdom, dictatorship, duchy, empire, republic, continent or continents we endured, survived, enjoyed, reveled in or delighted in, over the years.

But all the years and all of our lives, including those of the great men and great women who didn't get to finish the trip—Raymundo Veras, Adelle Davis, Evan Thomas, Mae Blackburn, Temple Fay, Edward LeWinn and others—have also produced a great many answers and among those answers were the answers required to trace these functions back to birth.

We found that each of these six human functions occurred in seven vital stages of the brain beginning at birth and ending at six years of age. We shall study them in detail.

We found that of these six exclusively human types of intelligence, the most basic was mobility intelligence.

Most startling of our discoveries was the fact that excellence in these six forms of intelligence was not *inherited*, as the world had believed was the case, but that excellence in all of them was *acquired*. Happiest of all was the discovery that since they were a product of what *happened* to a baby, high mobility was available to every child whose parents wished to give him or her physical excellence.

The six unique human functions are separate, distinct, and different from each other. They are, however, completely interrelated to and, to a high degree, dependent upon each other, not in the six areas themselves, but in each of the seven stages.

It is useful in understanding this to imagine each of these six functions as if it were a sphere such as a cannon ball. Now imagine that the six of them were chained to each other by a three-foot length of chain so as to form a circle on the ground.

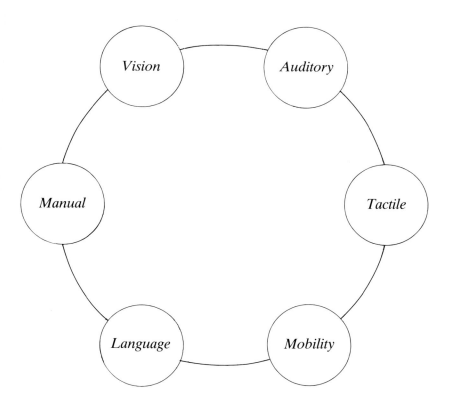

It would be apparent that it would not be possible to lift any one of these spheres very high off the ground without to some degree pulling up the others as well. This is true in life and in inverse proportion to age. As an example, it is not possible to raise a child's ability to move without to some degree raising his ability to see, as well as improving his manual, auditory, tactile and language functions.

Tiny kids want to learn everything there is to learn, and they want to do so *right now*.

Jennifer Patell, twelve months old.
Photo by Jennifer's parents.

6
THE PRINCIPLES OF MEASURING PHYSICAL INTELLIGENCE

There are seven significant stages in a child's life between birth and six years of age. These are the result of seven succeedingly higher levels of the child's brain coming into play successively as brain growth develops.

These seven brain stages govern the child's functions in each of the six uniquely human abilities.

For convenience, we have designated these seven stages I through VII.

We found that these seven stages occur in average children at approximately the same time and at the ages shown in Figure 1, on page 36.

The human brain may be divided anatomically into four separate and distinct sections. (See diagram of The Institutes' Developmental Profile inside the front cover or back cover.)

These four anatomically distinct sections, starting at the bottom are as follows:

STAGE I

MEDULLA

Medulla: (Latin; marrow.) The medulla is the lowest portion of the human brain and lies *over* the spinal cord and *under* the pons and connects them. The medulla is actually divided into two continuous parts. These are the medulla spinalis, which is actually the spinal cord, and the medulla oblongata, which is the lowest part of the human brain and which lies entirely inside the skull.

These two parts of the medulla operate almost as one and are looked upon as one in functional terms. The medulla is shown in red on the diagram of the human brain and the functions that are the primary responsibility of the medulla are colored red on the Developmental Profile.

VII	Child	72 Months	
VI	Little Child	36 Months	
V	Tiny Child	18 Months	
IV	Baby	12 Months	
III	Tiny Baby	7 Months	
II	Infant	2.5 Months	
I	Newborn	Birth	

Figure 1.

STAGE II

PONS

Pons: (Latin; bridge.) That portion of the brain *above* the medulla and *below* the midbrain. The pons contains fiber tracts that connect the medulla with the cerebellum and with upper portions of the brain.

The pons is the portion colored orange on the diagram of the human brain. The pons exercises primary control over those human functions which are colored orange on the Developmental Profile.

STAGE III

MIDBRAIN

Midbrain: That portion of the brain *over* the pons and *under* the cortex, which connects the pons with the cortex.

The midbrain is the part of the schematic drawing of the brain colored yellow. It exercises primary control over those functions shown in yellow on the Developmental Profile.

STAGE IV

INITIAL CORTEX

Cortex: (Latin; rind.) The outer or topmost layer of the brain, consisting principally of neurons. Neurons are the nerve cells that are the structural and functional units of the nervous system.

The human cortex is a vast section of the brain which may not be subdivided in an anatomical sense into distinct stages.

However, we have divided it into four *functional* stages which, while not anatomically distinct, are most certainly developmentally distinct in children and which probably reflect the order of human development since man first appeared on earth.

While we have represented these stages schematically for purposes of clarity as if they were ascending levels in anatomical terms, it is wise to remember that this is not true in a literal anatomical sense.

Stage IV (the initial cortex) is the part colored green on the schematic drawing of the brain. The initial cortex exercises primary control over those functions shown in green on the Developmental Profile.

STAGE V

EARLY CORTEX

Stage V is the part of the schematic drawing of the human brain colored blue. The early cortex exercises primary control over those functions shown in blue on the Developmental Profile. These are essentially the functions of early man.

STAGE VI

PRIMITIVE CORTEX

Stage VI is the part of the schematic drawing of the human brain colored indigo. The primitive cortex exercises primary control over those functions shown in indigo on the Developmental Profile. These are essentially the functions of primitive man.

STAGE VII

SOPHISTICATED CORTEX

Stage VII is the part colored violet on the schematic drawing of the human brain. The sophisticated cortex exercises primary control over those functions shown in violet on the Developmental Profile. These are essentially the functions of modern man as he exists today.

We found that while all of these brain levels exist in a newborn baby at birth, they become functional in successive order from the lowest level of brain (medulla) at birth to the highest level (sophisticated cortex) at six years of age in the *average* child.

THE ELEMENTS OF THE PROFILE

With these pieces of knowledge it was then possible to create a chart containing the six vital and unique human functions to be measured, the levels of brain responsible and the ages at which those functions occurred in average children. Such a chart would look like Figure 2.

By adding the following elements to our chart we then developed what is now well known internationally as The Institutes' Developmental Profile.

The elements added are:

1. A diagram of the human brain with its successive stages of development drawn in.
2. The actual brain function itself in each of the forty-two blocks.
3. A color code to distinguish each of the brain stages and its functions. Since there are seven we decided to use the seven successive colors of the visible-light spectrum, starting at the bottom with the longest visible rays (red) and ending at the top with the shortest visible rays (violet). No artist has yet topped the rainbow for pure beauty of colors.

The full Institutes' Developmental Profile is shown on the inside front and back covers of this book.

The Profile has been used by the staff of The Institutes for the Achievement of Human Potential and many other professional people to measure tens of thousands of children ranging from severely brain-injured to superior.

The Profile actually measures a child's *chronological age* (C.A.) which is a line drawn horizontally across the Profile at his exact age in months. This line shows us where the child *should* be, assuming him to be average.

				WALKING	TALKING	WRITING	READING	HEARING	FEELING
VII	Child	72 Months	Sophisti-cated Cortex						
VI	Little Child	36 Months	Primitive Cortex						
V	Tiny Child	18 Months	Early Cortex						
IV	Baby	12 Months	Initial Cortex						
III	Tiny Baby	7 Months	Midbrain						
II	Infant	2.5 Months	Pons						
I	Newborn	Birth	Medulla and Cord						

Figure 2.

The child is then measured in each of the six functions at the level where he *actually is*. This is called *neurological age* (N.A.).

The Profile has been used with children from scores of nations for the purpose of measuring the child's ability at a point in time so that it may be compared with his ability at a different point in time.

How do we accomplish this?

Let us imagine that on their babies' third birthdays, three mothers each learn about the program of The Institutes and decide they want their children to be intellectually, physically and socially excellent.

Each mother, having learned how to do so, measures her own baby on The Institutes' Developmental Profile before she begins the program.

First, each of the mothers draws a horizontal line from the left side of the Profile to the right, through the bottom of Stage VI, that of the primitive cortex. This represents where he *should* be, as compared to *average* children. This line represents his *chronological age* (thirty-six months).

Now each of the three mothers measures her child in each of the six functions, and draws a line exactly where he actually *is* in these six functions.

For the sake of clarity and illustration, let us suppose that each of the mothers finds that line to be a straight line across the Profile (this is actually very unlikely, since an individual child tends to grow at *different* rates in each of these areas, representing the amount of *opportunity* he has had in each of these six areas).

Nonetheless, for the purpose of clarity, let's assume that each of the lines is perfectly straight across the Profile from left to right, but each is at a different level. This represents each child's *neurological age.*

Child *A's* line goes across the Profile precisely at the bottom of Stage VI. This child's neurological line matches precisely his chronological line, and therefore his neurological age (thirty-six months). matches precisely his chronological age (thirty-six months) and he is exactly like his precisely thirty-six-month-old peers. He can be said to be precisely average in all of the things that matter to human beings. To state it differently, his functional ability or I.Q. would be precisely 100.

Let us suppose that child *B's* line crosses the Profile at exactly the bottom of Stage V. If such is the case, this child's line matches exactly the line of the average eighteen-month-old child, and therefore child *B* has a neurological age of eighteen months. His *neurological* age (eighteen months) is exactly half his *chronological* age (thirty-six months). To state it differently, his functional ability or I.Q. would be precisely 50.

Let us suppose that child *C's* line crosses the Profile at exactly the bottom of Stage VII. If such is the case, this child's line matches exactly the line of the average seventy-two-month-old child and therefore child C has a *neurological* age of seventy-two months. His *neurological* age (seventy-two months) is exactly twice his *chronological* age (thirty-six months.) To state it differently, his functional ability or I.Q. would be precisely 200.

Each of these mothers now knows *precisely* where her child stands in relation to other children of the same age.

If one examines the Profile closely, one will realize that each of the stages

	STAGE	VISUAL	AUDITORY	TACTILE	MOBILITY	LANGUAGE	MANUAL	
72 mos. Child "C"	VII							N.A.
36 mos. Child "A" "A","B","C"	VI							N.A. C.A.
18 mos. Child "B"	V							N.A.
12 mos.	IV							
7 mos.	III							
2.5 mos.	II							
1 mo. Birth	I							

Figure 3.

is divided from the others by a *line* (which in itself has no thickness) but that the stages themselves actually represent an *area* of substantial breadth.

The average child will spend two-and-a-half months in the areas of function controlled by the medulla, four-and-a-half months in the areas of function controlled by the pons, five months in the areas of function controlled by the midbrain, six months in the areas of function controlled by the initial cortex, eighteen months in the areas controlled by the early cortex, thirty-six months in the areas controlled by the primitive cortex, and the rest of his life in the areas controlled by his sophisticated cortex.

It is important to note that as a tiny child enters each new area of function as a result of each successively higher level of brain coming into play, the lower level of brain that he has just left will continue to control those functions for which it is responsible.

The result of this is that he acquires new function as he reaches each new brain level without in any way forsaking or losing the already acquired function. As an example, the child who is able to walk in cross-pattern (which is a function of the primitive cortex) at Stage VI does not lose his ability to crawl (which continues to be a function of the pons) at Stage II.

Now the parents understand the principle that by comparing a child's *neurological age* in mobility with his *chronological age* in mobility we can determine his *mobility intelligence*.

That gives us:

1. The ability to compare his mobility competence with that of his peers, and thus to determine whether he is below average, average or above average in mobility.
2. The ability to compare his mobility intelligence at one time with his mobility intelligence at a later time and thus to determine whether he is growing more slowly than he was earlier, growing at the same rate, or growing faster than he was earlier.

Now that the reader understands the *principles* of measurement, he or she will be able in subsequent chapters to learn the precise details of how to measure and become skilled in doing so.

Most important, now that we understand the principles of measurement (without which there can be no science) we can explore how to *multiply* physical intelligence.

The Institutes' Mobility Development Scale

BRAIN STAGE		TIME FRAME	MOBILITY
VII	SOPHISTI-CATED CORTEX	Superior 36 Mon. Average 72 Mon. Slow 144 Mon.	**Using a leg in a skilled role which is consistent with the dominant hemisphere** *Sophisticated human expression*
VI	PRIMITIVE CORTEX	Superior 18 Mon. Average 36 Mon. Slow 72 Mon.	**Walking and running in complete cross pattern** *Primitive human expression*
V	EARLY CORTEX	Superior 9 Mon. Average 18 Mon. Slow 36 Mon.	**Walking with arms freed from the primary balance role** *Early human expression*
IV	INITIAL CORTEX	Superior 6 Mon. Average 12 Mon. Slow 24 Mon.	**Walking with arms used in a primary balance role most frequently at or above shoulder height** *Initial human expression*
III	MIDBRAIN	Superior 3.5 Mon. Average 7 Mon. Slow 14 Mon.	**Creeping on hands and knees, culminating in cross pattern creeping** *Meaningful response*
II	PONS	Superior 1 Mon. Average 2.5 Mon. Slow 5 Mon.	**Crawling in the prone position culminating in cross pattern crawling** *Vital response*
I	MEDULLA and CORD	Superior Birth to .5 Average Birth to 1.0 Slow Birth to 2.0	**Movement of arms and legs without bodily movement** *Reflex response*

GLENN DOMAN
and
The Staff
of
The Institutes

THE INSTITUTES FOR THE ACHIEVEMENT OF HUMAN POTENTIAL
8801 STENTON AVENUE
WYNDMOOR, PA 19038

7

MULTIPLYING PHYSICAL INTELLIGENCE

Can you actually *multiply* a baby's physical intelligence?
Indeed you can.
How?

You can multiply a baby's physical intelligence by doing the following things:

1. By making sure that he has the fullest opportunity to learn *all* of the wonderful things there are to learn in each of those seven stages as he is taking his developmental journey through the brain.

2. By making sure he doesn't *waste* a moment of his life while he is *enjoying* to the *fullest* his journey to maturity.

How, precisely, do you do that for him?

That is, of course, what this book will discuss in detail, but let's have a quick look at the map of the territory he will cover during his six-year odyssey, beginning at birth and ending when his brain growth is virtually completed, during his sixth year of life.

What we have just seen in The Institutes' Mobility Development Scale is a map of his journey through the Mobility Stages, and here are the possibilities:

1. His journey can be an average one, which is to say he will complete his journey having done the usual things in the usual time and having spent the first six years of his life in the doing of them. He will have entered Stage VII at the age of seventy-two months (and finished touring it at eighty-four months), there to remain with average physical skills for the rest of his life unless some physical, occupational, social or other demand later requires him to ski, climb mountains, parachute or perform some other above average physical function. If such a requirement should occur later, the length of time he takes to learn the new function, the degree of difficulty he encounters, the amount of determination he has to exhibit and the level of skill he attains will all be determined by how above average, average or below average he became physically in those all-important first six years of life.

2. His long trip can be a poorer than average one if through lack of knowledge on his parents' part or other circumstances, he receives less than usual opportunity for mobility and thus does less than the usual things in longer than the usual times which are spent in doing them. If such should prove to be the case, he will have arrived at the end of his sixth year of life without having *completed* all of the physical abilities required of a child by life. If such is the case, he will go through life less physically gracefully and less easily. If special requirements of a physical nature are placed on him as an adult, he will learn how to perform them less easily, will require greater time to learn them and greater determination, and will, in the end, perform them less well. He is unlikely to become an athlete or to excel at sports. He will probably tend to avoid them.

3. His journey can be a superb one: a pilgrimage to the highest levels of the human cortex, an expedition to high adventure; which is to say he can enjoy it beyond measure, learn *all* there is to learn in *all* the areas he will traverse and finish the trip in record time, giving him all the period between when he actually finishes and the eighty-four months of physical brain growth that are available to the average child.

If such is the case, he will go through life gracefully and without effort in a physical sense. As an adult, he need not worry whether he can learn to scuba-dive, water-ski, ski-jump, parachute, run marathons, play tennis, or do aerials, since he probably could have done some of these well when he was five. If as a child he missed some physical activity such as mountain climbing and wishes to learn it as an adult, he will learn it quickly, easily, with little effort, and become as skillful as he wishes to become. He will enjoy physical activities.

How can we make *sure* he will make the trip easily, thoroughly and quickly?

By giving him *opportunity*.

What opportunity? We shall cover in detail the precise opportunities which will make him physically superb at each of the brain stages and in each of the areas which contribute to his physical intelligence: mobility, manual competence and balance.

We shall also point out the things which are to be avoided as hindering his progress toward physical superbness.

Perhaps as important, we shall show the parent *precisely* and *in detail* how to measure the child's growth in mobility and manual intelligence *at every point along the way.*

SECTION TWO

MULTIPLYING YOUR BABY'S PHYSICAL INTELLIGENCE

BY
DOUGLAS DOMAN
AND
BRUCE HAGY
WITH
GLENN DOMAN

Newborns lying on their backs facing the ceiling are *upside down*. They are in a position of total helplessness. Put *your* baby on his *tummy, right-side up*.

Bruce and Tegan Hagy. Tegan is eight weeks old. Photo by James Kaliss.

8
NEWBORNS—RIGHT-SIDE UP OR UPSIDE DOWN

All newborns and tiny babies spend most of their time lying on some surface. For most of them this is a baby carriage, an infant seat, a crib, a walker, a swinging seat, a stroller or a playpen; all of these are restrictive and prison-like. They either prevent the baby from moving at all (in the case of the carriage or the crib) or vastly restrict his movement (in the case of the playpen).

Yet even this is the smaller of the problems we have inadvertently created for our babies.

Even more important is the fact that we almost invariably keep them upside down.

Newborns lying on their backs facing the ceiling are *upside down.* They are in a position of total helplessness.

The almost universal restriction on the newborn's ability to move has resulted from some original errors. If one begins by making a basic error, one can then follow the error by all sorts of procedures which would be correct if it had not been for the original error.

Most babies, beginning with newborns and going up to almost a year of age, spend all of their sleeping hours and a major part of their waking hours upside down and therefore in a position that is both helpless and useless. Human beings are the only creatures that make this mistake.

One sees it most clearly in a hospital nursery. Watch the newborns lying on their backs and notice the totally random, useless and purposeless movements of their arms and legs. If the newborn has fingernails that are long enough he may scratch his face or even his eyes. Surely neither nature nor the baby intends this to happen. Then why does it? The answer is simple. He is upside down : he is as helpless as a brand-new Rolls-Royce would be in the same position.

How did we make the original error of putting our children upside down? Let's ask the nurse why these newborns are on their backs, face up.

We will be told that the babies are on their backs so that the nurse can tell at a glance whether or not they are breathing.

Why would they *not* be breathing?

It all begins with the original error. What is the original error?

At the moment of birth, the baby emerges, having lived for the previous nine months in an environment that has a temperature of just about 100 degrees Fahrenheit.

We bring him into the world in a room which has a temperature of about 70 degrees Fahrenheit for the simple reason that this is the temperature which best suits us. *This* is the original error.

The baby would, of course, freeze in this temperature that suits us.

To keep him from turning blue in a temperature 30 degrees colder than the environment in which he has grown, developed, and thrived for nine months, we must wrap him up very warmly in clothing and blankets.

Now we have added the complication that he might smother in all the blankets we have wrapped him in to keep him from freezing.

Now we must keep him upside down so that we can see his face in order to make sure that he doesn't smother.

Now he is helpless. Belly-up is a classic position of helplessness. It is the position of exposure. It is the position of vulnerability.

All because of an original error.

How *might* it be?

Well, it depends to a large degree on what the word *nursery* actually means.

If the word *nursery* means "a room for the nurses," then we've got it right and we ought to keep it the way it is.

If, on the other hand, the word *nursery* means "a room for the newborns and infants," then we ought to make a room suitable for them.

A *true* nursery would have a temperature of about 90 degrees so that it would be natural to the baby. It would also be more humid so that his skin would not dry out. He could therefore be unrestricted by clothing and blankets and could be practicing movement by being right-side up, which is to say, prone. How would the nurses survive in such an environment? It would seem reasonable that since this room is for newborns, the nurses might wear bikinis. That would make the nursery even more attractive, at least for the dads.

It would also make it a lot happier and more productive place for the newborns to be.

Human babies are the only creatures who are *kept* upside down. Has anyone ever seen a colt, calf, puppy, or kitten lying on its back with its legs up in the air?

How might things be with babies in mobility if we stopped doing cultural things which are stifling and started dealing wisely with our babies at birth?

Do you want to see such foolishness as scratching his own eyes come to a halt? Fine, turn him right-side up instead of on his back and watch it all make sense. Now, as he lies in the prone position, with his soft underbelly protected by the floor and his back protected by his bony skeleton, as nature intended, we will see the reasons for the arm and leg movements. Now, face down as he was intended to be, with all his brain mechanisms right-side up, we see all the movements of arms and legs become great propulsive movements intended to move his body forward. It is as natural and sensible as what occurs if you take a turtle who is upside down, thrashing its arms and legs about, and turn it right-side up.

Was the baby *really* intended to be face down instead of face up?

Put him face down and watch all those random and useless arm and leg movements become crawling movements. We may love to watch him face up, but *he* wants to get *moving* along the ancient road to walking, and that road begins here.

It is also precisely the fact of being face down on the floor that gives him the need for the function of holding his head up to see, and the structure required to do so.

Are there any societies in which babies do have an opportunity to move freely at birth?

Glenn Doman describes one such:

I remember the first time I was visiting Eskimos in the Arctic in the late 1960s. I was feeling just a touch adventuresome and a bit swash-buckling to be in a temperature of 54 degrees below zero. Then for the first time in a number of years I thought about my "Aunt" Gussie Mueller, who was my mother's closest girlhood friend. In 1920 or 1921 Aunt Gussie had gone to Point Barrow, Alaska and spent several years there as a nurse in a hospital unit. I believe that it was as close to the North Pole as any non-Eskimo woman had ever been. I remember that until I was grown-up, I believed that Aunt Gussie had long hair all over her body except her eyes, nose, and mouth. My only memory of her had been from photos of her at Point Barrow in a huge fur parka and mukluks which had seemed to me to be growing on her.

Aunt Gussie visited The Institutes in the middle 1970s and I was wise enough to make a tape of her telling about her nursing experiences with the Eskimos of Point Barrow in the early 1920s.

This is the story she told:

Among this particular tribe of Eskimos it was common for the Eskimo women to have babies while on the trail. Igloos used on the trail while hunting were very warm inside and when a mother had a baby she would do so in a kneeling position; the baby was born onto the warm fur rugs that covered the floor of the igloo.

Primitive women the world over have their babies in either a kneeling, a squatting, or a sitting position astride a hammock. This is a far more sensible position in which to have a baby since the "civilized" position of being supine with legs cocked up is more painful and more difficult for mother and baby alike. This position hampers the musculature required to help the birth process and does not even use gravity to assist.

When the U.S. Hospital Team arrived we insisted on stopping such "primitive" practices and insisted on the Eskimo women having their babies in the hospital we had built, and in the usual civilized manner. The Eskimo women reluctantly agreed to this but absolutely insisted that at birth the newborn be placed naked and prone on the naked mother's hip — at which time the newborn would find his way up his mother's body by crawling and would find his way to the breast where he would feed.

In our society the average infant does not begin to crawl until two-and-a-half months of age. We may now conclude that in mobility Eskimo newborns are genetically superior to other babies, or we may conclude that we non-Eskimos deny our babies the opportunity to move early enough.

We prevent them from doing so by swaddling them in clothing that makes movement difficult or impossible.

We extend this error by putting newborns in carriages, cribs and "playpens" which are, in fact, prisons.

Most important (in a negative way), we put them entirely upside down so that movement is impossible in any event.

What *should* we do?

We should create an ideal mobility environment for them at each stage of their mobility development.

How to do that is described precisely in each of the following chapters.

When the day comes that your newborn's reflexive movements push him one inch or two forward on the floor, your spirit should erupt with the joy of having witnessed your newborn move independently for the first time in his life. Sweep him up into your arms and have a joyous celebration!

Joia Ingram is sixteen days old and displays random arm and leg movements typical of a newborn at Stage I in Mobility. Her mom, Van Ingram, is an

The Institutes' Mobility Development Scale

BRAIN STAGE		TIME FRAME	MOBILITY
VII	SOPHISTI-CATED CORTEX	Superior 36 Mon. Average 72 Mon. Slow 144 Mon.	**Using a leg in a skilled role which is consistent with the dominant hemisphere** *Sophisticated human expression*
VI	PRIMITIVE CORTEX	Superior 18 Mon. Average 36 Mon. Slow 72 Mon.	**Walking and running in complete cross pattern** *Primitive human expression*
V	EARLY CORTEX	Superior 9 Mon. Average 18 Mon. Slow 36 Mon.	**Walking with arms freed from the primary balance role** *Early human expression*
IV	INITIAL CORTEX	Superior 6 Mon. Average 12 Mon. Slow 24 Mon.	**Walking with arms used in a primary balance role most frequently at or above shoulder height** *Initial human expression*
III	MIDBRAIN	Superior 3.5 Mon. Average 7 Mon. Slow 14 Mon.	**Creeping on hands and knees, culminating in cross pattern creeping** *Meaningful response*
II	PONS	Superior 1 Mon. Average 2.5 Mon. Slow 5 Mon.	**Crawling in the prone position culminating in cross pattern crawling** *Vital response*
I	MEDULLA and CORD	Superior Birth to .5 Average Birth to 1.0 Slow Birth to 2.0	**Movement of arms and legs without bodily movement** *Reflex response*

GLENN DOMAN
and
The Staff
of
The Institutes

THE INSTITUTES FOR THE ACHIEVEMENT OF HUMAN POTENTIAL
8801 STENTON AVENUE
WYNDMOOR, PA 19038

9
MULTIPLYING YOUR BABY'S PHYSICAL INTELLIGENCE

STAGE I, THE MEDULLA AND CORD

Mobility Competence

CLASS: Newborn.
BRAIN STAGE: Medulla.
PROFILE COLOR: Red.
FUNCTION: Movement of arms and legs without mobility.
AVERAGE AGE: This function is present in an average newborn at birth.
DESCRIPTION: Starting at birth and improving until two and a half months of age, the average infant is able, when placed in the prone position, to move his arms and legs, but is unable to move from point A to point B.

He has movement of his parts, but he does not have mobility.

PURPOSE: The purpose of the ability to move arms and legs without mobility is to perfect this reflex ability and to bring it under *volitional* control as an indispensable prerequisite to crawling.

To state it differently, the purpose is to promote brain growth in the medulla to the point where the next higher level of brain, the pons, can take over *its* function, crawling.

When the newborn is placed on the floor in the *belly-down position,* the random movement of arms and legs will begin almost immediately. These random movements are entirely reflexive in nature and occur without thought.

These reflexive movements entail the flexion and extension of arms and legs and the movement of hands and feet. The newborn's brain is learning precisely how it feels to move his arms and legs. When he is placed face down on the floor (the prone position), instead of being on his back (the supine position), he will inevitably find himself pushing his hands and feet against the floor.

With repetition and practice, he perfects these movements of arms and legs, the movements become propulsive in nature and, pushing against the floor, he will find that these random movements will push his body backward, to the right, to the left, or forward. He will find that, since his head and his eyes are in front of his body, it is advantageous to *reproduce* those movements that result in pushing him forward. He has learned *how it feels* to move forward.

Knowing how it *feels* to perform any act—from the simplest to the most complex—is the prerequisite to doing it well.

Since this is so, the newborn has now learned the most important lesson in movement and has now done all the homework necessary for him to begin crawling, and to move to Stage II.

Some newborns will learn these lessons very quickly and move through this stage very quickly, having learned all there is to learn in a very short time. These newborns will have a very high mobility intelligence.

Other newborns will move through this vital area of brain growth very slowly, learning what is to be learned very poorly. These babies will have a low mobility intelligence.

What will make this dreadfully important difference?

The Brain Grows by Use

Brain growth and development are a pure product of use. The greater the use of the sensory pathways and the motor pathways of the brain in a given period of time, the greater is the physical brain growth that takes place. *The brain grows by use in exactly the same way as the muscles grow by use.*

There are a great number of brilliant neurophysiological experiments with animals that prove this to be so beyond question. Prominent among them are those by Boris Klosovskii a half century ago, by David Krech in more recent times and by Marian Diamond and many others at the present time. The work of The Institutes with thousands of children demonstrates clearly that what the neurophysiologists have demonstrated with animals is true in a very practical way with human beings.

The brain grows by use because *function determines structure* (just as lack of function results in lack of structure).

How quickly a newborn learns to move his arms and legs purposefully rather than randomly will determine how quickly and how well the musculature he uses in doing so will develop and, much more importantly, how well and how quickly the sensory and motor areas of his brain that *control* such functions will develop.

This is a result of how *often* he has the opportunity to do so. It is fascinating and perhaps most important to realize that the younger he has an ideal floor environment to move on, the fewer number of times it is necessary to do so in order to bring about the brain growth and development required to reach the next higher level of brain function.

This is demonstrated conclusively by the tragic and all-too common a story of the baby who has been secretly chained by psychotic parents to a bedpost in an attic and who remains there for many years. When at last discovered, such a child is without speech, intellect or physical function.

In a recent case, a nine-year-old girl had been confined in a closet all her life and when discovered was not only found to be speechless and without intellect, but was physically the size of a two-year-old.

She was *not* locked in the closet because she was an idiot, but was instead an idiot because she was locked in a closet.

Sane parents do not chain children to bedposts in attics even if they *are* idiots. They seek help.

The brain grows at a staggering speed from conception to birth, at a tremendous speed from birth to thirty months, at a high speed from thirty months to six years, and extremely slowly thereafter.

It is easy to see, therefore, that from birth through six years of age, every succeeding year of life gives *less* brain growth than the preceding months.

It hardly seems necessary to point out that the earliest months, weeks and days are the most precious of all.

How then can parents be sure that their newborns, infants and babies have the very best chance to use these abilities as early as possible and as often as possible?

How quickly the newborn will perfect the movement of his arms and legs and move on to the next stage of his mobility development is a product of the amount of opportunity he has to be on his stomach, on the floor.

If we increase the number of hours a newborn is free on the floor while a newborn, we decrease the number of days he is on the floor as a baby.

Even more important, we will also speed his brain growth and development by doing so.

The glorious (in its presence) and tragic (in its absence) fact is that brain growth is a result of use.

NOT ONLY IS THIS TRUE IN THIS, THE FIRST BLOCK OF THE INSTITUTES' MOBILITY DEVELOPMENT SCALE, BUT IT IS TRUE IN EVERY ONE OF THE SEVEN BLOCKS.

This is arguably the most important piece of information this world has yet discovered. What has happened as a result of using this invaluable knowledge is that parents of thousands of children all over the world have increased the brain growth of their children and, as a consequence, literally *multiplied* both the intelligence and the competence of their children.

How did they do this? Quite simply.

By putting their children on the floor with greater frequency and duration than the average child.

The less a child is on the floor, the more difficult movement becomes.

The problem compounds itself because newborns can rapidly gain weight. When you look at it mathematically, what happens to the baby is awesome. It is common that by two months of age the average baby has gained 2.6 pounds, which is 34 percent above his body weight at birth.

That would be like the average woman of 125 pounds gaining 43 pounds in two months. How would *you* feel about going out for a jog having gone from 125 pounds to 168 pounds in two months? Would you feel like moving a lot under these circumstances?

Our culture teaches that a fat baby is a healthy baby.

But Institutes' babies, because they are given the opportunity to move, are big and heavy, but never fat. Grab one of our babies by the arms or legs, and you feel muscle! No rolls around thighs, belly and arms. Because our babies are moving right off, all the breast milk they take in is converted to muscle, not fat. Handsome, more capable babies are the result.

There would be absolutely nothing wrong with any newborn spending as many as twenty-four hours a day on the floor—in truth, it would be a *splendid* idea.

Arnold Gesell, that early studier of babies, said long ago, "The floor is the child's athletic field." Well said.

Gesell, who saw the floor as a prime means of allowing the child maximum physical development, neither knew, nor had any reason to know, that even more important than the physical growth was the brain growth and development that resulted.

It is particularly important, therefore, that newborns be given the opportunity to move immediately, at birth.

At The Institutes, all of our mothers put their newborns on their tummies at birth (which is something we learned from the Eskimos and Aunt Gussie).

Wherever the birth may occur—in the delivery room, the birthing unit, or at home—our moms arrange in advance with their obstetricians and midwives that, at the moment of birth, their naked babies will be placed on their naked tummies.

The babies then and there have the chance to move on the warm, smooth, pliable surface of Mom's tummy to her breast. Dozens of our mothers have described the joy of seeing their newborns move at birth.

This process is not as startling as it may seem. By only eight weeks of fetal life, the embryo has well-defined arms and legs. Not only that, but he moves his arms and legs as he "swims" across mother's uterus. Not until later, at about four to four-and-a-half months of fetal life, does Mom begin to feel him moving.

But, as all mothers know, with each day of pregnancy the movements of the baby become more apparent until, of course, moms begin to complain of their babies "kicking" here and "slugging" there!

Both Mom and Dad love to place their hands on Mom's tummy and feel the baby moving constantly, as if to say, "Let me out!"

Babies, at birth, have been in training for crawling for seven months! All those intrauterine arm and leg movements are so that at birth they can start moving. The musculature and structural development in utero coupled with the neurological control system make the capacity to move existent at birth. It is a continuum—prenatal through to postnatal!

Of course, it's not as easy as it may seem to give a newborn opportunity to crawl at birth. Putting baby on Mom's tummy at birth is the easy part.

Many midwifery manuals now recommend it; however, if you are staying in the hospital, it becomes increasingly more difficult for your newborn to have opportunity to move. Nurses conspire to keep the newborns near them, on their backs, in the nursery—why not? Who *doesn't* love them? However, you must arrange to outsmart those kindly nurses!

The fact is this: babies are born with everything they need to move. The sooner they get to use their abilities, the more rapidly they develop, but each day that passes with their being denied the opportunity to move, the longer it will take them to do so.

Now let's see how to create an ideal opportunity for your newborn to learn to move and thus develop his brain using the three sensory pathways and three motor pathways. . . .

In creating this ideal opportunity, three words become your key to success: *frequency, intensity,* and *duration.*

Frequency:	How often during the day you do each activity.
Intensity:	In mobility, this means how far he moves; in manual competence, it means how much weight he bears; in balance, it means how vigorously you do each activity.
Duration:	The length of time you do each activity.

See how sensible and sane this recipe for your baby's superb physical development is—simply do *everything* you do with him in a physical sense with *increased* frequency, intensity and duration, and you will soon have a most physically competent child.

THE MOBILITY COMPETENCE PROGRAM—STAGE I: INGREDIENTS FOR SUCCESS

We begin by creating an ideal environment for your baby, one in which the movement of his arms and legs can occur freely with the greatest opportunity for converting random movement of limbs into a means of forward propulsion.

This ideal environment is the floor—not just any floor, but a floor that is:

1. Safe
2. Clean
3. Warm
4. Smooth
5. Pliable
6. Flat

You can make your baby's environment *safe* by making sure that he has no access to open or uncovered electrical outlets, so that he cannot shock himself. Check to see that there are no lamps or other items of furniture that he might grab and pull over onto himself inadvertently, and that there are no splinters on furniture, floor, or any surface he may touch.

It's obvious you will not want to have unprotected heaters of any sort about on which he might burn himself. It's a good idea to get accustomed to checking the safety of his environment now, while he's making his random movements, so you're in the habit of doing so when he's moving somewhere on purpose!

You can make your baby's environment clean by wiping the surface he crawls on with a disinfectant that will not irritate his tender skin. Mild soap and water are always best for cleaning purposes, and rubbing alcohol is quite sufficient for disinfecting.

If we are to give the newborn freedom to move his arms and legs, we cannot confine him in blankets or restrictive clothing. Instead, *we must warm his immediate environment.*

In cold climates, windows and doorways should be sealed carefully to eliminate all drafts.

The floor surface itself should be warm.

If the floor is by its nature cold, place one or more infrared bulbs as high in the room as possible so as to cover the greatest amount of floor space (and protect your baby from burn from a bulb placed too close to him). While the wattage is high, they are much less expensive to buy and work much more efficiently than space heaters, since they heat the surface on which they shine rather than the intervening air. They will warm both the floor and your newborn.

The newborn's floor should be smooth.

This is particularly important because we want to make it as easy as possible for him to learn to move. The smoother the surface on which your baby is placed, the easier it will be for him to move as a result of his reflexive arm and leg movements. His body will slide easily in response to the reflexive pulling and pushing movements.

Surfaces covered with naugahyde, leatherette and vinyl are smooth, thus minimizing friction and making movements easier. They provide a skin-like surface that permits the newborn's elbows and knees to get traction. Very *slippery* surfaces such as linoleum can sometimes be *too* smooth, and thus the newborn slips and slides too much.

The naugahyde-type material must be pulled tightly across a hard surface, such as plywood, and glued or stapled down, or it will fold over itself as the newborn moves his arms and legs; these folds create little "hills" that are impossible for a newborn to get over.

Up to the time of birth, newborns have been living in a pliable world that "gives" as they move about, bending and straightening their arms and legs in utero. They find it easiest to move on a similar, *pliable* surface. Pliable vinyl and naugahyde can be stretched across and secured directly on top of carpeting. The advantage is twofold: the carpet helps provide insulation so the floor is warmer; and the cushion of the carpet provides just enough pliability to facilitate traction but not so much as to create "valleys" for the baby to crawl out of, or "hills" to be climbed.

Since the objective is to make movement as easy as possible for your newborn, *the floor needs to be flat* (level). Your newborn should not be trying to move up any slopes since this would be too difficult and discourage his efforts to move.

An ideal way to make movement easy is by using an infant crawling track.

The Infant Crawling Track

Over the years we have developed a single environment that incorporates *all* of the preceding requirements as well as some additional advantages. It is called the Infant Crawling Track.

The track is wide enough to enable newborns to move their arms and legs easily, yet narrow enough to enable them to push off the sides with their feet. This makes movement easier.

Because the track is straight, the newborn moves forward and doesn't waste time circling to the left or right, which is common for newborns to do. These circling movements can frustrate babies, because they can neither predict nor control where they're going.

The track is made of plywood or hardwood, with one inch of foam rubber covering the inside of the sides and the floor. Naugahyde is secured to the foam rubber, and the result is a well-insulated, pliable surface.

The protective sides also create a barrier against drafts and protect the newborn from being accidentally bumped by adults and older children while he is on the floor.

The surface is easily cleaned and stays cleaner because of the protective side.

The instructions for constructing a crawling track are included at the end of this book, in the section called "Equipment You Can Build and Make for Your Baby," in Appendix I, pages 250 and 251.

How quickly your newborn learns to crawl, and thus to develop his brain, is an unadulterated product of how splendid his environment for mobility is, and how much time he gets to spend in that environment.

It is important, therefore, that Dad makes his crawling track before Baby is delivered. (Too many parents have regretted waiting till the last minute. Once the baby is born, there's usually no time for Dad to be running off to the basement or seeking out carpenters.)

An added advantage to the crawling track is its portability.

All of our parents make one section of their track short and portable. It can easily be moved into any room in the house, or put in the trunk of the car for trips. You take your own clean, warm, safe floor with you, wherever you go!

One Japanese lady on our staff delivered her baby in a Philadelphia hospital, and took the three-foot-long, portable part of the track with her. The morning after the birth, the track lay beside her on her bed with her son,

Yuuki, crawling in it. The nurses were astonished by the innovation.

Miki explained that the Japanese live on the floor, and the tracks are an old Japanese custom (creative geniuses, these staff moms of ours!) You may find it equally helpful to discover and adopt the track as an old custom of *your* baby's ancestors.

Because all of our newborns are "Eskimo babies" and crawl at birth, the quantity of their daily crawling constantly increases.

The more they have opportunity to crawl, the closer they come to actually using crawling as a means of transportation.

Our newborns increase the quantity of their daily crawling by about *one foot a day!*

In other words, they crawl a total of one foot the first day after birth, a total of two feet the second day, a total of ten feet the tenth day, and so on. This guide has worked well, and has been most effective.

If you wish to *speed* the process even more, or if your newborn proves to be a slow mover as some are, owing to a number of reasons, you might like to give him the assistance of gravity by using a section of his crawling track as an inclined plane. The use of *the inclined plane* happened first in the late 1940s when the staff of The Institutes invented it to speed the mobility development of completely paralyzed babies.

When infants are not able to move, it is because gravity is too strong for them to defy. The force of gravity pulls us all down to the earth's surface every minute of our lives, creating friction and weight. The inclined plane, in the form of an inclined crawling track, enlists the force of gravity to aid the infant, rather than to defeat him.

We can use one section of his crawling track as an inclined plane by raising one end and producing a gentle incline.

Now, gravity pulls the baby down the track, becoming a friend rather than an enemy. The slightest movement of arms and legs creates forward movement. Formerly unsuccessful arm and leg movements become purposeful propulsive movements. As a result, forward crawling is developed much more rapidly than is usual.

Keep your newborn's track inclined until he begins to crawl on the flat floor, when the incline will no longer be necessary.

Adjusting the angle of the track is important.

The objective is to make movement successful. Obviously, if one end were lifted high enough, the newborn would simply *slide* forward. This would frighten him, and teach him nothing.

The angle should be only high enough to make it easier for him to move. It should actually be the smallest one which will result in a tiny bit of forward motion anytime he uses his arms or legs in a propulsive way.

Whether you use the inclined plane in *addition* to the crawling track or just the crawling track, he will learn to move his arms and legs purposefully and thus begin crawling.

Sleeping on the Floor

We have also discovered that newborns move a great deal in their sleep.

This is not so surprising, considering that newborns sleep many hours a day. *Just before they fall asleep, during their sleep, and just as they awake are all prime times for newborns' crawling.*

How often has a mother gone into her baby's room, only to find him scrunched against the headboard of the crib?

How did he get there? He crawled!

Years ago, the staff and moms realized this. Now, as it turns out, it has become more and more the style for couples to put their mattress on the floor, and to sleep on the floor.

At The Institutes, parents place their newborn's crawling track on the floor next to their own bed.

Although the prime purpose of this is to permit the baby much greater opportunity to crawl, moms also find this arrangement most convenient for them.

The newborn is right there under the watchful eyes of his parents, and there is no need to jump up and check on his well-being. Nursing during the night is greatly simplified—just turn over, pick your baby up, and nurse! Sit up and change him, then put him back in the track!

It's easier, safer, and *superb* for his mobility.

During the first few months of life, it was not uncommon for Marlowe Doman (Douglas Doman's son and Glenn Doman's grandson) to crawl five to ten feet a night.

What the MOBILE Baby Should Wear . . .

Swaddling babies in many layers of clothing makes it difficult (if not impossible) for them to move their arms and legs. Such a situation is just the opposite of what we are proposing: unlimited opportunity to move arms and legs so they can develop bodily movement.

Your newborn should wear a minimum amount of clothing so that his arm and leg movement is not in the least restricted.

He needs to receive the tactile stimulation of feeling his skin against the track surface, and to feel his body moving on the floor.

A diaper and a short-sleeved T-shirt are the best of fashion in this instance! Wearing only these two things permits him to use the "rubbery" consistency of his skin to get traction on the smooth floor surface. At the same time, you don't want too much traction; keep the T-shirt and diaper on so his heavy chest and tummy still slide along the floor. The real power in crawling comes from digging the toes and knees into the floor and pushing off, so toes and knees must remain bare.

"Become Japanese for a While"

The final and now most important point about the ideal floor environment (considering you've done everything the right way up till now,

64

Newborns move a great deal in their sleep. Just before they fall
asleep, during their sleep, and just as they awake, are all
times for newborns to crawl.

Newborn Isolda Maauad sleeps in her track on the
floor next to her parents, Federica and José.

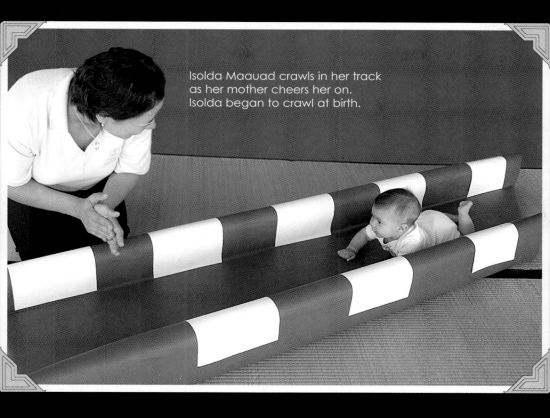

Isolda Maauad crawls in her track
as her mother cheers her on.
Isolda began to crawl at birth.

Begin early—be a cheerleader for your child when he's on the floor and in his crawling track!

The crawling track is raised high enough
to make crawling easier for Isolda.
She crawls down the track with her
mom's encouragement.

and why wouldn't you?) is that your newborn's attitude toward the floor will be a direct reflection of your own.

If you regard the floor as a strange and alien place for your newborn, he will find it strange and alien. Moreover, if your newborn learns that Mom and Dad are absent when he is on the floor, he will associate the floor with loneliness and isolation.

You are everything to your new baby—love, warmth, nourishment, protection, happiness and information. If your newborn is on the floor, you should be, too. *You can't expect your newborn to like the floor if you don't.* Be with your baby on the floor. Become Japanese for a while. Eat, sleep, play, teach, and do everything on the floor. If you are enthusiastic about your baby's being on the floor, and see it as the best place for him to develop physically, then he will reflect that attitude.

And when the day comes (which may well be the first day of your newborn's life) that his reflexive movements push him one inch or two forward on the floor, your spirit should erupt with the joy of having witnessed your newborn move independently for the first time in his life. Sweep him up into your arms and engulf him in such a joyous celebration that his only reaction can be, "Wow, I can't wait to get back down there and do it again so that this happens to me another time!"

This heroic feat is the first step toward the next stage of his mobility development.

BUT IF, AFTER ALL WE'VE SAID, YOU STILL DON'T FEEL COMFORTABLE ABOUT HAVING YOUR NEWBORN ON THE FLOOR, YOU SHOULD DEFINITELY NOT PUT HIM THERE.

Mothers and dads should never do anything with their babies that they are not entirely comfortable with themselves. They should follow their own instincts and not do anything they don't want to do with their babies, because *we know it won't work!*

One thing we know. We know babies.

Babies are smart enough to know when Mom is comfortable and when she's not. Even newborns sense this and, if she's uncomfortable, do not enjoy what they're doing—*whatever it is,* if Mom's uncomfortable, then Baby won't do it happily or well.

By the way, providing opportunity to move on a surface that would make movement difficult (a compromise such as a soft bed or a thick shag carpet) would not only waste valuable time, but would teach the newborn that movement is much more difficult than in fact it is!

But let's assume that you're like the great majority of the other readers of this book, and feel entirely comfortable about keeping the baby on the floor (and can hardly wait to start with your own baby right now). By combining all of the elements that are guaranteed to make your baby successful: a good, warm, clean, pliable, flat, smooth, safe environment; a T-shirt and diaper for "best-dressed" attire; and getting right down there on the floor with him AND ENJOYING IT, you can get off to the very best start. Add to these ingredients for success the basics of *frequency, intensity* and *duration,* and we have the ideal program to help your baby learn to move!

Frequency:	We propose that *at least* ten times a day you get down on the floor with your newborn and encourage and cheer him on as he moves.
Intensity:	Watch how far and how fast your baby crawls on the floor—the crawling track can easily be marked on the sides every six inches, to monitor his movements.
Duration:	A newborn should have a *minimum* of four waking hours daily to move in his track or on the floor. Ideally, he should also spend all of his sleeping hours in the track.

THE GOAL AT THIS LEVEL IS FOR YOUR NEWBORN TO CRAWL TWO TO THREE FEET NONSTOP ON THE FLAT FLOOR OR TRACK.

Conclusions

Remember that getting to Stage II of brain growth is an unadulterated product of how often your newborn has opportunity to try to crawl and is rewarded, which is to say, loved for his effort.

Remember also that if we are going to state a child's mobility intelligence, we have to measure his mobility competence against that of other kids his age. If your child is functioning, in a mobility sense, at five weeks of age in precisely the same way as does an average infant of ten weeks, then we should have to call this a mobility intelligence of 200.

Does it seem unlikely that such a simple process as we have described could, in so short a time, bring about such a dramatic result? If it seems so, you will be interested in knowing that by using the precise same process, increased *only* in frequency and duration, thousands of our mothers of brain-injured kids have brought their own children from the total paralysis of brain injury to Stage II of mobility competence.

The more you give your newborn opportunity to do so, the more physically effective he will be, the more his brain will develop, the higher his mobility intelligence will be, and the sooner he will arrive at Stage II and the use of his pons.

When a newborn actually begins to crawl as a means of transportation, which is to say that crawling goes from being a simple bodily function to becoming a means of getting about, his newborn days are just about over. He has learned about all there is to learn about mobility from the medulla.

A good indicator is that he can, and does, crawl two to three feet with only a brief stop here and there. This does not happen in a flash, but may require ten minutes' time. When this happens, you color him orange (on the Profile) and record the fact that he is now operating from that level of the brain known as the pons. These are all the credentials he needs to continue his newfound function of crawling until he perfects it.

If he is exactly two-and-one-half months old, he has a mobility intelligence of exactly 100. Now you can find *your* baby's exact mobility intelligence by consulting the chart that follows.

Of course, you should expect this only if you purchased this book before your baby was born and have followed it very carefully up to this point.

Regardless of his age, it is a giant accomplishment to crawl for the first time. *He has made the largest single mobility gain he will ever make.* He has gone from the immobile world of the plant kingdom to the exciting and mobile world of the animal kingdom.

Rejoice in his mobility.

	Mobility Intelligence	
	LEAVING STAGE I, THE MEDULLA **ENTERING STAGE II, THE PONS**	
AGE (in weeks)	**MOBILITY** **INTELLIGENCE ****	**OUR ADVICE**
Three	361	World's record?
Four	271	You are doing
Five	217	a superb job.
Six	180	
Seven	155	
Eight	135	Keep up the
Nine	120	splendid
Ten	108	job you are doing!
Ten and one-half (2½ mos., or 74 days)	100	He is exactly average.
Eleven	98	Give him more
Twelve	90	opportunity to move.
Thirteen	83	
Fourteen	77	Give him a lot
Fifteen	72	more opportunity.
Sixteen	67	Give your child immediate
Seventeen	63	and extraordinary opport-
Eighteen	60	unity to move, move, move.
Nineteen	57	
Twenty	54	
Twenty-one	51	
Twenty-two	49	If your child is below 50 in manual intelligence, waste no time in seeking professional help.

* The child's mobility intelligence is determined by dividing the average age at which a child reaches this stage by your child's age, e.g., 74 days (average child enters Pons) divided by 42 days (age at which your child performs this function). 74 ÷ 42 days = 1.8 *or* M.I. = 180.

Do you remember when, as a child, your mother dressed you up to go out and play in the snow?

First the "long-johns," then the corduroy pants, then the flannel shirt—next, two pairs of socks followed by a wool sweater and full snowsuit—then the scarf around your neck, the beanie cap with the snowsuit hood over it and tied beneath your chin; finally, the shoes and rubber boots that took forever to pull on—and last, the mittens with clips that attached them to the jacket.

You'd go outside and walk around like the Abominable Snowman! It took a half an hour just to learn how to move in that outfit. Let's not do that to our babies on the floor. Let's keep the environment warm so they're free to move and explore the world they want so desperately to learn about.

The Institutes' Manual Development Scale

GLENN DOMAN
and
**The Staff
of
The Institutes**

BRAIN STAGE		TIME FRAME	MANUAL COMPETENCE
VII	SOPHISTI-CATED CORTEX	Superior 36 Mon. / Average 72 Mon. / Slow 144 Mon.	**Using a hand to write which is consistent with the dominant hemisphere** *Sophisticated human expression*
VI	PRIMITIVE CORTEX	Superior 18 Mon. / Average 36 Mon. / Slow 72 Mon.	**Bimanual function with one hand in a skilled role** *Primitive human expression*
V	EARLY CORTEX	Superior 9 Mon. / Average 18 Mon. / Slow 36 Mon.	**Cortical opposition bilaterally and simultaneously** *Early human expression*
IV	INITIAL CORTEX	Superior 6 Mon. / Average 12 Mon. / Slow 24 Mon.	**Cortical opposition in either hand** *Initial human expression*
III	MIDBRAIN	Superior 3.5 Mon. / Average 7 Mon. / Slow 14 Mon.	**Prehensile grasp** *Meaningful response*
II	PONS	Superior 1 Mon. / Average 2.5 Mon. / Slow 5 Mon.	**Vital release** *Vital response*
I	MEDULLA and CORD	Superior Birth to .5 / Average Birth to 1.0 / Slow Birth to 2.0	**Grasp reflex** *Reflex response*

**THE INSTITUTES FOR
THE ACHIEVEMENT OF
HUMAN POTENTIAL**
8801 STENTON AVENUE
WYNDMOOR, PA 19038

MULTIPLYING YOUR BABY'S PHYSICAL INTELLIGENCE

STAGE I, THE MEDULLA AND CORD

Manual Competence

CLASS: Newborn.
BRAIN STAGE: Medulla.
PROFILE COLOR: Red.
FUNCTION: Grasp reflex.
AVERAGE AGE: This function is present in an average newborn at birth.
DESCRIPTION: At the time of birth, the newborn's hands are almost always clenched into fists, and the opening and closing of them is entirely random.

If one inserts one's index finger into a newborn's hand and the other index finger into the other hand, the newborn will clench the fingers tightly. This is known as the grasp reflex.

If the adult now slowly lifts his arms, the newborn will continue to maintain his grasp on the adult fingers; it is possible to lift him entirely off the bed or floor in this way. He clings to the fingers much in the manner of a baby gorilla clinging to his mother's hair and body. He does so for the same reason.

However, as Sir W. S. Gilbert pointed out about a century ago, "Things are seldom what they seem."

The newborn appears to be determined to hang on. Such is not the case. The truth is that he is incapable of letting go.

Is the grasp reflex without purpose? Good grief, no! Like all reflexes, it is of great importance.

PURPOSE: The newborn is functioning at the reflex level of the medulla precisely *because* he has not yet reached high enough levels of brain control to perform useful acts at a conscious level. This is *why* the grasp reflex exists.

It is there precisely so that he can hold on to his mother without conscious thought, exactly as the bird holds onto the branch it is sleeping on. Because the bird is asleep, it must do so reflexively, rather than consciously.

The significance of the grasp reflex is not the ability to grasp an object, but rather, the *inability to let go*.

It is a developmental reflex. This means that as higher brain stages mature, the grasp reflex will be replaced by the ability to grasp and let go.

The newborn must now use the grasp reflex over and over again. The more he uses it, the more quickly brain growth will take place to the next higher level of brain. That brain level is in place and waiting for the circuitry to be completed.

How many times does he have to use this grasp reflex in order to produce brain growth to the next stage?

The reason we don't know is because there are two variables:

1. How *often* does he do it?
2. How *early* does he do it?

We know that the *earlier* he does it, the *fewer times* it is necessary to do it.

Now let's see what happens to our *average* newborn. What *are* the accidents that cause him to do it at all?

There are several.

Any time his hand happens to be open and something brushes his palm, the grasp reflex will operate and he will close his hand around it. Mother's hair is a good example. As every mother knows, any time her hair happens to fall into his hand, Mother has her hair pulled.

It happens with bed covers and his own clothing.

Mother herself induces the grasp reflex, since she loves to put her finger into his tiny hand, seeing it as a miracle in itself—which it is. However, her action is an accident in terms of knowing what will cause his brain to grow.

Other visitors and family members will do the same thing for the same reason Mother did it. Every time it happens, he is one step closer to achieving brain growth to the next higher level, but all by accident, loving or otherwise.

It's clear that newborns who are most loved by their mother, family and friends also have the most attention paid to them. Thus such babies have the accident happen more often and are therefore the "brightest" babies.

It is equally obvious that the newborns who are the least loved have the least attention paid to them, and as a result, have the accident happen fewer times. These babies are the "dullest" babies.

Now let's see what is actually happening from the newborn's point of view. In order to develop his medulla fully, and then proceed with the development of the brain level of the pons, the accident has to happen often enough.

In order to pass from the lower level of the medulla to the higher level of the pons, he must be able to "let go" and "let go" on purpose.

Every time he has the opportunity to use his grasp reflex by holding on to hair, blanket or fingers, he is developing his medulla more, and therefore coming closer to the level of the pons.

What is *more*, every time he grasps these kinds of objects, they are sooner or later pulled out from his fingers, thus telling his brain what it feels like to "let go."

So, all the time the newborn is progressing further toward the next higher brain level by using his grasp reflex, he is also practicing "letting go."

All you need do is give him unlimited opportunity to use his grasp reflex. Suppose you decide you are going to devote a total of ten minutes a day to making your newborn a manual genius. That's easy.

Ten times a day for one minute, you pick him up in your arms and devote one minute to giving him opportunity for grasp reflex. First rate.

Lay him down on his back on a flat surface, such as a bed, and put each of your thumbs into each of his hands. Let him get a good grip. Let him hold on for five seconds. If it takes about three seconds to get your thumbs into his hands and five for him to hold on, you'll be able to do it about seven or eight times in one minute.

That means he'd have about seventy or eighty grasp reflexes a day *on purpose.*

And, there would still be all the accidents.

Getting Ready for Brachiation

There's one final thing you can do, starting at birth: you can begin a program of manual competence that will lead to an accomplishment called *brachiation.*

When we human beings got up on our feet a long time ago, and thus into the totally upright position, we no longer needed our hands, either to act as front paws or to swing through the trees. We took a significant step forward.

We could now use our hands in a skilled role, to become very efficient in the use of tools.

So—we traded in the old model of holding on to the branches and swinging with our hands (which we call brachiating) for the new model of walking on our feet. As we have said, it was a great step forward.

However, in making the splendid trade, we also made a mistake. In order to get the new model, it was not really necessary to trade in the old one. We could have eaten our cake and had it as well.

There are advantages in being able to brachiate. It is a splendid exercise for human beings to be able to swing by our hands from rung to rung on an overhead ladder. Yet we do it very poorly indeed.

Glenn Doman remembers that as an infantry parachute officer during World War II, he was required to cross streams swinging from rung to rung on an overhead ladder. He says rather ruefully that he inevitably ended up sitting "in those damned creeks."

However, two-year-olds in The Evan Thomas Institute can traverse a twelve-foot ladder with joy.

At Stages I *and* II, the Manual Competence Program for brachiation is exactly the same program—it stimulates your newborn's grasp reflex at Stage I and develops vital release at Stage II.

It's a part of the program dads especially seem to love to do!

THE MANUAL COMPETENCE PROGRAM—STAGE I: INGREDIENTS FOR SUCCESS

Here's Dad's job—one that will begin a process leading to brachiation as well as providing opportunity for use of the grasp reflex. (In preparation, Dad should get a $\frac{3}{8}''$ or $\frac{3}{4}''$ wooden dowel, one foot and a half long.)

You'll remember that we already have Mom getting ready to pick her newborn up with her thumbs. Some newborns prefer dowels; some prefer to grasp Mom's or Dad's thumbs. Whichever your child chooses, watch him carefully, and lower him if he is slipping.

With the newborn lying on a bed in the supine position (on his back), Dad or Mom puts thumbs or dowel in the baby's hands and pulls the baby's upper body a few inches from the bed. Dad should do this as often as time permits and as he enjoys doing it!

Frequency:	Do a minimum of ten sessions a day with your baby.
Intensity:	After one to two weeks of gradually lifting him higher and higher off the surface he is lying on, he will begin to be able to bear some of his own weight.
Duration:	Always lower your newborn to the bed as soon as you feel his grip loosening or see the expression on his face change from delight to concern. After a few tries, you'll be expert at determining how long is just enough. He is now supporting his own weight by hanging by his arms. It is the first step toward brachiation.
	Each session should take only one minute. In a minute, however, you could get seven to eight grasp reflexes on your thumb or dowel, since each grasp only may last five to ten seconds initially.

Remember, you are beginning your program in an environment that is clean, warm and safe for your baby, so there is very little need for clothing other than a T-shirt and diaper. A newborn trying desperately to learn to deal with his own body weight for the first time needs everything going for him; his T-shirt and diaper weigh little, provide freedom of movement and will allow your baby to succeed in learning to hang with joy.

Since you will have made certain your baby never falls, and always starts out on a soft surface such as a mattress for extra protection, you will also have thought about the size and texture of the dowel—not too large for his hands to close around completely, and not too rough for his hands or so smooth that gripping becomes difficult. (A dowel fresh from the hardware store is normally of good texture.)

Most important, be sure to tell your baby in a joyful and very proud voice how great he is every time he hangs on—and every time he lets go! *You* will establish your newborn's reaction to hanging on to your thumbs or a dowel. You won't want to show fear or concern since you will have taken all precautions to avoid the need for them. Instead, you'll be motivating him to attempt ever more challenging physical feats in the future. Obviously, if you don't express the sheer joy of his accomplishments, his desire to try will be a lot less than it could be!

YOUR GOAL IS FOR YOUR BABY TO HANG FOR TEN SECONDS FROM YOUR THUMBS, TAKING 50 PERCENT OF HIS WEIGHT.

Conclusions

If you have done all these things and have enjoyed them every time you did them with him, your newborn will develop his medulla very quickly and superbly and at an early age will have reached the next brain level, the pons.

Obviously, every time he had an opportunity to grasp (a reflex function of the medulla) he also had to let go (a conscious function of the pons).

At first he didn't let go at all but instead had the object he was grasping actually pulled from his grasp, either by another person or by his own weight.

As he used the grasp reflex more and more and his grasp reflex relaxed, the object began to fall from his hand by accident.

With increasing opportunity to *use* his grasp reflex and consequently increasing opportunity to *drop* the object grasped, he began to understand how it *felt* to let go and began to reproduce that feeling of *opening* his hand.

When, for the first time, he actually *opens* his hand (as opposed to simply letting go), he has crossed the line which separates the function of the medulla and the function of the pons.

By simply observing him, his mother will see distinctly that he is now *opening* his hand for the purpose of letting go.

Color his brain stage orange; he is operating at the brain level of the pons in manual competence. In each subsequent chapter there will be a section on manual competence similar to this section telling you precisely how to continue to develop his manual competence and therefore his manual intelligence. The more you give him opportunity to perform the function, the better and quicker he will do it.

If your child is already older, then you must read all the stages and fit him in at the highest level of which he is capable.

If your baby is *exactly* two and one half months old, he has a manual intelligence of *exactly* 100. If not, you can now find his precise manual intelligence by consulting the chart that follows.

Manual Intelligence
LEAVING STAGE I, THE MEDULLA
ENTERING STAGE II, THE PONS

AGE (in weeks)	MANUAL INTELLIGENCE **	OUR ADVICE
Three	361	World's record?
Four	271	You are doing
Five	217	a superb job.
Six	180	
Seven	155	
Eight	135	Keep up the
Nine	120	splendid
Ten	108	job you are doing!
Ten and one-half (2½ mos., or 74 days)	100	He is exactly average.
Eleven	98	Give him more
Twelve	90	opportunity.
Thirteen	83	
Fourteen	77	Give him a lot
Fifteen	72	more opportunity.
Sixteen	67	Give your child immediate
Seventeen	63	and extraordinary
Eighteen	60	opportunity to develop
Nineteen	57	his manual competence.
Twenty	54	
Twenty-one	51	
Twenty-two	49	If your child is below 50 in manual intelligence, waste no time in seeking professional help.

* The child's manual intelligence is determined by dividing the average age at which a child reaches this stage by your child's age, e.g., 74 days ÷ 42 days = 1.8 *or* M.I. = 180.

Billions of average children have followed the ancient pathway from immobility at birth to walking, running and jumping in cross-pattern at six years of age, happily, instinctually—and without the foggiest notion of the profound effect it would have on every phase of their lives.

For a minority of them (about one in twenty), the trip is not happy and instinctual, but heroic and harrowing, and ranges from difficult to simply impossible. These are the brain-injured children who, given the opportunity, fight with endless determination and unique courage to conquer the seven stages of mobility and manual development that average children achieve so joyfully and blithely.

However, it is the little brain-injured children who began our programs paralyzed who have made it as clear as clear can be that virtually anyone can be physically excellent.

As we have said, if your child is older as you begin reading this book, or is one of the children we so lovingly refer to as "hurt" kids, you must not expect him to fit in exactly at all of the stages we have outlined at the earliest possible times. Perhaps, sadly, he will hardly "fit" there at all. If he is older and well and willing, have him help you teach your younger children how to crawl and creep and brachiate; he will be all the better for it.

If he is a brain-injured child, he stands to benefit much more than his "average" young neighbor next door; however, a very important book, WHAT TO DO ABOUT YOUR BRAIN-INJURED CHILD (Glenn Doman, Doubleday and Company, 1974 and The Better Baby Press, 1987) may serve as the next book you will want to read before implementing a home program—and you may want to write to us as well, for additional information about the frequency, intensity and duration of the program he may need. You will have a special reason for keeping this in mind as we continue through the following stages of our programs—it is your child who has the most to gain from the knowledge we will be presenting. We know you will use it wisely and well.

The best part about doing the balance program with your baby is that it's going to be as much fun for <u>you</u> as it is for <u>him</u>.

Carry your baby around, holding him carefully, with one hand supporting the back of his head and the other hand holding his bottom.

Move your baby up and down and back and forth, and from side to side as well.

Take him around the house, telling him where he is and what things are, and stopping occasionally to talk about what you both can see outside the window.

A BALANCE PROGRAM FOR THE NEWBORN

The Russian neurophysiologist, Boris Klosovskii demonstrated more than a half century ago that newborn kittens and puppies had greatly increased brain growth in the first ten to twenty days of life when exposed to very gentle vestibular stimulation. These kittens and puppies actually had 22.8 percent to 35.0 percent more brain growth in the balance areas of their brains than did their litter mates, who had not received such gentle stimulation.*

These activities are extremely gentle and quite pleasurable for newborns. (Marlowe Doman would consistently stop crying in the first weeks of life if certain vestibular activities were begun. It was clear almost immediately which ones were his favorites.) All of the activities we are about to describe can be done safely and enjoyably with your newborn.

Obviously, you will want to *exercise extreme care* and make certain the area you use is free from obstructions. *Be sensitive* to your baby; keep your eyes on him. *Hold him carefully* for those activities for which he needs to be held. *Start gradually,* slowly and calmly, and build up the activities in stages. (This means carefully building up the length of time involved.)

Always tell your newborn what you are going to do, before you do it.
Explain to him what you are doing, while you do it.

Always stop before he wants to stop. That way, he'll always be looking forward to the next session!

You can dress your newborn in as little or as much clothing as his environment warrants—just be sure you can grasp him securely with whatever he has on.

The best part about doing the balance program with your baby is that it's going to be as much fun for you as it is for him. All over the world we have observed parents (especially fathers) developing their babies' balance. We have observed this from the world's most sophisticated capitals to the most primitive jungles and deserts of the world. In both extremes of civilization parents and kids enjoyed it equally as much. Fathers toss their babies up into the air and then catch them. Moms bounce their babies on their knees. Both activities, so simple and so easily done, stimulate the balance, or vestibular, areas of the brain.

All parents have their own favorite bouncing and rough-housing activities but we've listed fifteen specific ones that stimulate the balance areas of the brain in recognition of the three dimensions in which we all live. Enjoy these activities; you might just have had to invent your own if we hadn't created these for you:

1. **Carry your baby around.** Carefully hold your baby in this way: hold your hands palm up; with one hand, support the back of his head; with the other hand, hold his bottom. Now simply carry him around, moving him gently through the air and up and down. Move him up

---

* B. N. Klosovskii, *The Development of the Brain,* translated from the Russian and edited by Basil Haigh (New York: Macmillan Co., 1963).

and down and back and forth, and from side to side. Take him around the house, talking to him and telling him where he is and what things are. Let him look out the window.

2. **Lie on your back and move Baby through space.** This is another activity that we didn't have to invent: we observed parents doing it all over the world. Lie in bed on your back. Hold your newborn on your tummy. Grasp him firmly, with one hand on each of his sides, under his armpits. Raise him up directly over your chest, so that you and he are eye-to-eye. Tell him he is an airplane. Gently "bank" him to his right and left and raise him up and down before he comes in for a "landing" on your chest.

3. **Rock in a rocking chair.** Here's another age-old technique for calming babies; sit in a rocking chair and hold your newborn in the vertical position in your arms. Rock back and forth.

   Then, put your newborn on his tummy across your lap and rock back and forth again.

4. **Rock on a pillow.** Rocking and pitching (number 5, ahead) were some of Marlowe Doman's favorite activities as a newborn. He did these very effectively on a waterbed (with Mom and Dad's help), but these things can also be done well on a pillow.

   Place your baby on his tummy on a large pillow. Have him facing either toward or away from you. Now, gently pick up the side of the pillow with your left hand so that he rocks to the opposite side. Pick up the other side of the pillow with your right hand, and he will rock back to the left again.

5. **Pitching.** Rotate your newborn (still on the pillow) 90 degrees, so he now faces one of your hands, and his feet are extended toward your other hand. Continue to pick up alternate ends of the pillow and now your baby is "pitched" from head to toe!

6. **Accelerating on a mat—forward and backward.** This was Marlowe's favorite activity. Apart from the movement, he loved the sound that the mat made on the carpet. For him it was guaranteed to stop fussing.

   Buy an inexpensive changing mat (they have plastic covers and foam rubber padding and are useful for changing your baby on the floor). Double it over to give it more rigidity and place it on the floor. Put your newborn on it, on his tummy.

   His body should be perpendicular to you (i.e., his head at your right hand, his feet at your left hand). Now, with your right hand, pull the mat to the right. He moves forward. Then, with your left hand, pull the mat to the left. He moves backward. He accelerates forward and backward.

7. **Accelerating right and left.** Rotate the mat 90 degrees so that your newborn is facing you. Pull the mat with your left hand so that he moves to his right and then pull with your right hand so that he moves to the left. This is called acceleration right and acceleration left.

Always tell your newborn what you are going to do, <u>before</u> you do it.
Explain to him what you are doing while you do it.

Lie on your back and move your baby through space.

Isolda Maauad is moved through space by her mother, Federica Maauad.

"Pitch" your baby from head to toe.

Isolda is pitched head to toe on a pillow by her mom.

Rock your baby from side to side and back and forth.

Isolda is rocked side to side on a pillow by her mom.

Accelerate your baby forward and backward.

Federica accelerates her daughter backward and forward on a mat.

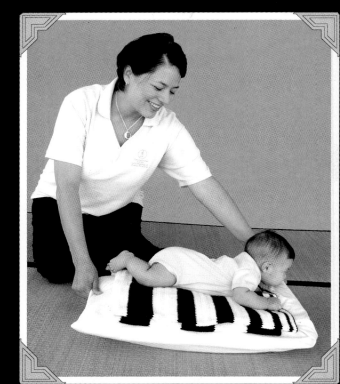

Isolda's dad accelerates her to the left and the right.

...otate your baby horizontally.

...rica rotates Isolda clockwise and counterclockwise.

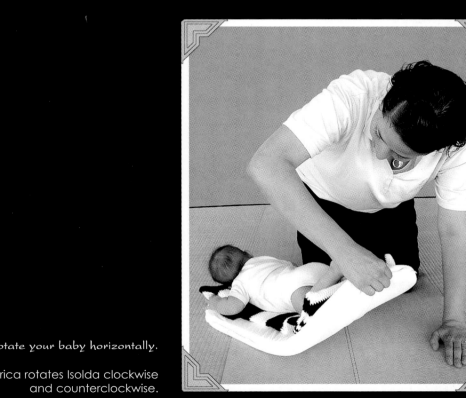

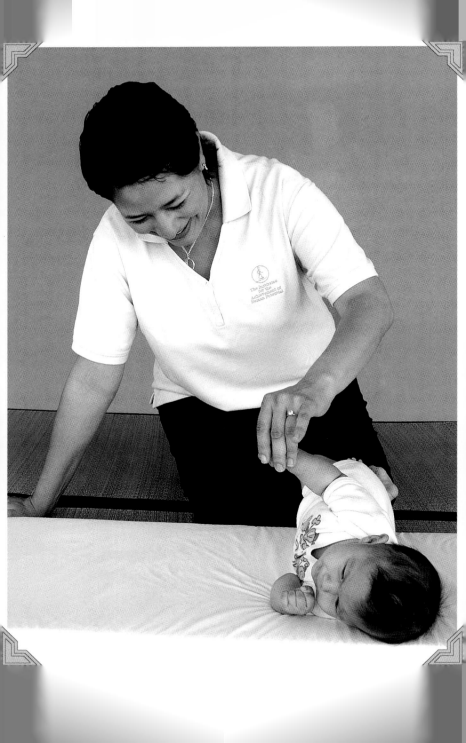

8. **Horizontal rotation clockwise.** Place your newborn on his tummy, lying lengthwise on the mat. His head should be close to the edge. Take the other end of the mat and rotate it clockwise.

9. **Horizontal rotation counterclockwise.** Repeat as above, only this time reverse the direction of the rotation to counterclockwise.

10. **Horizontal spin, prone position.** Stand up and place your newborn over your shoulder on his tummy and spin around, being careful not to get dizzy enough to lose your own balance. Alternate your spinning direction clockwise and counterclockwise. (See page 132.)

11. **Horizontal spin, left side.** Repeat as above, but with your newborn placed on your right shoulder on his left side, so his tummy is against your neck. Spin both clockwise and counterclockwise.

12. **Horizontal spin, right side.** Repeat the directions as above, but this time place your baby on his right side on your left shoulder. Spin both clockwise and counterclockwise.

13. **Pitching up and down.** Standing or kneeling with your newborn in the face-up position, carefully hold his head with one hand, his bottom with the other. He is in a semi-vertical position. Gently lift him up to eye level, and then gently lower his head. Your newborn tilts from a vertical position to a horizontal position, then to his head being lower than his toes. Repeat.

14. **Rolling.** This is a superb balance activity that combines nicely with an activity to develop manual competence. Put your newborn on his back on the floor. Kneel down on your knees at your baby's feet, positioned so that his toes touch your knees. Let him grasp the index finger of your left hand in his right hand. Say "pull" and gradually pull his right hand with your left hand, so that he rolls over onto his left side and then onto his tummy.

    Now let him grasp your right index finger with his left hand. Hold his hand over his head and pull him so he rolls over onto his right side and then his back. *Be careful when doing this that you don't put his left arm in an uncomfortable position.* Continue in this fashion, rolling him over, first to his left and then to his right.

15. **Trot about with your baby.** Carefully hold your newborn to your body and gently trot through the house. He will feel your body moving up and down as you carry him about. As he develops and gains control of his head and back, you can run faster and vary the positions in which you hold him. He is seeing the world move past him in yet another new and different way.

Carefully hold your newborn to your body and gently trot through the house.

Federica Maauad clasps Isolda closely to
her body as she trots about.

Doing the Basic Balance Program with Your Newborn

Frequency:	A good daily program consists of doing each one of the fifteen activities at least once a day.
Intensity:	Move slowly and carefully with all activities. If, by chance, your newborn isn't enjoying an activity (or if you get fatigued), you are probably going too fast. Slow down.
Duration:	Begin with about fifteen seconds of each of the activities and gradually and carefully build up to forty-five seconds for each of them.

Always stop before he wants you to stop.
Total time for daily program: Ten minutes.
Your newborn will love these activities.

STAGE I
DAILY CHECKLIST FOR MOTHER

1. The Mobility Program

____ **Frequency:** At least ten opportunities to be on the floor daily, to be cheered and encouraged to move.

____ **Intensity:** Watch how far and how fast he travels (the sides of his track can be marked every six inches, for instance).

____ **Duration:** A *minimum* of four waking hours daily to move in his track on the floor. (Ideally, he should spend all sleeping hours in his track.)

____ **GOAL:** FOR YOUR NEWBORN TO CRAWL TWO TO THREE FEET NONSTOP ON THE FLAT FLOOR OR TRACK.

Mother's comments: My newborn began to crawl at age _____ .

2. The Manual Program

____ **Frequency:** Ten sessions a day of opportunity to hang from your thumbs or the dowel.

____ **Intensity:** After one or two weeks of gradually lifting him higher and higher off the surface he is lying on, let your baby begin to bear more and more of his own weight.

____ **Duration:** About one minute each session, or seven to eight chances for grasp reflexes—until his grip loosens, or he begins to look concerned; a total of ten minutes a day.

____ **GOAL:** FOR YOUR NEWBORN TO HANG FROM YOUR THUMBS OR THE DOWEL FOR TEN SECONDS, BEARING 50 PERCENT OF HIS OWN WEIGHT.

Mother's comments: My newborn began to hang for ten seconds, bearing half of his own weight at age _____ .

3. The Balance Program

____ **Frequency:** Do each one of the fifteen basic activities at least once a day.

____ **Intensity:** Move *slowly* and *carefully* for all activities; do not tire your child. If in doubt, *slow down*.

____ **Duration:** Begin with fifteen seconds for each of the activities, building gradually and carefully to forty-five seconds. Total time per day: ten minutes.

____ **GOAL:** TO HAVE YOUR NEWBORN LOVING TO DO THESE ACTIVITIES WITH YOU, WHILE YOU ALWAYS STOP BEFORE HE'S READY TO.

Mother's comments: _____

_____

There is a very strong relationship between being able to crawl and creep and being able to converge vision at near point. The Xinguano baby who does not have the opportunity to be on the ground to crawl and to creep (because it is dangerous for him to be there), and thereby to learn to converge his eyes, grows up to be very good at far-point vision. This is to say that he is able to control his eyes in such a way as to bring them together on an object fifty feet away. Thus he successfully forms a visual triangle with a two-and-a-half inch base (the distance between his eyes) and a fifty-foot altitude (the distance from his eyes to the toucan in a tree fifty feet away) and brings the bird to the ground with an arrow.

However, this same Xinguano does not develop near-point vision, which is to say he does not have the ability to form a visual triangle with a two-and-a-half inch base (the distance between his eyes) and an altitude of eighteen inches. *Near-point vision, which is materially aided by crawling and creeping,* is being able to converge one's eyes to come together within the distance from one's eye to one's hand. This is the distance at which we read; this is the distance at which we write; this is the distance at which we sculpt; this is the distance at which we write music. This is the distance from our eyes to a desk—so it is most properly said that *civilization is eighteen inches long.*

It would not be difficult to make a case for the point that the lack of floors in a primitive culture leads to a lack of crawling and creeping, which in turn leads to little or no near-point vision, which leads to no written language, which leads to no civilization.

We have often discussed the fascinating fact that if you show us a culture that had no floors we will tell you about its primitiveness.

If you show us a culture that had substantial floors, we will tell you about its civilization.

The Egyptian floors, the Greek floors, the Inca floors are still there to be seen. The people in these cultures did brain surgery and created beautiful art three thousand, two thousand and one thousand years ago.

Xinguano art and Bushmen art are so simple as to be almost insignificant.

Thus the ramifications of being denied this opportunity for mobility, the opportunity to crawl and creep, will have vital effects in other areas: vision is one of them.

The Institutes' Mobility Development Scale

BRAIN STAGE		TIME FRAME	MOBILITY
VII	SOPHISTI-CATED CORTEX	Superior 36 Mon. / Average 72 Mon. / Slow 144 Mon.	Using a leg in a skilled role which is consistent with the dominant hemisphere *Sophisticated human expression*
VI	PRIMITIVE CORTEX	Superior 18 Mon. / Average 36 Mon. / Slow 72 Mon.	Walking and running in complete cross pattern *Primitive human expression*
V	EARLY CORTEX	Superior 9 Mon. / Average 18 Mon. / Slow 36 Mon.	Walking with arms freed from the primary balance role *Early human expression*
IV	INITIAL CORTEX	Superior 6 Mon. / Average 12 Mon. / Slow 24 Mon.	Walking with arms used in a primary balance role most frequently at or above shoulder height *Initial human expression*
III	MIDBRAIN	Superior 3.5 Mon. / Average 7 Mon. / Slow 14 Mon.	Creeping on hands and knees, culminating in cross pattern creeping *Meaningful response*
II	PONS	Superior 1 Mon. / Average 2.5 Mon. / Slow 5 Mon.	Crawling in the prone position culminating in cross pattern crawling *Vital response*
I	MEDULLA and CORD	Superior Birth to .5 / Average Birth to 1.0 / Slow Birth to 2.0	Movement of arms and legs without bodily movement *Reflex response*

GLENN DOMAN
and
The Staff
of
The Institutes

THE INSTITUTES FOR THE ACHIEVEMENT OF HUMAN POTENTIAL
8801 STENTON AVENUE
WYNDMOOR, PA 19038

10
MULTIPLYING YOUR BABY'S PHYSICAL INTELLIGENCE

STAGE II, THE PONS

Mobility Competence

CLASS: Infant.
BRAIN STAGE: The Pons.
PROFILE COLOR: Orange.
FUNCTION: Crawling in the prone position culminating in cross-pattern crawling.
AVERAGE AGE: Two and a half months.
DESCRIPTION: At some time during his first few months of age, the well infant learns to use the movement of arms and legs (which developed earlier) to push himself forward with his belly actually in contact with the floor. This is called crawling.

He may still move in circles a good deal and he may sometimes move backward, but he's got the mobility bit in his teeth and he's on his way.

He is a long way from being a skilled crawler, but he has certainly earned his learner's permit.
PURPOSE: Crawling is pure movement. It is movement for movement's sake.

When a baby begins to crawl, he will have learned one of the most important lessons life has to teach, and he will have crossed the border from the kingdom of the vegetable world to the kingdom of the animal world. He can now get from point A to point B even though point A and point B may be only two or three feet apart, and it may take him some time to do so.

> Crawling is of a vital nature. His movements at Stage I were totally reflexive and he could not have moved a significant distance even to save his own life. Now at Stage II he can. He could now actually save himself by moving away if a fire or life-threatening set of circumstances occurred.
>
> Now he needs all the experience he can get. The amount of *experience* he gets is an unadulterated product of the amount of *opportunity* he has to practice in an ideal environment.

When the infant learns that he can actually get from place to place by crawling, he will learn that going forward is the most efficient way to accomplish this, and he will do so. The infant may, in the beginning, move in no recognizable pattern. He may then crawl by moving his arms forward together, while pushing his legs. He may then support his weight on his arms while pulling his legs forward. This is called an *homologous* pattern of movement. It is frog-like.

He may move by reaching forward with his right arm and leg simultaneously, while pushing with his left arm and leg simultaneously. He may then reverse the process. This is called an *homolateral* pattern of movement.

In the well infant all these early patterns will eventually be abandoned in favor of the ultimate pattern of movement, which is called *cross-pattern*.

In this, the most sophisticated pattern, the infant moves by using his right arm and left leg to push himself forward, while simultaneously moving the left arm and right leg forward in order to support his weight on them in preparation for the next forward movement. He will then use his left arm and right leg to push himself forward, while simultaneously moving his right arm and left leg forward.

This cross-pattern is the most efficient form of moving forward on the ground.

THE MOBILITY COMPETENCE PROGRAM—STAGE II: INGREDIENTS FOR SUCCESS

The *quality* of his movement will rest upon the nature of the environment itself.

His floor will need to be as before:
1. Safe
2. Clean
3. Warm
4. Smooth
5. Pliable
6. Flat

It is a great accomplishment to crawl for the first time — it is the largest <u>single</u> mobility gain a child will ever make.

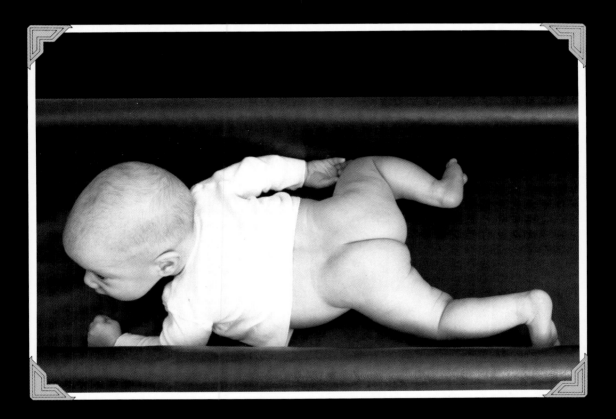

Here, at not yet three months of age, Spencer Doman (Douglas' youngest son) crawls in a cross pattern. His left arm is forward and his right leg is coming forward. At this point, Spencer has crawled a total of more than 110 feet per day, both on the floor and in his crawling track.

These things, taken together with opportunity to crawl, will determine how *well* he will crawl and, as a consequence, how he will conquer crawling in all its various forms: without pattern, homologously, homolaterally, and finally, in cross-pattern—beautifully, skillfully, and synchronously.

We must see that our babies waste not a single day, hour, or minute dawdling uselessly, imprisoned in a playpen, crib, or other jail, during the precious time their itinerary allows them to take their journey through the vital functions governed by the pons.

Other than by a car seat (which is a mighty good idea), if an infant must be restricted, the best place is in Mom's or Dad's arms!

The rest of the restrictive devices one sees are *dreadful* for babies and tiny children—playpens, infant seats, swing sets, jumping devices and walkers. They are all *prisons* of one sort or another.

These devices deliberately *immobilize* babies.

The children in our International School often run in beautiful Fairmount Park, near The Institutes. As we run with them, we are often confronted with a bizarre sight—an infant strapped into a stroller, his eyes wide and attentive, his arms reaching out in frustration. He wants to get out, see the trees, feel the leaves—*LIVE!*

The situation is upside down. Let's *release* kids, so they can learn. The adults can sit in the strollers and rest!

If the problem were actually only that these devices were restrictive, they might be tolerable.

Unfortunately, the problems they present actually compound themselves.

Infants who cannot walk are "designed" to live in a horizontal world parallel to the earth's surface—namely, the floor.

They don't have the muscle structure to support their bones, the bone structure to support their body weight, or the mechanism to balance their bodies in the *vertical* position.

However, adults live in a vertical world, standing perpendicular to the earth's surface. It is *convenient* for us constantly to take our babies out of a horizontal world to be in a vertical position with us. Sitting is a vertical rather than a horizontal position.

The problem is gravity.

Gravity is a ubiquitous and powerful force that can take the soft, pliable bones of an infant and literally *bend them into abnormal positions.*

Today, school children are regularly tested for scoliosis: a deformed, curved spine. The incidence of scoliosis appears to our staff to be increasing, because we see babies more and more frequently being compromised by restrictive devices.

Next time you're out, look at infants' postures as they sit in strollers, swingsets and so on. Their bellies stick out, their shoulders hunch forward, their backs are curved.

The problems, however, don't even stop there.

All the restrictive devices *deny* and *limit* opportunity for moving, crawling and creeping. Not only is *mobility* denied, but so are *crawling* and *creeping,* which are vital to the development of the medulla, pons, and midbrain respectively. These parts of the brain develop less (and more slowly) because movement is denied.

Particularly affected is the opportunity to develop convergence of vision and, in the end, reading, because convergence is not fully developed.

Bare Elbows, Knees and Feet

As was the case in Stage I, your baby's elbows, knees and feet should still be bare so that he gets the best possible traction on the smooth floor where you'll place him. Overdressing an infant will only restrict his arm and leg movements and decrease his ability to get the proper traction. Once again, the T-shirt and diaper combination are what the most "mobile" babies should wear!

YOU Should Be on the Floor

Your infant has two great desires right now: to be with you, and to use his newly found form of transportation to explore his world. *You* should use these two great desires to help your infant expand his quantity of crawling. Remember, in order for your infant to feel comfortable on the floor, you should be there also.

One of his greatest joys will be to crawl after you, to go where you are going. Your infant will love to crawl up to you to receive your warm praise and embrace. This is your very best method of expanding his crawling world. It won't do *you* any harm either!

Give Your Baby Opportunity to Explore His World

You can now expand your infant's crawling by giving him things toward which he wants to crawl. Obviously, if you place your infant on the floor and immediately surround him with all the things that interest him, then he will have no reason to go anywhere.

That great genius, Temple Fay, long ago wrote us a letter in which he included what is probably the clearest and most important neurological statement ever made in a single paragraph. You can apply it to every level of mobility development described in this book. If you do, you will be a very wise parent indeed.

Temple Fay was responding to the question of how man himself developed.

"Which came first," asked Temple Fay, "the chicken or the egg? You may be sure that *first there was a need, and then there was a facility.* Nature is an opportunist. Can you blame her for wanting to put *words* to *song* and not merely *sounds* to *tone?*"

There is probably no greater neurophysiological statement contained in a single sentence than his "First there was a need, and then there was a facility."

We must make absolutely certain that we supply our children generously with needs, so that they may develop their brains and the appropriate facilities to satisfy those needs.

Give Your Baby NEEDS

Take his favorite objects and initially place them on the floor a few feet from him where he can easily see them. Place them at a distance you know he can travel in a reasonable length of time, such as ten or fifteen minutes. As your infant becomes more proficient at crawling, make the distance greater.

Always place the objects that are attractive to him *out of his reach,* but never out of his *range.*

In this manner, you can continually expand the distance that your infant crawls so that it becomes ever greater.

Always make sure the reward is worth the effort.

Make sure your infant always has the opportunity for a brief period of time to *enjoy* the object he crawls to get.

He must receive a reward for his effort. Of course, your hugs and kisses, your enthusiastic praise, and the caresses and encouragement of his family mean more to your baby than anything else.

For this reason, we must add just a simple word of caution here: be careful not to fall into a habit that can trap even the most enthusiastic parents.

The scene is this: everyone is on the floor and everything is going great. Your infant is *loving it.* He crawls to the teddy bear, and just as he reaches it, Dad backs the teddy bear up three feet. Baby struggles to crawl to it again, and just as he gets to it, Dad backs it up again. . . .

It won't take too long for your bright young infant to figure out how *unrewarding* this game is. He'll simply stop playing it. Set the goal, cheer him to it, and let *him* have it before anyone else touches it!

How long it takes him to speed properly, successfully and completely through the pons will be a product of the opportunity we provide him for crawling. The more your infant crawls, the closer he gets to creeping. Opportunity has been the key factor up to this point. Now that you've provided your infant with maximum opportunity, distance becomes of prime importance. The greater quantity of movement your infant accumulates, the more purposeful his crawling will be, the faster his crawling will be, and the sooner he will acquire the strength and balance to get up on his hands and knees.

Sometimes, at this stage, babies cry when crawling.

This is *good,* not bad.

They're crying for a reason. The fast, deep respiration of crying actually gives them the additional oxygen they need to make easier the movement of their arms and legs for crawling.

Crawling, for an infant, is the equivalent of an adult going out for a distance jog. If your breathing did not become faster and deeper, because of your jogging, then there is no way you could run. Infants need deeper, faster breathing in order to crawl, and crying aids this process.

If you're a careful observer of babies, you will have noticed that when an infant who's lying on the floor spots an object in front of him and wants to get it, he will start to breathe more deeply. He needs this increased respiration to get his arms and legs cranking!

Most of our infants here cried sometimes at this stage. Benjamin Newell, pictured at the beginning of this chapter, cried very little.

Newborns and infants uniformly cry less and less as their movement becomes more and more purposeful.

The objectives, then, at this point are:

Frequency: Your infant should have a minimum of fifteen opportunities to move a day. (Obviously, as he crawls more and more purposefully, he will demand the freedom to move and explore the world.)

Intensity: This is determined by how far he moves now. Gradually his distances will expand from feet traveled to yards traveled. Your correct judgment in placing objects always out of reach but never out of range becomes absolutely essential here.

Duration: The length of time of each session will vary in the beginning from the few minutes it takes for him to achieve his objective to possibly half hours at a time when your infant is crawling around for his own reasons. In general, *we recommend a minimum of four hours a day on the floor* and *a maximum of eighteen* if your baby is sleeping on the floor, or in an infant crawling track.

AT THIS STAGE OF MOBILITY, A FAIR GOAL IS TO HAVE THE INFANT ABLE TO CRAWL A FOOT FARTHER EACH DAY THAN HE CRAWLED THE DAY BEFORE.

The long-term objective is for the infant to crawl 150 feet in a day. Most infants will begin to get up on their hands and knees before they reach 100 feet of crawling in a day. If your infant does not, keep working toward 150 feet and you'll see him push up.

In order to speed his process toward his next level of brain development by accomplishing the next level of mobility, that of *creeping,* we must now alter, gradually, the surface upon which he crawls.

It is easy to crawl on a smooth surface, which is why we have given him such a surface.

It is more difficult to crawl dragging one's belly on a lightly-textured surface.

It is *most* difficult to crawl on a *deeply* textured surface.

THEREFORE:

We now provide him with a less smooth surface, such as a carpet with a very short pile, to crawl on. He will find it a disadvantage to crawl, dragging over the textured surface, but much more advantageous and easier to do if he supports more of his weight on his arms and legs and less of his weight on his belly. Soon he will learn this and move as quickly and as far on the relatively clinging surface as he used to on the smooth surface.

THEREFORE:

Since we wish to encourage him as soon as possible to move up to the *next* higher brain level, we now provide him with a crawling surface that is more deeply textured; it is slightly more difficult to crawl on a thick carpet.

So we place him on such a carpet. He will find that crawling is more difficult because his abdomen must be *pulled* across the surface. If he is ready for this step, he will succeed in crawling by putting even more weight on his arms and legs and less on his abdomen.

If, after several days of opportunity to crawl, he does not succeed in doing so on this surface, it is an indication that he is not quite ready. Put him back on the very short pile carpet to become a little more skilled at crawling and try again in a week or so!

If (as is likely) he succeeds in crawling on the deeper-pile carpet, let him continue to do so until his crawling is once again easy and quick.

Once he is proficient on the thicker pile, he can begin to crawl on even a deep shag carpet.

Getting Up on His Hands and Knees

Now your infant will often experiment with getting up into a quadruped position (on his hands and knees). He will lean forward and backward, and he will lean to the left and the right.

Sometimes in performing these experiments, he will fall down.

Isn't it nice that the deep shag carpet will cushion his fall?

He'll get right up and try all over again.

By now, of course, your baby is crawling freely all over the house, from the smooth floor of the kitchen through the luxurious carpets in the living room.

Between two and three months of age, Marlowe Doman gradually pushed up off the floor more and more.

First he got up on his elbows, then he was able to get onto his hands, and then his elbows began to straighten as his arms strengthened. At about this time, he purposefully crawled to his tape recorder while music played, or to a colorful ceramic cat given to him by a Japanese friend.

One evening after his evening swimming session in the bathtub, we let out just enough water (as usual) so that while he lay on the tub bottom, his shoulders were covered.

On that particular evening, he was very, very active.

His dad (Douglas Doman) held his head out of the water.

With great effort, he heaved himself up onto his knees with fully extended arms.

He was in the quadruped position!

He was wildly excited. He did it several times. The next day, lying on the carpet, he got up again and then again.

All before his third-month birthday!

We moved the track out of his room. He had graduated from it.

Older Children and Opportunity

So many hundreds of mothers have asked us the same question that this small aside seems worth the writing.

As they read chapters like these about initial movement, *crawling* and then *creeping,* they often become concerned about their older children. It occurs to them that perhaps their older children did not have enough opportunity on the floor as infants. This is vital and perceptive thinking on a mom's part, and many mothers express this concern.

A splendid solution to this problem is to encourage those children to encourage your baby to crawl and creep by crawling and creeping with him.

Crawling and creeping play an important and seldom-recognized role in the development of human vision, speech and intelligence—facts we learned in the treatment of brain-injured children during more than forty years of achieving function in thousands of such children.

Conclusions

When an infant can manage to push himself up on his hands and knees, and thus assume the quadruped position with some degree of regularity, his infant days are just about over. He has learned just about all that the pons has to teach him and he is headed straight for his new school in the midbrain.

After he has gotten steady in the position that leads to creeping, he will begin to experiment with moving while on his hands and knees. He will lose his balance frequently and revert back to crawling when he really wants to get somewhere "right now," but still he'll persevere with his attempts to creep, and sooner or later he'll get his learner's license for creeping by creeping one to two feet on all fours. He's only a beginner, but he has crossed the line into the yellow area of function controlled by the midbrain.

These are all the credentials he will need to continue to develop this stage he has reached.

If you began the program the day your baby was born and paid a great deal of attention to mobility, he may be as young as three and a half or even *two* months of age, when he first gets up on his hands and knees.

If he is *exactly* three and a half months old when he first gets onto his hands and knees, he has a mobility intelligence of exactly 200. If he is exactly seven months old, he has a mobility intelligence of 100. Now you can find *your* baby's exact mobility intelligence by consulting the chart that follows.

At whatever age he reaches it, it is a huge event in his life when he first gets into the quadruped position. He has climbed to a status far beyond all the creatures of the earth who have not learned to defy gravity to the degree of pushing themselves up off the earth's surface.

	Mobility Intelligence **LEAVING STAGE II, THE PONS** **ENTERING STAGE III, THE MIDBRAIN**	
AGE (in months)	**MOBILITY INTELLIGENCE**	**OUR ADVICE**
Two	349	World's record?
Three Four	232 174	You're doing a superb job!
Five Six	140 116	Splendid job.
Seven (213 days)	100	Exactly average.
Eight Nine	87 77	Give him more opportunity.
Ten Eleven Twelve Thirteen	69 63 58 53	Give your child immediate and extraordinary opportunity to move, move, move.
Fourteen	49	If your child is below 50 in mobility intelligence, you should waste no time in seeking professional help.

How long it takes your child to speed properly, successfully and completely through the pons will be a product of the opportunity we provide him for crawling.

The more *your infant crawls, the closer he* gets to creeping.

Opportunity *has been the name of the game up until this point.*

Now that you've provided maximum opportunity, distance becomes of prime importance. *The greater the quantity of movement your infant accumulates, the more purposeful his crawling will be, and the sooner he will acquire the strength and balance to get up on his hands and knees.*

The Institutes' Manual Development Scale

BRAIN STAGE		TIME FRAME	MANUAL COMPETENCE
VII	SOPHISTI-CATED CORTEX	Superior 36 Mon. / Average 72 Mon. / Slow 144 Mon.	**Using a hand to write which is consistent with the dominant hemisphere** *Sophisticated human expression*
VI	PRIMITIVE CORTEX	Superior 18 Mon. / Average 36 Mon. / Slow 72 Mon.	**Bimanual function with one hand in a skilled role** *Primitive human expression*
V	EARLY CORTEX	Superior 9 Mon. / Average 18 Mon. / Slow 36 Mon.	**Cortical opposition bilaterally and simultaneously** *Early human expression*
IV	INITIAL CORTEX	Superior 6 Mon. / Average 12 Mon. / Slow 24 Mon.	**Cortical opposition in either hand** *Initial human expression*
III	MIDBRAIN	Superior 3.5 Mon. / Average 7 Mon. / Slow 14 Mon.	**Prehensile grasp** *Meaningful response*
II	PONS	Superior 1 Mon. / Average 2.5 Mon. / Slow 5 Mon.	**Vital release** *Vital response*
I	MEDULLA and CORD	Superior Birth to .5 / Average Birth to 1.0 / Slow Birth to 2.0	**Grasp reflex** *Reflex response*

GLENN DOMAN
and
The Staff
of
The Institutes

THE INSTITUTES FOR THE ACHIEVEMENT OF HUMAN POTENTIAL
8801 STENTON AVENUE
WYNDMOOR, PA 19038

MULTIPLYING YOUR BABY'S PHYSICAL INTELLIGENCE

STAGE II, THE PONS

Manual Competence

CLASS:	Infant.
BRAIN STAGE:	The Pons.
PROFILE COLOR:	Orange.
FUNCTION:	Vital release.
AVERAGE AGE:	Two and a half months.
DESCRIPTION:	By the end of the tenth week of life, the average infant has started to let go of objects which up to now had been held in the palm of his hand as a result of the grasp reflex over which he exercised no volitional control. At first he does so sporadically and more often drops the rattle or other object in his hand by accident than on purpose. But, as he develops his pons by continuing to grasp objects reflexively, and to let go of them consciously, his vital functions continue to improve.
PURPOSE:	At birth he picked things up entirely by accident when the palm of his hand happened to close around them reflexively. It was not that he could hold on, but rather that he could not let go, a function that he will continue to improve as he continues to gain control over his pons functions. He can now let go of a painful or dangerous object (for example, something hot or sharp). He is on his way toward uniquely human hand control. Letting go is a vital function.

It is vital to remember that the Developmental Profile describes things as they *are* with children.

This book describes how they *should be* and *can be*.

How we are going to use your baby's manual abilities in a very practical way to achieve physical excellence and grow his brain is a first-rate example.

Bear in mind that all babies are born with the total ability to support their own weight with their hands and arms, and there is absolutely no need for them to give up that ability as we humans as a species have done.

We traded the old model of swinging through the trees for the new one of using our hands in a skilled role, with tools, but we could have had our cake and eaten it, too. Your baby can have it all!

THE MANUAL COMPETENCE PROGRAM—STAGE II: INGREDIENTS FOR SUCCESS

Your infant has reached Stage II of his manual development. Begin now, when he's lying on his back on the bed, to put your thumbs in his hands, as before. This time, however, be prepared to grab his hand with your fingers so that you can be sure he does not let go, *which he is now capable of doing*.

Hanging from Fingers or a Dowel

Let him grasp your hand, raise him to the sitting position, and then to the standing position. If you feel his grip loosen, gradually but quickly lower him to his back. Your fingers are there to hold him just in case he slips. Once he stands, you may be surprised to feel him supporting some of his weight with his legs. Excellent. If he is still holding on, you can now actually lift him off the bed.

He's hanging all by himself.

Of course, you're smiling and watching him, ready to lower him when his grip loosens. Finally, lower him back on to the bed. You can use a ¼″ dowel in place of your finger as you become more confident of your infant's ability to hang on.

Not merely is hanging a splendid exercise to improve manual competence and coordination (and thus to grow the brain in manual pathways), but equally important is the opportunity to actually improve the brain's nutritional environment by creating a larger chest that supplies more oxygen, the primary food of the brain, to the brain.

Now replace his wooden dowel with a dowel suspended in a doorway, as seen on page 253 in the Appendix.

Make sure the dowel is strong enough to support your infant's weight.

The bar across the doorway should serve you well.

You will use it until your child becomes an independent brachiator. Even after he brachiates, he will enjoy playing on it.

It is very easy to suspend a dowel across a doorway. Measure your infant from the tip of his finger to the tip of his toes, and add two inches so he is sure to just clear the ground. Screw a strong frame of inch-thick wood to the doorway to firmly support the dowel. Be prepared for your child's growth by

Add a bit of a thrill!

Hanging from fingers or a dowel is not merely a splendid
exercise to improve manual competence and coordination,
but equally important is the opportunity to enrich the brain's
nutritional environment by enlarging your child's chest and
providing more oxygen to the brain.

Maria enjoys hanging from her mother's thumbs.

adding a half dozen holes above the original one. These holes should be separated by three inches from the center of the hole to the center of the hole above.

You are now ready to begin teaching him to hang by his own hands on purpose (rather than because he couldn't let go, which was formerly the case).

Kneel down, "Japanese style," facing your baby. Put his hands around the bar across the doorway exactly as you did on the bed. He may actually be able to support his own weight but, for safety's sake, you should hold your hands at his hips. Be sensitive—you'll be able to tell if his grip loosens, so that you can hold on to him firmly.

Begin with your infant hanging only two seconds each session. (You can measure approximately two seconds by saying, "One one-thousand, two one-thousand," at a fairly good speed.)

Don't try to compare the effort that it takes you to hang by your hands with the effort it will require from him. It is much easier for him. He never gave up the ability to do it, as you probably did long ago. He is an "expert" in hanging on, and he weighs practically nothing compared to you.

Once again, only a T-shirt or loose-fitting polo shirt and a diaper are needed.

The ideal thing, of course, is to be prepared to hold *him* so that he never drops.

As you both become quite expert at this game, and your mutual confidence grows, it will begin to get boring for both of you—and that is a cardinal sin.

Add a Bit of a Thrill

Now it's time to add a bit of a thrill for both of you.

Being extremely careful, now, when you actually see his grip loosen, let him drop an inch or two before you catch him.

His first reaction will be an instant of astonishment, thrill, and maybe a bit of indignation. He will probably either laugh or cry.

Whichever *he* does, *you laugh and tell him how great he is.*

Tell him how much fun it is. He'll take all his clues from you. If you scream in terror, so will he. If you laugh, he will laugh . . . after a bit. In the end, because you never permit him to be in any real danger, even for an instant, his natural trust in you will grow even greater.

Let's start a program now that incorporates the following and works up to the expert "fun" we just told you about:

Frequency: You can begin with a high frequency (let's say fifteen sessions a day). This can be divided between hanging from the dowel seven to eight times and hanging from your thumbs seven to eight times. *It's best to do both activities and it's only going to take a few seconds each time.* You should be guided by which situation provides the greatest success for your baby.

Intensity: The intensity of your program is determined by the weight of your child. The heavier he is, the more intensely he'll have to hold on. The lighter he is, the less effort it will take.

Duration: We talked about beginning with your baby hanging for two seconds each session, and you know how to measure that time. There are some important considerations about "duration" we'd like to tell you about.

Especially in the beginning, you must place great emphasis upon frequency, graduated emphasis on intensity, and very small emphasis upon duration.

Stop before he's ready to, and he'll be looking forward to your next session. We want to make your infant *extremely* fond of hanging by his arms.

All you need to do is make absolutely sure he succeeds.

You do so by telling him how beautifully he's done it, how great he is, how very clever he is, and how much you love him. You give him a big hug every time he does it.

Don't worry about the fact that he does not yet understand the words. He'll get the message, loud and clear.

In terms of how to approach it, the answer is "gently."

In terms of how to deal with him, the answer is "sweetly and lovingly."

In terms of results, the answer will be "splendid."

As he gets better and better at hanging, and looks forward more and more to doing it, in order for him to get his greatest reward—your love, appreciation and approval—you can begin slowly to increase the duration to ten seconds and more.

Never get to as long as a minute, no matter how good he gets. Hanging on a full minute for a well infant is both hard work and—what is ever so much worse—boring.

At fifteen or thirty seconds of hanging, you keep him from being bored by telling him enthusiastically how great he is while he is hanging.

Hardly anyone alive gets bored by being told, by someone he loves, how great he is.

We'll bet it will be easy for you to praise your eager little "expert at hanging" with all the warmth, joy and enthusiasm you're sure to feel for his efforts. That's his reward for playing this great game with you, and there's nothing he wants more than to have your love and approval! *

---

* Parents who wish to understand this in an absolutely thorough way might wish to study a chapter from Glenn Doman's book *What to Do About Your Brain-Injured Child* (New York: Doubleday & Co., 1974). We recommend reading Chapter 25, titled "On Motivation."

Interestingly enough, that chapter deals precisely with motivating a young child to hang on to a bar. While it was written for parents of hurt children, it applies equally to well children and actually deals with how to motivate any child in any situation.

AT THIS STAGE OF MANUAL COMPETENCE (SINCE AS YOU GRADUALLY REDUCE THE SUPPORT YOUR INFANT NEEDS TO HOLD ON, HIS ABILITY TO DO SO IS INCREASING), <u>THE GOAL</u> IS FOR HIM TO BE ABLE TO SUPPORT 100 PERCENT OF HIS BODY WEIGHT FOR AT LEAST TEN SECONDS.

Conclusions

As your infant's very practical program of manual competence continues, his hands, elbows and shoulders will become visibly more developed, since his time in that extraordinary stage of the brain called the pons will have served him well.

The ability to hang, and a good deal of hanging, will speed the day when he's able to pick up objects in his hands.

He will now have good control over opening and closing his hands. He will soon begin to use these two abilities to attempt to accomplish a third and much higher ability. He will use these now controlled abilities to *pick up* objects *on purpose*.

The ability to do so is called *prehensile grasp*. He does it by opening his hand to encompass an object in his palm and then to purposely close his fingers around it. This is no function of the infant's pons, but is instead a function for the baby's midbrain.

His infant days are over.

If you began this program the day your baby was born, and paid a great deal of attention to manual competence, he may be as young as three and a half months, or even younger, when he begins to pick up objects.

If he is exactly seven months old, he has a manual intelligence of exactly 100.

Now you can find *your* baby's exact manual intelligence by consulting the chart that follows. Of course, you should expect the very high intelligence levels at very early ages *only* if you purchased this book before your baby was born and have followed it very carefully up to this point.

Regardless of his age, it is a huge event when he first successfully picks up an object on purpose. He has climbed to a level of brain function and status far beyond all the creatures of the earth who do not have the precious possession of useful hands.

Manual Intelligence
LEAVING STAGE II, THE PONS
ENTERING STAGE III, THE MIDBRAIN

AGE (in months)	MANUAL INTELLIGENCE	OUR ADVICE
Two	349	World's record?
Three	232	You're doing a superb job!
Four	174	
Five	140	Keep up the splendid job
Six	116	you are doing!
Seven (213 days)	100	He is exactly average.
Eight	87	Give him more opportunity.
Nine	77	
Ten	69	Give your child immediate
Eleven	63	and extraordinary
Twelve	58	opportunity to develop
Thirteen	53	his manual competence.
Fourteen	49	If your child is below 50 in manual intelligence, waste no time in seeking professional help.

A BALANCE PROGRAM FOR THE INFANT

Your baby is still only a few months old and so continues to need the vestibular (balance) program for newborns we explained in great detail in the last chapter.

Everything we outlined there, all the requirements for building balance at Stage I, remain the same throughout Stage II as well.

All those programs may now be carried on with increased frequency, intensity and duration. They are ideal to help your infant become a creeper!

Frequency: Fifteen times a day do each of the initial balance activities discussed in Chapter 9.

Providing you and your infant are enjoying them (which is very likely), feel free to do as much as you want.

Intensity: Your infant should be quite accustomed to the activities by now. You can accelerate the speed at which you spin, rock and pitch and move him through all the activities.

Duration: Now increase the length of time of each session from forty-five seconds to a full minute. You can go up to about a minute, but do remember to stop before your baby wants to!

Often, concerned parents tell us their eight- to twelve-month-old babies have been crawling for several months, but are not interested in creeping—or, parents will say their babies have been able to get onto their hands and knees, but just don't move forward. In most instances, within just a few weeks of beginning a solid initial balance program, babies are beginning to creep, and shortly thereafter are creeping everywhere.

More important, your baby will consider these vestibular activities the highlight of his day.

Remember that the newborn's balance program is a requirement for proper preparation of your baby's balance, vision and body structure for the more sophisticated balance program described in our next chapter and make these activities the highlights of your day, too!

STAGE II
DAILY CHECKLIST FOR MOTHER

1. **The Mobility Program**

___ **Frequency:**   A minimum of fifteen opportunities to crawl daily.

___ **Intensity:**   Watch to see how far your infant crawls—from feet traveled, at first, to yards traveled.

___ **Duration:**   A minimum of four hours a day on the floor to a maximum of eighteen (if your infant is sleeping on the floor, or in his track).

___ **GOAL:**   FOR YOUR INFANT TO CRAWL A FOOT FARTHER EACH DAY THAN HE CRAWLED THE DAY BEFORE. LONG-TERM GOAL: 150 FEET A DAY.

Mother's comments: My infant began to crawl 150 feet a day at age _____ .

2. **The Manual Program**

___ **Frequency:**   Begin with fifteen sessions daily, divided between hanging from your thumbs and hanging from the dowel.

___ **Intensity:**   Depends on your baby's weight: the heavier he is, the harder he'll have to hold on.

___ **Duration:**   Begin with your baby hanging two seconds each session. Especially at the beginning, place great emphasis on *frequency,* graduated emphasis on *intensity,* and *very small* emphasis upon duration. As he gets better at it, build slowly to fifteen to thirty seconds. *Never* quite get to as long as a minute.

___ **GOAL:**   FOR YOUR BABY TO BE ABLE TO SUPPORT 100 PERCENT OF HIS BODY WEIGHT FOR AT LEAST TEN SECONDS.

Mother's comments: My infant began to support all his body weight and hang for ten seconds at age _____ .

3. **The Balance Program**

___ **Frequency:**   Do each of the initial balance activities from Stage I fifteen times a day. (If you and your baby are enjoying them a lot, do them as often as you want.)

___ **Intensity:**   Now you can move as quickly as you and your child want to move; he should be quite accustomed to the activities by now.

___ **Duration:**   Increase each session to forty-five seconds and then to one full minute—continuing to stop *before* your baby wants to!

___ **GOAL:**   TO HELP YOUR INFANT BEGIN TO CREEP, PRE-PARING HIS BALANCE, VISION AND BODY STRUCTURE FOR MORE SOPHISTICATED BAL-ANCE PROGRAMS.

Mother's comments: _____
_____ .

The Institutes' Mobility Development Scale

GLENN DOMAN
and
The Staff
of
The Institutes

BRAIN STAGE		TIME FRAME	MOBILITY
VII	SOPHISTI-CATED CORTEX	Superior 36 Mon. Average 72 Mon. Slow 144 Mon.	Using a leg in a skilled role which is consistent with the dominant hemisphere *Sophisticated human expression*
VI	PRIMITIVE CORTEX	Superior 18 Mon. Average 36 Mon. Slow 72 Mon.	Walking and running in complete cross pattern *Primitive human expression*
V	EARLY CORTEX	Superior 9 Mon. Average 18 Mon. Slow 36 Mon.	Walking with arms freed from the primary balance role *Early human expression*
IV	INITIAL CORTEX	Superior 6 Mon. Average 12 Mon. Slow 24 Mon.	Walking with arms used in a primary balance role most frequently at or above shoulder height *Initial human expression*
III	MIDBRAIN	Superior 3.5 Mon. Average 7 Mon. Slow 14 Mon.	Creeping on hands and knees, culminating in cross pattern creeping *Meaningful response*
II	PONS	Superior 1 Mon. Average 2.5 Mon. Slow 5 Mon.	Crawling in the prone position culminating in cross pattern crawling *Vital response*
I	MEDULLA and CORD	Superior Birth to .5 Average Birth to 1.0 Slow Birth to 2.0	Movement of arms and legs without bodily movement *Reflex response*

THE INSTITUTES FOR THE ACHIEVEMENT OF HUMAN POTENTIAL

8801 STENTON AVENUE

WYNDMOOR, PA 19038

11
MULTIPLYING YOUR BABY'S PHYSICAL INTELLIGENCE

STAGE III, THE MIDBRAIN

Mobility Competence

CLASS: Tiny Baby.
BRAIN STAGE: The Midbrain.
PROFILE COLOR: Yellow.
FUNCTION: Creeping on hands and knees culminating in cross-pattern creeping.
AVERAGE AGE: Seven months.
DESCRIPTION: At some time prior to one year of age the crawling infant makes a very important discovery. He finds he can push himself up on his hands and knees and move forward with his belly raised off the floor. This is called creeping.

He will very often return to crawling if he wants to get somewhere quickly and surely because, in the beginning, he will still be a much better crawler than he is a creeper.

For a short period, he may creep by moving his arms forward together, putting his hands down together, and pulling his legs up together. This looks like a rabbit hopping, and is called homologous creeping.

He may creep by moving his right arm and leg forward simultaneously, anchoring them down and then pulling the left arm and leg forward simultaneously. This is called homolateral creeping.

PURPOSE:

Finally he will move to the highest and most efficient form of creeping. Now he will rest on his left hand and right knee while he moves his right hand and left knee forward. He will then rest on his right hand and left knee while he begins the process again. This is called cross-pattern creeping and is the highest and most efficient form of creeping.

While crawling is movement for movement's sake, creeping is a *goal-directed* function.

The medulla is in control of *reflex* function, and the pons is responsible for *vital* function, but his newly reached midbrain is responsible for *meaningful* function.

The tiny baby now creeps across the room, not merely to get across it but instead to get the cracker that awaits him as his reward.

What good would it do for him to be able to creep purposefully across the floor if he could not see the cracker clearly and recognize it for what it is (a visual responsibility of the midbrain)?

What would it avail him to recognize the cracker and to get across the room, if he could not pick the cracker up with his hand when he arrived at the other side?

But the world of creeping is one your tiny baby has just entered, and he is far from skilled. Once again we can say that, at the best, right now he has his learner's permit for creeping.

How Creeping Occurs

Before he was ninety days old, Marlowe Doman had mastered the quadruped position. He would get up onto his hands and knees, get his balance, shuffle his hands and knees, and, in the process, move about two inches. Then—in an homologous pattern—he would lunge forward and land on his tummy. He would be another six inches closer to his objective. He would then get up and start all over again.

During that week, he fussed if he was put on the short, looped-pile carpeting in the hallway. Obviously he didn't appreciate "biting the dust" on that hard carpet.

He discovered that to creep he needed two new skills. First, he had to have a new ability to coordinate the functions of his shoulders, elbows, wrists and fingers with his hips, knees, ankles and toes. (Most especially was this true of his knees and elbows.)

Second, he learned that if he was now to move with his belly raised from the ground, he would be dealing directly with gravity in a new way. Now, for the first time, he would be off the floor and, consequently, capable of falling down. He needed, therefore, to develop a sense of balance, and this he did. He got up and crept.

Now that *your* tiny baby has begun to creep, you are faced with a number of options.

1. You can make it *difficult* for him to creep by giving him little opportunity to do so and a difficult environment in which to do so. In this case, his ability to creep will develop very slowly and, as a result, so will *all* his bodily systems. Most important of all, his brain growth will be slowed down.

2. You can simply *allow* him to creep, so that his opportunities to do so will be accidental, neither being denied the possibility to creep, nor encouraged to do so. Since this is what has traditionally happened to the average tiny baby, his mobility development will be average, his bodily systems will have average growth and so will his brain.

3. You can, if you like, give him an ideal situation in which to creep, great *encouragement* to do so, and a perfect environment in which to do it. In that case, you will give him a superb opportunity to pass through the yellow territory of the midbrain learning everything there is to learn in that fascinating land, but wasting not a moment along the way.

Let's follow the last option and see where *you* might lead *your* tiny child . . .

THE MOBILITY COMPETENCE PROGRAM—STAGE III: INGREDIENTS FOR SUCCESS

It is hard to *crawl* on a thick carpet, but it is easy to *creep* on a thick carpet.

It is hard to *creep* on a smooth surface (it hurts); therefore your baby needs a thick carpet as his surface for creeping.

Remember, your floor is still clean, warm and *safe*.

"Safe" now takes on greater implications. Your tiny baby's mobility is expanding. As it does, you must remove objects or pieces of furniture that are unstable. Your tiny baby's range of mobility is increasing every day. You should now "batten down the hatches" as it were, making sure all tables, lamps, and other pieces of furniture are secure, and removing all table lamps or other objects from table tops. Stairways and stairwells must be protected.

It becomes increasingly important for your tiny baby to have "room to roam." He has learned he can get to *objects* he wants and now he needs the opportunity to learn he can go to *places*. Mobility is for transportation. Your tiny baby is learning what mobility is all about. He has a lot of problem-solving to do.

Margeaux Jackson, nine months old, of The Evan Thomas Institute Off-Campus Program, moves in a fluid cross-pattern. Her left hand and right knee are forward. Her right hand and left knee are behind. (Margeaux started creeping at five months and was standing within a month's time.)

He'll creep up to a wall and need to learn how to turn around; he'll creep into a corner and have to "back out"; even creeping across a threshold into a different room provides a challenge.

Let him conquer his world. Given opportunity, he'll do it in no time.

At this point, we should remind you of a few possible pitfalls to be avoided: not only do hard floor surfaces such as linoleum and hardwood hurt if you slip on them, and slow a creeping baby down, but they can also reduce his "sure-kneed-ness."

Try to keep him in rooms where there is a minimum of furniture and a maximum amount of open space.

Creepers Need Pants

It's time now to put on your baby's long pants (to protect his knees) and socks (to protect his feet). Everything should be comfortable and loose-fitting. This is not an activity for dresses; little girls can be slowed down considerably at this point if they are wearing skirts of any sort. No matter what you do, the skirt gets caught under the wearer's knees and trips her up while creeping.

Encourage Your Baby to Explore

Providing you've given your tiny baby "room to roam," and dressed him properly, he'll utilize his natural desire to explore and learn about the world. You can encourage his thirst for exploration by placing interesting items in far corners of the room and, as his distance expands, into other rooms and eventually to the far corners of the house and outdoors!

You'll learn quickly what your tiny baby likes and what he'll find irresistible to chase—items such as balls or trucks—and your household pet!

If the place he creeps in and to is not *one hundred percent safe*, then you will find yourself nagging him about all the things not to touch there. Make sure the environment is safe beforehand.

Make sure the environment is clean, but do keep in mind that there is just no way to make it sterile. If you become a "hygiene maniac," you'll reduce your baby's time on the floor. Don't spend so much time scrubbing it that you and your baby can't enjoy some time together down there!

Going for Distance

The distance your baby creeps daily remains essential to rapid midbrain development. His total quantity of creeping should be growing daily. This is not difficult—to the contrary, it becomes easier. Your tiny baby's thirst to learn about everything makes him want to creep everywhere. His speed increases constantly. His respiration develops with his mobility.

As he creeps for long periods without stopping, his respiration develops precisely as it does for adults who go out and jog several miles.

Breathing adapts to the duration of the physical activity and even, deep breathing is the result. People without that respiratory adaptation can't jog several miles. The function of running and, in your baby's case, the function of creeping, creates the necessary respiratory structure.

Frequency: Begin with many, many, many *brief* sessions of creeping—twenty, thirty or more brief opportunities throughout the day. As his ability to creep nonstop distances increases, so will his skill as a creeper.

Intensity: When your tiny baby begins to creep, he will move only a few inches at a time. With more and more opportunity to creep (as in "Frequency," above), his nonstop distances will increase to measurement in feet and yards.

Intensity will be determined by how quickly your baby is able to creep and, obviously, his speed will develop markedly as he becomes an increasingly accomplished creeper.

Duration: Frequency and duration are inextricably tied together. As duration increases, frequency decreases. Duration of sessions will be very short as your baby starts to creep and become increasingly longer as he demands opportunity to explore his world.

He should have a minimum of four hours a day of opportunity to creep, and a maximum of as many hours as you can provide.

THE GOAL AT THIS LEVEL IS FOR YOUR BABY TO REACH A TOTAL OF FOUR HUNDRED YARDS OF CREEPING IN A DAY.

Yes, we said four hundred yards. Four hundred yards is almost one-quarter mile. How will your little baby *ever* creep that much?

It seems a lot.

However, for years now, we have kept accurate records of our creepers' accomplishments. Babies given adequate opportunity have been known to creep *four times* that much!

The parent's next question is, "How is creeping distance measured?" That's a fair enough question. Obviously, you can't follow your baby around with a yardstick.

Here are two ways it can be done:

One way is to know the dimensions of your rooms and halls and keep a checklist of the approximate number of times your baby crosses the room or heads down the hall. Once the habit of recording the distance is established, it's not too difficult to keep a record.

The other way is to make a concerted effort, once every week or so, to record accurately an average day's distance. That way you know approximately what distance your baby is covering.

The more he creeps, the closer he is to total midbrain development. The more he creeps, the closer he is to walking. (Incidentally, we've never seen a baby who can creep four hundred yards who can't pull himself to a standing position holding onto a piece of furniture.)

Conclusions

Now your baby is a truly confirmed creeper. He creeps in cross-pattern. He goes wherever he pleases. His movement is now entirely goal-directed. He creeps to get the cracker. He creeps out to the kitchen in order to be with you while you cook dinner. But, primarily, he creeps everywhere to learn about the fantastic world that surrounds him and about which he wants to learn absolutely *everything—right now!*

He has crept his way through the midbrain and is approaching the level of the cortex. He has gained a great deal of knowledge and an incredible amount of ability while doing so. His creeping has been responsible for finishing the functional development of his midbrain and has provided the stimulation required to begin activation of the cortex.

Now that your baby has perfected his creeping so that he moves over virtually every surface, expertly, quickly, easily and confidently, he will begin a new and very daring experiment.

His midbrain is now matured by all the creeping he has done. He turns his eyes upward and gets a look in them which is both dreamy and determined. He creeps to the sofa, puts his hands on the seat, and pulls himself to an upright position. His days as a full-time creeper are coming to an end. Now he is getting hard to hold down.

He begins to pull himself erect on every table, hassock, chair and sofa he can reach. The day arrives when he gets a firm grip on the table, pulls himself to his feet and, holding on to the edge, walks its whole length.

He is *cruising*. Cruising isn't an end in itself, but it *is* a beginning—the beginning of walking.

One day, after much cruising, he will get to the end of the table and appraisingly eye the sofa just four free steps away. He has a walking imperative that he has come by honestly through all his human ancestors. Those four steps from the table to the sofa are in some respects the longest journey he will ever take. He takes it.

He has crossed the line that separates the highest area of midbrain function from the lowest level of cortical function.

He is walking.

He is, to be sure, a rank amateur when it comes to walking, but he has a proper and certified learner's permit that those few unassisted steps have earned him. These are all the qualifications he will need to continue to develop the walking areas of his initial cortex.

If he is exactly twelve months old, he has a mobility intelligence of exactly 100. If he is younger, or older, you can find *your* baby's mobility intelligence by consulting the chart that follows.

At whatever age he reaches this exalted stage of beginning to walk on his legs, and in the upright position, it is an event for great celebration.

He has begun his ascent into that area of nature's domain reserved exclusively for human beings.

Mobility Intelligence
LEAVING STAGE III, THE MIDBRAIN
ENTERING STAGE IV, THE INITIAL CORTEX

AGE (in months)	MOBILITY INTELLIGENCE	OUR ADVICE
Four	300	World's record?
Five	240	You're doing
Six	200	a superb job!
Seven	171	
Eight	150	
Nine	133	Splendid job!
Ten	120	
Eleven	109	
Twelve	100	Exactly average.
Fourteen	85	Give him more opportunity.
Sixteen	75	
Eighteen	66	Give your child immediate
Twenty	60	and extraordinary
Twenty-two	54	opportunity to move, move, move.
Twenty-four	50	If your child is at 50 or below in mobility intelligence, waste no time in seeking professional help.

The more a baby creeps, the closer he is to walking. When your baby reaches the exalted stage of beginning to walk, it is an event for great celebration.

Margeaux (still nine months old in this photo and able to stand since the age of six months) gets ready to take some steps to her mom, Judith Jackson.

The Institutes' Manual Development Scale

BRAIN STAGE		TIME FRAME	MANUAL COMPETENCE
VII	SOPHISTI-CATED CORTEX	Superior 36 Mon. / Average 72 Mon. / Slow 144 Mon.	**Using a hand to write which is consistent with the dominant hemisphere** *Sophisticated human expression*
VI	PRIMITIVE CORTEX	Superior 18 Mon. / Average 36 Mon. / Slow 72 Mon.	**Bimanual function with one hand in a skilled role** *Primitive human expression*
V	EARLY CORTEX	Superior 9 Mon. / Average 18 Mon. / Slow 36 Mon.	**Cortical opposition bilaterally and simultaneously** *Early human expression*
IV	INITIAL CORTEX	Superior 6 Mon. / Average 12 Mon. / Slow 24 Mon.	**Cortical opposition in either hand** *Initial human expression*
III	MIDBRAIN	Superior 3.5 Mon. / Average 7 Mon. / Slow 14 Mon.	**Prehensile grasp** *Meaningful response*
II	PONS	Superior 1 Mon. / Average 2.5 Mon. / Slow 5 Mon.	**Vital release** *Vital response*
I	MEDULLA and CORD	Superior Birth to .5 / Average Birth to 1.0 / Slow Birth to 2.0	**Grasp reflex** *Reflex response*

GLENN DOMAN
and
The Staff
of
The Institutes

THE INSTITUTES FOR THE ACHIEVEMENT OF HUMAN POTENTIAL
8801 STENTON AVENUE
WYNDMOOR, PA 19038

MULTIPLYING YOUR BABY'S PHYSICAL INTELLIGENCE

STAGE III, THE MIDBRAIN

Manual Competence

CLASS:	Tiny Baby.
BRAIN STAGE:	The Midbrain.
PROFILE COLOR:	Yellow.
FUNCTION:	Prehensile grasp.
AVERAGE AGE:	Seven months
DESCRIPTION:	At this stage, the tiny baby gains the ability to go beyond merely holding on as he did at the level of the medulla, or merely letting go as he did at the level of the pons.
	He can now actually open his hand *for the purpose* of closing it on an object and picking it up. This is called prehensile grasp. He has sufficient skilled function of shoulder and elbow to allow him to place his hand in the position required to grasp an object on purpose and to use it.
	He is not yet able to use his thumb and forefinger to pick up *little* objects, but he *can* use the entire hand to pick up a larger object between his fingers and the palm of his hand in the manner of the great apes.
PURPOSE:	He has reached this still higher function because his brain development and growth have now reached the midbrain. His continuing growth *through* the midbrain will be a direct result of how many times he will have opportunity to pick up objects of the proper size, shape and texture to be "pick-up-able." In a manual sense, he has outdistanced all the other creatures of the earth, save the great apes.

The function of prehensile grasp is now his, and is a goal-directed rather than a life-saving function. The tiny baby himself is now very goal-directed. He has the visual, auditory and tactile knowledge to *appreciate* without yet fully *understanding* his newfound ability to pick things up for eating, investigating, studying or simply banging them about.

He's learning at an astonishing speed.

THE MANUAL COMPETENCE PROGRAM—STAGE III: INGREDIENTS FOR SUCCESS

At the previous stage of manual function, you were beginning to give your infant the ability to bear some of his weight momentarily.

Now that he can use his hands, you are ready to take the next step. This step is for him to hang by his hands, supporting his own weight for greater periods of time.

We're going to be getting your baby ready to hang independently for longer periods of time, and to instill in him a burning desire to begin brachiating!

Continuing to Use the Bar

Continue to use the bar in the doorway that you used throughout Stage II. Of course, for fun, your baby should continue to hold on to and hang from your thumbs. This will keep his ability to hang independently intact. This is very important in light of his constant growth and weight.

Hold him with your hands clasped firmly around his hips and waist so he is facing you. Lift him to a height where he can grasp the bar easily. As he holds on, lower the rest of his body until his arms are completely straight. Keep your hands in the same position, holding him firmly. Now, move his hips and swing him back and forth a little bit, as if he were swinging from rung to rung on an overhead ladder (which he will soon be doing, when we start the very important job of teaching him to brachiate).

Make sure the floor under the dowel is softly covered with a thick pile carpet and, preferably, a gym or tumbling mat. Obviously, it would not be a good idea to have either the dowel, or later, the brachiation ladder, over a concrete floor. A fall that hurts, even though from only a few inches, might discourage your baby from brachiating for a good, long time.

Frequency: Do fifteen sessions a day.
Intensity: Gradually decrease your support until he is supporting all of his own weight while you continue to swing him.
Duration: Twenty seconds at a time.

Because of the manual development created by these "hanging" sessions, your tiny baby will begin to be able to pick up smaller and smaller objects with greater and greater ease.

You, of course, will continue to supply him with smaller and smaller objects and more and more opportunity.

As the objects become smaller and smaller, you must watch him more and more carefully, because as surely as the good Lord made little green apples, the objects will go into his mouth.

You, as a consequence, must make *absolutely sure* that any small objects that fit into his mouth are, in point of fact, edible.

He must have an ample supply of small food that is acceptable to you from a dietary standpoint (i.e., crackers, biscuits and bits of soft fruit, such as banana).

Getting Ready to Brachiate

Now we are ready to start whetting your baby's appetite for brachiation!

Brachiating, you will remember, is the ability to swing from bar to bar on an overhead ladder just as apes swing from branch to branch on a tree. We will teach the baby in two ways initially:

1. *Teaching him how by having the other members of the family demonstrate* (for all of *you,* this means beginning *right now!*) and
2. *Teaching him how by helping him to do so himself.* (For him, it means watching *your* fun, hanging and swinging from his dowel in the doorway, and becoming *very eager* to brachiate himself. He gets his chance, next chapter, in Stage IV!)

Absolute Requirements for Success

Once moms and dads understand that brachiation enhances the growth of the chest and thus creates a better structure for breathing, they really *want* their kids to succeed in brachiating. But how?

We're going to supply you with *all* the *different* methods we've learned since 1968. These methods *we* learned from parents, and we're sure there are so many others we haven't heard about that each mom will find or invent one that suits *her* kid best.

There are, however, three factors that are inherent in all of the successful methods:

1. *You must have a proper brachiation ladder in your house.*
2. *Brachiation must be done frequently throughout the day.*
3. *Your kid must love to brachiate!*

A "proper brachiation ladder" means "built according to specification for the size of your kid"—one that's solid and doesn't wobble. It should also be adjustable, so it can be raised to adult height for Mom's and Dad's daily trips.

"In your house" means that it is available twenty-four hours a day for use. Use is not limited by weather conditions or how long it takes to get to the ladder.

If you don't have a brachiation ladder, *stop everything until you've got one.* You will find a detailed description of how to build a brachiation ladder in Appendix I of this book. By having a proper brachiation ladder in place all of the time, you can make brachiation a way of life for your family.

Now, at any time, you have a virtually foolproof approach to teaching guaranteed: Mom, Dad, and older sisters and brothers can *show* the prospective brachiator how it's done by giving him an honest example:

1. Brachiating *independently* with feet off the ground.
2. Brachiating frequently daily.
3. Brachiating AND ENJOYING IT.

Providing all of you, or at least some of you, do this, you've got it made, because if someone else in his family can do it, your tiny baby will naturally want to do it. Perhaps, for a couple of weeks, later on, he will change his mind and *not* want to brachiate. He'll just be testing the water.

Don't stop.

Providing you continue every day to set the right example, he will definitely come around. Make the pleasure you feel in doing it obvious. If you, and your older sons and daughters *love* to brachiate, you will find you have younger ones who can't *wait* until they can do it, too!

Brachiate Frequently Throughout the Day

Brachiation must be done frequently throughout the day.

Frequently.

Frequently.

Frequently.

Frequently, because initially brachiation can be done for a minute or two, maximum. Longer periods will cause the hand muscles to become exhausted. Therefore, brachiating for *many* brief periods every day is the key.

Throughout the day.

Throughout the day.

Throughout the day.

Throughout the day—spread the sessions through the course of the day to give the hands and skin (yours, and at the next stage, your baby's) maximum time to recuperate and toughen.

Your Kid Must Want to Brachiate

There is simply no way to succeed if your child doesn't want to do it.

Brachiation requires a conscious decision, and the determination to get oneself along that ladder!

We know you'll encourage this by being very careful *not* to give your child the impression that brachiation is fun for him, but not for you. He'll get his chance at it next chapter, and you'll want to have him chomping at the bit to get there!

THE GOAL AT THIS LEVEL IS FOR YOUR CHILD TO HANG FOR TWENTY SECONDS ONE HUNDRED PERCENT TOTALLY INDEPENDENTLY, AND TO HAVE A BURNING DESIRE TO ACTUALLY BEGIN BRACHIATING!

Conclusions

Your baby is now a confirmed picker-upper, and his trip through the midbrain is coming to a close since he can now pick up virtually anything that will fit in his hand and that can be grasped by his fingers pressing against his palm.

Now a very subtle thing begins to happen. You have been accustomed to seeing him picking up the cracker from his high chair tray using his prehensile grasp. *Now* if you watch him carefully, you will, upon occasion, see him almost accidentally trap a very small piece of cracker between his thumb and forefinger and, with some amount of surprise, pop it into his mouth.

This new act is called cortical opposition and is a function of the exclusively human cortex.

Only human beings have a human cortex, and only human beings have true cortical opposition.

When he has accomplished this highly skilled act by accident often enough to get the "feel" of it (and thus to do it on purpose), he will have crossed that wonderfully important line that separates the highest functions of the midbrain from the lowest functions of the human cortex.

Average children cross that line in manual competence at one year of age.

He does *not* have to be able to brachiate to get credit at Stage IV. *If you've worked ahead* and started brachiating a little, it's a wonderful *bonus*.

AGE (in months)	MANUAL INTELLIGENCE	OUR ADVICE
Manual Intelligence **LEAVING STAGE III, THE MIDBRAIN** **ENTERING STAGE IV, THE INITIAL CORTEX**		
Four	300	World's record?
Five	240	You're doing a
Six	200	superb job!
Seven	171	
Eight	150	
Nine	133	Splendid job!
Ten	120	
Eleven	109	
Twelve	100	Exactly average.
Fourteen	85	Give him more opportunity.
Sixteen	75	
Eighteen	66	Give your child immediate
Twenty	60	and extraordinary
Twenty-two	54	opportunity to develop his manual competence.
Twenty-four	50	If your child is below 50 in manual intelligence, you should waste no time in seeking professional help.

THE PASSIVE BALANCE PROGRAM
FOR BABIES FOUR MONTHS OLD OR OLDER

Important Prerequisites

If you have, from birth, consistently and daily done the balance program for newborns and infants, then by around four months of age, you can begin gradually to change your baby from the newborn program to this one. The transition should take about two months.

If your baby has never had a balance program, begin with the program for newborns as instructed previously.

The activities listed ahead are more sophisticated than those of the newborn and infant because they provide a more varied environment in which to develop balance.

If it were conceivable to combine all the activities into a single activity, it would almost be as if a child could be suspended in midair and spun (as the earth spins on its axis) on all axes and rotated (as the earth orbits the sun) through all orbits. As a result, the baby's brain could then experience and feel its relationship to gravity in all possible positions, rather like an acrobat. Such opportunity would provide a basis for the baby to understand any gravitational situation that he might encounter.

Do everything with him you can do to approach that situation.

These activities, like the previous program, are passive from the baby's standpoint. All the work is done by the parents and the baby just needs to be there, enjoying it.

They add another degree of sophistication because they can be done with greater intensity than can the initial balance programs. As a result, more vestibular (balance) information is delivered to the brain in less time.

From the baby's standpoint, these activities are even more enjoyable than the previous ones. Babies dislike static situations, but they love new challenges and new experiences.

These activities involve more "flying through the air."

They happen more quickly and intensively.

You'll find every baby and kid within a hundred yards gravitating in your direction whenever they hear you're about to start your balance program—so be ready for the crowds!

Ingredients for Success

Safety is our prime concern—your baby's safety, and yours as well.

All the previous safety requirements remain in effect and require even more thoughtfulness and vigilance on your part. If the environment where you're considering doing the activities is cluttered with furniture or objects on the floor, clean the area up first and then do them. Obstacles like these represent hazards to your footing and to your tiny baby's swinging.

Be careful, be sensitive, start gradually, tell your baby what you're doing, and stop before he wants to stop.

Neck collars are in order for the Passive Balance Program activities.

Maria wears her collar with a chuckle and a smile.

Neck Collars Are in Order

It's important to be particularly careful of the babies' necks, so neck collars are definitely required.

A very soft towel, folded many times, and wrapped loosely around the infant's neck (as if it were a thick collar on a turtleneck sweater), will keep his head in a stable position.

We found it even better and easier to make a neck collar, so we've described how to do so in the Appendix of this book. (See how proudly Benjamin Newell wears his in the accompanying photograph.) Page 252 in the Appendix shows you how to make one.

Use the neck collar for every single one of these balance activities.

In order for their babies to enjoy wearing the collar, moms have found it helpful to wear it first themselves for several days. When you do so, your baby will want to wear one—just like you!

Make sure any clothing your child has on isn't so loose that it may catch on something as you spin around. When you hold on to him, don't hold him by socks or shoes (these may slip off); hold him by the bare ankles.

Demonstrate YOUR Enthusiasm

As in beginning any new activity, you will want to demonstrate *your* enthusiasm so that your child is confident.

Begin gradually. Proceed with short durations (perhaps only a few seconds), and increase the time and speed of the activity bit by bit.

Do the already familiar activities with even more speed, energy and verve (intensity).

Don't do any of these activities unless you're completely comfortable with them. If you're uncomfortable, your kid will sense this and he will not enjoy doing them.

Don't do any of these activities without being one hundred percent confident you can do them safely.

If you are concerned about any of the activities, don't talk about it in front of your child and don't do them. Tiny babies have a sort of built-in radar that picks up on your attitude every time!

THE PASSIVE BALANCE PROGRAM ACTIVITIES

Horizontal Spin

1. *Prone Position.* Place your baby over your shoulder on his tummy (as in the photograph) and spin around, being careful not to get dizzy enough to lose your own balance. Alternate the direction in which you spin between clockwise and counterclockwise.
2. *Left Side.* Repeat the spin, only place your baby on his left side on your right shoulder so his tummy is against your neck. Spin both clockwise and counterclockwise.
3. *Right Side.* Repeat the spin, only place the baby on his right side on your left shoulder. Spin both clockwise and counterclockwise.

Horizontal spin,
prone position:

Beatriz Diaque starts a
horizontal spin with Maria.
(Please note: she's wearing
her neck collar for all of
these passive balance
activities.)

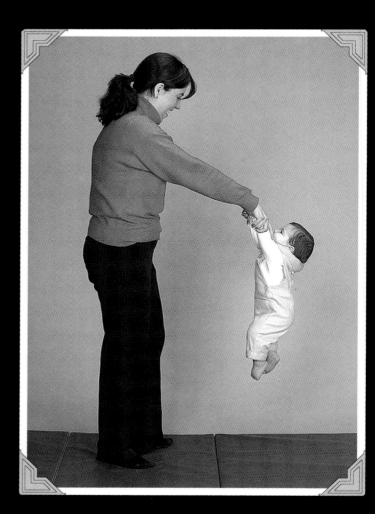

Horizontal rotation,
prone position, head in:

Beatriz rotates Maria horizontally
in the prone position,
with her head facing inward.

Rocking

The rocking activities you did with your newborn and infant have prepared your baby for a more sophisticated version:

4. *Rocking Supine Position.* Hold the baby by his wrists with his face up (supine), while your spouse holds him by the ankles. Pick him up and rock him exactly as if he were in a cradle. This activity gives him more stimulation and can be done faster than would be the case if the baby were being rocked in the old-fashioned cradle (an ancient and still extremely wise procedure, too).

Remember when you were a kid and your parents would rock you back and forth and then throw you on the bed?

Remember how much *fun* it was?

Horizontal Rotation

When you did the newborn balance program, you did horizontal rotation on a mat. Your baby will be delighted to do the same activity now, "in the air":

5. *Horizontal Rotation.* Hold your baby's left wrist in your left hand and his left ankle with your right hand. Your baby should be prone. Pick him up and spin carefully around in a counterclockwise direction.

    Clockwise, do the following: hold your baby's right wrist in your right hand, and his right ankle with your left hand. Your baby should be prone. Pick him up and spin him around carefully in a clockwise direction. The faster you spin, the more your baby will fly up into a prone position. You can also use the same positions and reverse direction so that he is rotating "feet first."

6. *Supine Position.* At first, hold your tiny baby so he faces away from you. Hold your baby's left wrist in your right hand, and his left ankle with your left hand and spin around carefully in a clockwise direction. The baby is facing out so the faster you spin, the more he "floats" up into a supine position. Then reverse directions so he rotates feet first.

    To do it counterclockwise, hold your tiny baby's right wrist in your left hand, his right ankle in your right hand, and spin around carefully in a counterclockwise direction. Again, reverse direction so he rotates "feet first."

7. *Prone Position (Head In).* Hold your tiny baby by his hands and wrists, with him facing toward you. Then spin around with arms outstretched.
    Do this activity in both clockwise and counterclockwise directions.

Horizontal Pitching

8. *Horizontal Pitching.* When you held your newborn and pitched him up and down, he was "in training" for horizontal pitching. Now your baby is so big that both Mom and Dad will be needed for this activity! With your tiny baby lying face up (supine) on the floor, Mom takes his right wrist and ankle while Dad takes his left wrist and ankle, as in the photograph.

134

When you did the newborn balance program, you did horizontal rotation and pitching on a mat or pillow. Your baby will be happy to do these activities now, "in the air."

Horizontal rotation: Beatriz spins Maria counterclockwise.

Horizontal pitching: Beatriz and Juan-Pablo pitch Maria from a horizontal position, toward a vertical one.

Acceleration and vertical rocking

Acceleration (up and down):
Beginning by holding Maria firmly
under the armpits and then carefully
tossing her into the air, Juan-Pablo
waits to catch her and share the fun.

Vertical rocking (head down):
Beatriz holds Maria upside
down and rocks her back
and forth like a pendulum.

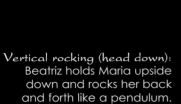

Now, swing the child to a head-up position, then back to a head-down position, very much in the manner of an older child on a playground swing.

Acceleration

9. *Acceleration (Up and Down).* Facing your tiny child, grasp him directly underneath his armpits. Now, throw him up in the air and catch him.
Be careful.
This activity (which is universally practiced by fathers, especially) is very valuable. The tiny baby actually experiences, momentarily, several times the usual force of gravity as you toss him up and he is accelerated through space. On the way down, he is in free-fall, until you catch him, as is an astronaut during re-entry.

In this particular balance and gravitational activity, the danger of missing your tiny child is present, and so special care must be exercised to begin carefully and to gradually become very skilled at doing it. Be guided to a large degree by how much your baby is enjoying it. If he is in any way apprehensive, go slowly. (Observe the action on page 135, and see Ben's happy smile!)

As we move forward to "vertical rocking with head down," we want to note beforehand that sometimes parents feel apprehensive about the idea of holding their baby upside down. This position, although not the usual one for an adult, is well known to almost every newborn. It's good to remember that within the last four weeks of a normal pregnancy, the newborn's head is engaged in the mother's pelvis. That means whenever Mom is standing up or sitting down, the fetus is upside down!

Our moms here at The Institutes have been doing this vestibular activity with their babies for more than two decades and all have found it safe and enjoyable. Now, of course, hanging upside down has become the new rage. Doctors and chiropractors recommend it for one of the plagues of adulthood: bad backs.

Babies *love* hanging upside down.

In the previous program for newborns and infants, you did pitching up and down. This was preparation for vertical rocking (head down):

10. *Vertical Rocking (Head Down).* Place your tiny baby on his back on a comfortable carpet on the floor. Standing up, you bend down and pick him up by the ankles, grasping him firmly. He should be facing toward you. When you are well positioned, gently rock him from side to side, as if he were a pendulum. Also, swing him back and forth between your legs. The photo clearly shows this action. When you return him to the floor, be careful to put him down on his back, *not* his tummy. This will protect his neck from injury, as will the neck collar he continues to wear for all these activities.

These ten activities constitute the passive balance program for your tiny baby; do them with the following:

Frequency: A good program consists of doing all of the preceding ten activities at least twice a day.

Intensity: Proper attention to the *intensity* of each activity is necessary to maintain proper safety procedures. *Begin each activity very slowly and carefully.*

Initially, there is no need for speed.

In fact, it is *disadvantageous* for the growth of the balance areas of the brain.

It is vital that the brain receives the full range of intensity of balance information from very slow to very fast movement.

Remember that we've told you the famous Russian neurophysiologist, Boris Klosovskii, proved in a classic experiment that the balance areas of the brain were between 22 percent and 35 percent larger in young animals provided with gentle balance stimulation.

He rotated his developing animals at the very slow rate of one revolution per minute; nevertheless, the results were superb.

Your tiny baby's structure will develop with function. Gradual increase of function (in this case, intensity) will gradually develop the structure he needs.

It is important to know that "starting" and "stopping" are as significant as motion. For example, for any of the spinning or rotating activities, if you spin ten times and pause, and continue another ten spins, it can be more productive than twenty continuous spins. Use *both* methods.

These guidelines are recommended for increasing intensity:

1. Move just fast enough to keep your tiny baby from hitting your body as you spin.
2. Move faster, but maintain your balance well. Stop if you feel the least bit dizzy.
3. Move more quickly, but sensibly. Hold your tiny baby firmly, but not tightly enough to make it uncomfortable for him.
4. Move fast enough during rotational and acceleration activities for your baby to feel a "flying" sensation.
5. Always stop before your baby wants to stop.
6. Always stop before *you* tire.

Duration: Begin with not more than fifteen seconds' duration for each activity for a month or two, then gradually increase to one minute per activity.

Total time for daily program: Twenty minutes.

STAGE III
DAILY CHECKLIST FOR MOTHER

1. The Mobility Program

___ **Frequency:** Begin with *many* brief sessions of creeping—twenty, thirty or more throughout the day.

___ **Intensity:** Your baby will begin by moving only a few inches at a time. With more opportunity, nonstop distances will increase to measurement in feet and yards.

___ **Duration:** Short, as baby starts to creep; increasingly longer as he demands opportunity to explore his world. A minimum of four hours daily, a maximum of double or triple this.

___ **GOAL:** FOR YOUR BABY TO REACH A TOTAL OF FOUR HUNDRED YARDS OF CREEPING IN A DAY.

Mother's comments: My baby reached a total of four hundred yards of creeping in a day at age _____ .

2. The Manual Program

___ **Frequency:** Fifteen sessions a day of hanging from a dowel.

___ **Intensity:** Gradually decrease your support until your baby is supporting all of his own weight while you continue to help him swing.

___ **Duration:** Twenty seconds at a time.

___ **Goal:** YOUR BABY HANGS FOR TWENTY SECONDS 100% TOTALLY INDEPENDENTLY (AND CAN'T WAIT TO BRACHIATE, THOUGH BRACHIATION REMAINS A SPLENDID "BONUS"!).

Mother's comments: My baby was able to hang for twenty seconds totally independently at age _____ .

3. The Balance Program

___ **Frequency:** Do all ten passive balance activities at least twice a day.

___ **Intensity:** Begin slowly and carefully. Provide the full range of intensity of balance information for your baby from very slow to very fast movement.

___ **Duration:** Begin with not more than fifteen seconds' duration for each activity for a month or two, then gradually increase to one minute per activity. Total time for daily program: twenty minutes.

___ **Goal:** TO DO ALL OF THE ACTIVITIES COMPLETELY SAFELY, WITH INCREASING FREQUENCY AND DURATION, AND GRADUALLY INCREASING INTENSITY.

Mother's comments: _____

_____ .

Our "Rules of Transportation"

For newborns, we use snuggle packs. These packs strap babies to Mom's front.

Backpacks are dangerous. Kids come to us brain-injured because they fell out of backpacks.

Frontpacks let you see your baby's face, they permit nursing, keep Baby warmer and put his legs in a good position for the natural grinding of proper hip sockets.

Our older babies are carried on their parents' hips until they can walk. Slings are now available commercially that permit babies to be carried on the hips so Mom's arms are free for use, and she can see her feet.

If a baby can walk a little, we let him walk a little, then we carry him, and so on.

If a baby can walk well, then we let him walk, walk, walk.

That's what walking's for.

The Institutes' Mobility Development Scale

GLENN DOMAN
and
The Staff
of
The Institutes

BRAIN STAGE		TIME FRAME	MOBILITY
VII	SOPHISTI-CATED CORTEX	Superior 36 Mon. Average 72 Mon. Slow 144 Mon.	Using a leg in a skilled role which is consistent with the dominant hemisphere *Sophisticated human expression*
VI	PRIMITIVE CORTEX	Superior 18 Mon. Average 36 Mon. Slow 72 Mon.	Walking and running in complete cross pattern *Primitive human expression*
V	EARLY CORTEX	Superior 9 Mon. Average 18 Mon. Slow 36 Mon.	Walking with arms freed from the primary balance role *Early human expression*
IV	INITIAL CORTEX	Superior 6 Mon. Average 12 Mon. Slow 24 Mon.	Walking with arms used in a primary balance role most frequently at or above shoulder height *Initial human expression*
III	MIDBRAIN	Superior 3.5 Mon. Average 7 Mon. Slow 14 Mon.	Creeping on hands and knees, culminating in cross pattern creeping *Meaningful response*
II	PONS	Superior 1 Mon. Average 2.5 Mon. Slow 5 Mon.	Crawling in the prone position culminating in cross pattern crawling *Vital response*
I	MEDULLA and CORD	Superior Birth to .5 Average Birth to 1.0 Slow Birth to 2.0	Movement of arms and legs without bodily movement *Reflex response*

THE INSTITUTES FOR
THE ACHIEVEMENT OF
HUMAN POTENTIAL
8801 STENTON AVENUE
WYNDMOOR, PA 19038

12
MULTIPLYING YOUR BABY'S PHYSICAL INTELLIGENCE

STAGE IV, THE INITIAL CORTEX

Mobility Competence

CLASS: Baby.

BRAIN STAGE: The Initial Cortex.

PROFILE COLOR: Green.

FUNCTION: Taking steps with arms used in a primary balance role, most frequently at or above shoulder height.

AVERAGE AGE: This function is present in an average child at twelve months of age.

DESCRIPTION: At just about one year of age the average baby makes a joyous, exciting and most momentous discovery. He discovers that he can pull himself to his feet holding onto a sofa, chair, or table.

He then discovers that he can, for an instant, let go without falling down.

Finally, he discovers the fabulous fact that not only can he stand independently, he can, moreover, take a few steps without falling.

At this stage, he will carry his arms at or above shoulder height, using them as a balance device much in the manner of a tightrope walker—and for precisely the same reason, since he and the tightrope walker are both concerned with the crucial issue of *not falling down*. At first the baby will often fall down. His initial steps will probably begin with his letting go of the furniture on which he finds support, launching himself forward in a projectile way, and generally ending up on the floor. He is unable to stop himself and stand still.

Oh well, he is close to the floor, he is well padded, and he is virtually without fear. In any case, he will learn a great deal from his falls. He will learn about inertia when he is unable to stop his projectile thrust forward (bodies in motion tend to remain in motion until disturbed from without). He will learn the remainder of the law of inertia when the family dog brushes past him while he is standing (bodies at rest tend to remain at rest until disturbed from without).

He will learn about gravity when he leans too far to the right, left, forward or backward and falls to the floor.

He will learn that these laws are immutable and that they *always* work and cannot be turned off by charm, tears, wailing, or screaming and because he is a baby and learns very quickly that he is *always* fined for disobeying these laws (he falls down) and that he is *always* rewarded for obeying them (he continues to stand or walk), he very quickly learns how to walk.

PURPOSE: It is in every way accurate to say that when Baby has taken his first steps without help from mother, father, furniture, or railing, he has taken out his first papers for full-fledged citizenship in the human race, shaky though he may be.

While each of the six uniquely human functions is truly unique and truly necessary to the full functioning of a human being, it does not necessarily follow that all are equally important. Developmentalists, neurosurgeons, behaviorists, etiologists and anthropologists may reasonably argue the respective merits of each of these, but almost all would agree that astonishing things happen when an individual human child succeeds, or when man himself first succeeded in getting onto his feet.

Of the many, many things that take place when a baby goes from being a quadruped to being an upright human being, the clearest and most important thing that happens is he frees his hands from the mobility role—but we shall return to that shortly, in our next discussion on manual competence.

From a mobility standpoint, he has acquired an ability that is given to human beings alone and is conferred upon him at conception when he acquired that generous gift of the genes of Homo sapiens. He walks upright.

Walking upright is the beginning, and it will lead to running, jumping, gymnastic grace, the beauty of ballet and all other physical activities that are strong and graceful and beautiful, and which spring from the proud, completely upright human stance.

Again, we as parents are faced with a number of choices, although now the child is a bit less of a victim if we make a poor or foolish choice. By taking his first tottering step, he has markedly reduced his dependence on others.

1. You can make it *difficult* for him to walk by giving him an environment in which walking is inconvenient, difficult, or even impossible. If you do so he will walk poorly and progress slowly, in which case he will develop slowly in a physical sense, and will have a low mobility intelligence. His brain will continue to grow but will grow more slowly.

or

2. You can *allow* him to walk in an environment in which walking is essentially accidental and average. If such is the case, he will develop as an average walker with an average mobility intelligence and an average brain in mobility areas.

or

3. You can give him an environment for walking as perfect as your circumstances allow. You can encourage him to walk often and well by giving him enthusiastic respect every time he does it successfully. You can walk with him using the principles of frequency, intensity and duration. If you choose to do *all* those things, and some others which follow, you can prepare him to walk easily, efficiently and even superbly, and by so doing, you will give him a superb base for all later physical accomplishments at the youngest possible age.

   You will also give him a high mobility intelligence and superb brain growth in all areas of the brain that have to do with mobility and its allied functions.

Let's keep following the last and best of these options. . . .

THE MOBILITY COMPETENCE PROGRAM—STAGE IV: INGREDIENTS FOR SUCCESS

Give your baby unlimited opportunity to walk, walk, walk.

By himself.

Adults tend to want to hold a baby's hand when he walks. We understand this. All parents, including all of us, experience a spark of amazement and love when we hold the perfect, tiny hands of our babies.

But, from the baby's standpoint, *at this stage*, holding his hand is doing him a disservice.

The balance mechanism (the vestibular part of the brain) needs *opportunity* to learn how to balance the baby for walking.

When we adults hold a baby's hand, our fully developed vestibular mechanisms balance *for* the baby. Unconsciously, *your* hand will make the necessary adjustments to keep the baby balanced.

Thus, he is *denied* the opportunity to learn to balance.

He can also develop bad habits.

Moms have often said to us, "But my baby *always* wants to hold my hand."

Of course—now he is *dependent* upon your balancing for him.

Look at it from his standpoint.

For a baby to hold an adult's hand and walk, he must raise one arm way over his head. This results in his being thrown off balance. Now he *must* hold on, or he'll fall over. Try walking around with one arm extended way over your head, and you'll get a real feeling for the *baby's* situation.

Once he's an accomplished walker, you can enjoy holding his hand as much as you and he like, because then it won't have anything to do with his balance development!

The ideal surface for the room in which he walks is smooth (such as a wood floor), but not slippery. A tightly woven carpet is better than one with plush, deep texture.

At first the room he's walking in should contain some low and stable furniture, to allow him to get to a standing position easily and then to move from one piece to another. *Make sure the corners and edges of the furniture are not sharp* so that if your baby falls, he doesn't hurt himself.

Some pieces of furniture should, at first, be within easy reach of each other so that he can easily and safely touch two pieces of furniture simultaneously, and step from piece to piece.

Gradually separate the furniture so he is taking two, three, or four steps to travel from one piece to the next.

As he learns to get up without the aid of furniture, and to walk without its help, even these pieces of furniture should be moved aside to give him the largest uncluttered area in which to walk.

Encourage your baby to walk longer and longer distances nonstop.

Give your baby unlimited balance information with increased frequency, intensity and duration.

As his walking becomes more and more surefooted, *begin to give him objects to carry in his hands*, as a preliminary step toward Stage V.

What the Walking Baby Should Wear

Your baby should be barefooted until he is reasonably surefooted. This is so that his ankle structure develops naturally, without artificial support.

The baby should be fully clothed, but in clothing that is lightweight and nonrestrictive, so that he can move with the greatest freedom. Putting long pants on to protect his knees from frequent spills is very wise.

It's obvious that putting many layers of heavyweight, tight-fitting clothing on your baby (even outdoors) will only weigh him down, restrict his movements and probably *guarantee* that he won't be able to make much progress.

Join Him in His Joy

The joy of walking and the opportunity to have your undivided attention and applause—these things will motivate your baby to walk. He will be thrilled at the new freedom he has found. When he walks, he will be brimming over with pride and he will be right to feel so prideful.

By all means, join him in his expressions of glee!

It is no mean accomplishment to walk upright.

Walking, like talking, is the miracle of miracles and almost never appreciated as the incredible thing that it is *except in its absence*. When the miracle of walking occurs in an average child, we accept it as natural, which it is, and take it totally for granted, which we should *not*.

It is only when this miracle does *not* happen that we appreciate the enormity of the accomplishment. Every parent alive whose baby does *not* walk (when at one year of age he is *supposed* to) appreciates the significance of the accomplishment. Parents whose children fail to accomplish this till-then-unappreciated miracle are then prepared to bring their child halfway 'round the world to The Institutes to learn how to *make* the miracle occur.

Ask any adult who is quadriplegic whether the ability to walk is a miracle or not. Ask him what he would *give* to walk.

Your baby fully appreciates the miraculous thing he has accomplished when, for the first time, *he walks*. Join him in his exultation. It is an exultation of life itself.

Walk with him at every opportunity.

And keep remembering, however hard it is for you to do, to permit him to walk by himself. It's so important. Let *his* balance mechanism do the work.

Sometimes he'll need to hold onto a railing, or even get down on all fours to climb up a step. What's important is that *his brain* is in charge. As his brain experiences these opportunities, he will learn how to conquer them.

Since babies will take many falls at this stage, it's obvious you must watch him like a hawk.

His craze for exploration will entice him to the stairs and other places you would rather he avoided. Be careful, be attentive.

At this stage, it's natural for babies to take many spills. This is part of the learning process. We have a tendency, when Baby falls, to instantaneously blurt out "Ahhh" or "Ooops," or more serious expressions of alarm. Almost always the baby is fine, and happy to get up and go on, but in time babies get the message that something *bad* must be happening, based on all the adult concern they hear. This is discouraging to the baby and often makes him cry.

When a baby falls and we can't catch him, we can discipline ourselves to be quiet, and help him up; if he's hurt, we can give him a hug and ask him if he's all right. Once he's okay *we keep right on going*.

Mom, Dad and Baby Play the "Walking Game"

The quantity of time your baby spends walking will directly determine how quickly he advances to the next stage. All parents instinctively understand this. Parents and baby play an age-old ritual: Mom stands up, stands Baby up, and gets him balanced. Dad stands expectantly, facing them, at a distance of a few feet. Baby walks to Dad.

The game continues and Baby improves. Mom and Dad gradually get farther and farther apart. It would not be unnatural for the reader to say, "But all well babies walk. Isn't this a great deal of fuss to make about a completely natural occurrence?"

Of course.

The point we've *missed* is that how *much* he walks, how *soon* he walks and how *well* he walks will result in brain growth to the next brain stage. They will multiply his mobility competence and intelligence—and that's what this book is all about!

The whole game is *expanding* the *duration* of the walking.

Mom, Dad and Baby are all very proud, and they try to play the game with great *frequency*. And the *intensity* of the game depends on how much and how far the baby walks. As we've said, the *more often* the game is played in a day, the *greater the distance* the baby travels and the resulting *increased quality of his walking*, the sooner the baby goes to the next stage.

Frequency: When your baby begins to take his first tentative steps, high frequency is imperative. Give him twenty to thirty opportunities to walk each day. Each session should consist of a step or two of walking followed by loving hugs and kisses. As he improves, the *number* of sessions will diminish to the point where he is on his feet most of the day.

Intensity: This will be determined by the distance your child walks without getting down. Obviously, as he develops, this will increase on an almost daily basis. Encourage him to gradually build up his nonstop walking distance toward the goals we will outline ahead.

Duration: The sessions will be very brief in the beginning—only a few seconds to get his balance and take a step or two. As his standing and nonstop walking ability improve, the duration of each session will become longer and longer.

Remember—always stop *before* your baby wants to. Be careful, because your excitement (and the baby's too) may affect your judgment. Don't let Baby wear himself out attempting to walk and walk. Baby should have a total duration of at least two hours a day to improve his walking.

The objective is to reach a total quantity of two hundred yards a day. This is not achieved all at one time. The quantity is arrived at by adding up all the two-, five-, fifty-, and seventy-five-foot walking sessions that your baby does during the day.

Nonstop walking, or walking without getting down or falling down, is equally important. The distance Baby walks nonstop is a guide to how rapidly his balance and breathing are adapting to his newfound mobility expertise.

THE GOAL FOR THE CHILD AT THIS LEVEL IS TO REACH FORTY FEET OF NONSTOP WALKING AND A TOTAL OF 200 YARDS IN A DAY.

We've never seen a baby who could do this who hasn't promptly progressed to Stage V. So—this goal represents your baby's ticket to the *next* stage.

Conclusions

Now your baby is an honest walker, not highly skilled, but a walker for all of that.

Now a subtle change will begin to take place. Its subtleness and gradualness belie its importance.

Up to now, your baby has relied on holding his arms up in the air for balance. His walking has been real, but precarious, and dependent on using his arms exclusively in a balance role.

Now he will begin to lower his arms *beneath* shoulder height, and to walk *without* using his arms in the balance job. It is not as significant that he does not need them for balance every second as it is that *he has now freed* his arms to use them, and his hands, as tools.

They are no longer front paws; they are now arms and hands.

Baby is on his way to full participation in the human race. You will know he has arrived when he begins to walk a few steps carrying things in his arms and hands.

He has developed his brain so well at the level of the initial cortex that he has taken the steps required to enter into the next higher brain level (which is demonstrated when he first begins to carry things in his arms while walking).

If he has had unlimited opportunity for mobility from the moment of birth, as well as sincere and warm-hearted praise from loving parents, he *could* arrive at the entrance to Stage V as early as six months. If he has, color him blue and give him a mobility intelligence of 300.

If he has had splendid opportunity, the praise he so rightly deserves from loving parents, and a great deal of practice, he may well arrive at *nine* months. Color him blue and give him a mobility intelligence of 200.

If he is *already* eighteen months when you read this book and has just arrived, give him a mobility intelligence of 100. If he is somewhat younger, or a bit older, *his* exact mobility intelligence is shown on the chart that follows.

However old he is, he arrives at the stage of the early cortex and crosses the border without needing his arms to balance him.

Now not only does he take a great many steps on his own, he actually walks across the border into the blue area of the early cortex.

Mobility Intelligence
LEAVING STAGE IV, THE INITIAL CORTEX
ENTERING STAGE V, THE EARLY CORTEX

AGE (in months)	MOBILITY INTELLIGENCE	OUR ADVICE
Six	300	World's record?
Nine	200	You're doing
Twelve	150	a superb job!
Fifteen	120	
Eighteen	100	Exactly average
Twenty-one	85	Give him more
Twenty-four	75	opportunity.
Twenty-seven	66	Give your child immediate
Thirty	60	and extraordinary
Thirty-three	54	opportunity to develop his manual competence.
Thirty-six	50	If your child is below 50 in mobility intelligence, you should waste no time in seeking professional help.

At birth a newborn has virtually no hip socket at all.

Instead, the head of the femur, which is the long bone of the upper leg, rests up against the shallow depression in the hip which will become the hip socket. As the baby who has the opportunity to do so crawls flat on his belly, his legs, flat on the floor, cause the head of the femur to dig into the hip bone, thus digging the hip socket in a lateral way. When the child gets up on hands and knees and begins to creep, the head of the femur now digs into the hip bone in a vertical direction, thus digging the hip socket into a universal joint that will permit the leg to move in many directions.

In cultures that permit newborns and tiny babies unlimited opportunity to move, there is little or no congenitally dislocated hip, and virtually no hip surgery. This may occur either because the babies themselves are permitted unlimited opportunity to crawl and creep (as is the case with our babies here at The Institutes) or it may occur because the mothers carry the babies on their hips, as is the case among the Xinguanos of Brazil, the Bushmen of the Kalahari Desert, and many other groups of primitive people.

In cultures where babies are permitted very limited opportunity to crawl or creep or in which babies are carried in backpacks, chest-packs or infant seats (which do not permit the babies' legs to move constantly), as is the case in most European and American cultures, there is less likelihood that well-developed hip sockets will be formed.

The Institutes' Manual Development Scale

BRAIN STAGE		TIME FRAME	MANUAL COMPETENCE
VII	SOPHISTI-CATED CORTEX	Superior 36 Mon. / Average 72 Mon. / Slow 144 Mon.	**Using a hand to write which is consistent with the dominant hemisphere** *Sophisticated human expression*
VI	PRIMITIVE CORTEX	Superior 18 Mon. / Average 36 Mon. / Slow 72 Mon.	**Bimanual function with one hand in a skilled role** *Primitive human expression*
V	EARLY CORTEX	Superior 9 Mon. / Average 18 Mon. / Slow 36 Mon.	**Cortical opposition bilaterally and simultaneously** *Early human expression*
IV	INITIAL CORTEX	Superior 6 Mon. / Average 12 Mon. / Slow 24 Mon.	**Cortical opposition in either hand** *Initial human expression*
III	MIDBRAIN	Superior 3.5 Mon. / Average 7 Mon. / Slow 14 Mon.	**Prehensile grasp** *Meaningful response*
II	PONS	Superior 1 Mon. / Average 2.5 Mon. / Slow 5 Mon.	**Vital release** *Vital response*
I	MEDULLA and CORD	Superior Birth to .5 / Average Birth to 1.0 / Slow Birth to 2.0	**Grasp reflex** *Reflex response*

GLENN DOMAN
and
The Staff
of
The Institutes

THE INSTITUTES FOR THE ACHIEVEMENT OF HUMAN POTENTIAL
8801 STENTON AVENUE
WYNDMOOR, PA 19038

MULTIPLYING YOUR BABY'S PHYSICAL INTELLIGENCE

STAGE IV, THE INITIAL CORTEX

Manual Competence

CLASS:	Baby.
BRAIN STAGE:	The Initial Cortex.
PROFILE COLOR:	Green.
FUNCTION:	Cortical opposition.
AVERAGE AGE:	Twelve months.
DESCRIPTION:	At Stage IV of Manual Competence, a baby is able to oppose his thumb to his forefinger and can, as a result, pick up objects too small to be picked up using prehensile grasp (i.e., bread *crumbs*, as opposed to a piece of bread). In order for a baby to do this, he must have developed his manual, visual and tactile understanding to the point where he is able to begin to understand the world in a manner unique to the human cortex.
PURPOSE:	While a baby initially uses his newfound function of cortical opposition in the relatively unimportant function of picking up crumbs, it is the fact that he is *capable* of picking them up that has such walloping importance. Nature has bigger things in mind for his future than to spend it merely picking up crumbs. She remembers a little boy named Thomas who ultimately used cortical opposition to take quill in hand to write the Declaration of Independence, and, earlier, a boy named Leonardo who ultimately used cortical opposition to take brush in hand to paint the Mona Lisa.

It's the beginning of big things.

THE MANUAL COMPETENCE PROGRAM—STAGE IV:
INGREDIENTS FOR SUCCESS

How quickly he will move through this stage while simultaneously learning all there is to be learned, and exploiting all the abilities there are to be exploited in the initial cortex, will be a pure product of how frequently, how intently, and how long he has opportunity to use his cortical opposition in every conceivable and sensible way. If we give him lots of opportunity, and encourage him to use his cortical opposition to do increasingly difficult things, we will also give him a high manual intelligence and superb brain growth in all of the areas of the brain that have to do with manual competence.

Your Baby Wants to Brachiate

Since you and Dad and your baby's brothers and sisters have already started to use your brachiation ladder, and haven't let your baby *touch* it, he is already clued into and intrigued by the "mystique" about it.

Introduce him to it as the truly great gift it actually is.

The "secret" to *teaching* brachiation is to begin by "spotting" each other.

At The Institutes, *everyone* brachiates—babies, tiny kids, big kids, families and staff.

Until each person (from babies to the most capable staff member) becomes highly skilled, he continues to be spotted. *Spotting* means that every person who is brachiating has a parent or staff member actually touching and protecting him while he does so. For a child first learning to brachiate, the term takes on a greater meaning. Just as in gymnastics, spotting is designed to help a gymnast through a new skill successfully without the spotter getting in his way.

Spotting in brachiation means helping your child brachiate along the ladder successfully.

It must be remembered that the bars are very close together, so that they can accommodate the tiny arm length of the baby. The adult will find it easier to grasp every second, third or fourth bar when brachiating.

As the person swinging becomes more and more skilled, he will skip more and more bars, because his swing will become easier.

The great secret of actually *doing* the brachiation is to *swing*. In swinging, the forward movement overcomes *inertia* and is easily utilized.

"A body at rest tends to remain at rest until disturbed from without. *A body in motion tends to remain in motion until disturbed from without.*"

The new brachiator tends to forget the second part of the law of inertia.

He almost always *hangs* from the first bar and then grabs desperately for the next bar, and hangs from that while he tries desperately for the third bar.

In so doing, his body is dead weight and works against him. He has to *pull* it with sheer brute force from bar to bar.

Instead, the brachiator must swing forward and backward (as well as from side to side), and in so doing, use his own momentum to pull himself forward exactly as we do in walking.

The person who is acting as the spotter for the brachiator must help him to get that swinging feeling by moving his hips in that normal way, as well as holding him to provide safety.

Introducing Your Baby to Brachiation

Now that you understand the importance of spotting and now that you can do a few bars (or maybe even the whole ladder) without groaning, and with some degree of honest pleasure and satisfaction, it's time to introduce your baby to this new and superb toy (tool).

He's been watching you get familiar with it and gets to see every member of the family performing on it, and being spotted.

You now perform for him on a regular basis for several days in a row and express your pleasure and pride in being able to perform this great accomplishment, as well as telling him what fun it is to do. Congratulate each other on every success.

He's watching, and he's willing and eager to have a crack at brachiating himself.

He's ready.

In the beginning, it may be helpful to use two people. Mom stands behind the child and performs the spotting function. Meanwhile Dad or big brother or sister stands in front of him and moves his hands from rung to rung in exact coordination with Mother's swinging his hips, so he gets the proper feeling right from the very beginning.

At first, you are supporting his entire weight. After a few times, eliminate the person in front moving your child's hands because he'll get the idea very quickly (which means that Mother must be ready at every instant to keep him from falling, should he suddenly let go of the ladder).

Mom can very quickly move to letting him support *some* of his weight and then move on to letting him support more and more until finally he is supporting all of his weight. She continues to hold his waist without supporting any of his weight, for safety's sake.

The ladder should be set at Mom's height. She can then easily and comfortably spot her child as he moves down the ladder.

It seems silly to have to insert this, but we must say again there is just no way to teach your child to brachiate without a brachiation ladder that's as much a part of his environment as breathing. You will simply not succeed using the steel ladder in the nearby park once a week or once a day, so please don't consider it.

Your baby needs frequent opportunity throughout the day, every day, to learn to enjoy what he is doing and to become successful at it.

In addition, you, Mom, or you, Dad, must be the spotter. Your baby trusts you more than anyone else. It is your example he wants to follow. If you turn the teaching of brachiation over to someone else, you are unlikely to have a baby who enjoys brachiating.

If the ladder is too high or too low for the spotter, whether Mom or Dad, spotting will be awkward. If you are bent over uncomfortably doing it, or up on your tiptoes supporting your child, the help you give will be clumsy, and your child will feel uneasy.

What the Well-Dressed Brachiator Should Wear

Because brachiation is an activity of grace and coordination, it requires loose-fitting clothing that does not restrict the free-swinging action of the body. Bulky outer clothing and too many layers of clothing also impede fluid movement. Wearing a coat would make brachiation darned near impossible— if not awfully uncomfortable!

T-shirts or loose-fitting polo shirts with shorts or long pants are great to wear. Pants with belts loops and/or pockets are a good idea for spotting purposes; the loops give you something specific to hold onto; even without belt loops, pants are a good idea. They are easier to hold onto than a diaper and are more secure.

A child who's learning to brachiate should never wear shoes. Bare feet or light sneakers are the best footwear. Heavy shoes such as hiking boots weigh the body down and clunk together as the body tries to swing. Save them for when you and your baby go hiking together!

Don't Make Brachiation Just for Your Baby

Remember not to start your child brachiating until the rest of your family has learned to do it. With a little bit of practice, all the members of the family will be able to brachiate to a greater or lesser degree. The kids, to a greater degree, the adults to a lesser degree.

Don't make brachiation just for your baby. It is a sure way to teach him to dislike it. Since brachiation requires a conscious effort, a real desire to want to do it, you will find your baby more willing to put forth the effort after having watched the rest of the family laugh their way across the brachiation ladder regularly.

You must exhibit genuine pleasure and zero apprehension while you're teaching your baby to brachiate. Remember that radar he's got? Babies sense apprehension better than anyone else does—just as they sense genuine pleasure.

You are giving your baby a simply splendid opportunity, and there is absolutely no reason for apprehension.

Don't forget to tell him how absolutely great he is, every single time he grasps another bar.

He is, isn't he?

He's performing a very difficult function, and he is, although we're inclined to forget it more and more, only a baby.

It's just that he's a very superior baby.

The Brachiation Program

Frequency:	Ten sessions a day of brachiating; five sessions of hanging.
Intensity:	Varying amounts of weight-bearing ranging from none in the beginning when you totally supported him through a gradual increase.
Duration:	A little bit *less* than the length of time he would *like* to do it, perhaps twenty to thirty seconds a session.

He's beginning to be a true brachiator.

In addition to brachiation, give your baby unlimited opportunity to pick up small bits of food that will in no way present a danger to him. Bits of cracker or soft fruit are still in order. Use food he cannot possibly choke on.

The more opportunity your baby has, the better his cortical opposition in both hands will become until he'll eventually be able to oppose his thumbs and forefingers to pick up small bits of food in both hands and will do so simultaneously.

THE GOAL AT THIS STAGE: THE END RESULT OF APPLYING THE MANUAL COMPETENCE PROGRAM WILL BE THAT YOUR BABY ENJOYS BRACHIATING WITH YOUR SUPPORT.

He should see moving down the full length of the ladder as sheer fun.

Conclusions

Your baby is by now a real expert at picking up tiny objects and he picks things up without conscious thought about the mechanics of doing it.

He is now so good at picking things up that he will begin to try to pick up a very small object in each of his hands simultaneously. At first, he will not succeed.

Sooner or later, he will begin—rarely, at first—to succeed in picking up two objects simultaneously, using cortical opposition in both hands.

He has entered the area controlled by the early cortex.

If you began this program when your child was born, and did it with some fair degree of enthusiasm, then the chances are good that your child is now nine months old and that would give him a manual intelligence of about 200.

If you began this program when your child was already three years of age, he had probably already reached this border when he was less than eighteen months old, you being who *you* are. That gives him a manual intelligence of over 100. If he is *exactly* eighteen months old, he has a manual intelligence of exactly 100.

However young or old he is, he is now operating above his initial cortex and is into his early cortex. It will be easy to find his exact mobility intelligence on the chart that follows.

He does *not* need to brachiate to get credit for manual competence at Stage V (or at any other stage); brachiating is a *superb bonus!*

Manual Intelligence
LEAVING STAGE IV, THE INITIAL CORTEX
ENTERING STAGE V, THE EARLY CORTEX

AGE (in months)	MANUAL INTELLIGENCE	OUR ADVICE
Six	300	World's record?
Nine	200	You're doing
Twenty	150	a superb job!
Fifteen	120	
Eighteen	100	Exactly average.
Twenty-one	85	Give him more
Twenty-four	75	opportunity.
Twenty-seven	66	Give your child immediate
Thirty	60	and extraordinary
Twenty-three	54	opportunity to develop his manual competence.
Thirty-six	50	If your child is below 50 in manual intelligence, you should waste no time in seeking professional help.

In the zoological world, the most famous of all the brachiators is the gibbon. Watching a gibbon in a zoo is an amazing sight. He can flash across the cage in an instant. He does so by swinging his arms, holding onto the ceiling of the cage itself or onto branches placed there for his use. Surely he brachiates across the cage as casually as we humans walk.

The gibbon's structure is a reflection of his function. He has long, powerful arms and a large chest. Gibbons are arboreal and use brachiation as their means of transportation. They swing from tree to tree and thus avoid the predators on the ground.

Ten years after The Institutes' staff had begun to teach parents to teach their children to brachiate, we found these very apt words in Carl Sagan's The Dragons of Eden:

> *Our arboreal ancestors had to pay attention. Any error in brachiating from branch to branch could be fatal. Every leap was an opportunity for evolution. Powerful selective forces were at work to evolve organisms with grace and agility, accurate binocular vision, versatile manipulative abilities, superb eye-hand coordination and an intuitive grasp of Newtonian gravitation. But each of these skills required significant advances in the evolution of the brains and particularly the neocortices of our ancestors.*
>
> *Human intelligence is fundamentally indebted to the millions of years our ancestors spent aloft in the trees. And after we returned to the savannahs and abandoned the trees—did we long for those great graceful leaps and ecstatic moments of weightlessness in the shafts of sunlight of the forest roof?**

* Carl Sagan, *The Dragons of Eden* (New York: Random House, Inc., 1977), p. 83.

THE PASSIVE BALANCE PROGRAM

The passive balance program described in detail in the previous chapter provided your baby with the development of balance he needed to learn how to walk. Now that this is accomplished, the process of taking him from being a brand-new walker at Stage IV to a more secure walker at Stage V is easy.

Continue with the same passive balance program that you have been doing. It contains all the opportunity for vestibular input that your baby needs. He is also getting superb brain growth as a result of the brachiation he's doing.

Frequency: Do the passive balance activities twice a day for a total of twenty sessions daily.

Intensity: This will be determined by the speed at which you move, spin, and put your child through these activities. After your baby has consistently done these activities for four months, you can gradually increase the speed of your spinning and swinging.

Duration: Do each session for one minute. The program will be twenty sessions for one minute, for a total of twenty minutes a day.

YOUR GOAL HERE IS TO PREPARE YOUR CHILD COMPLETELY FOR THE <u>ACTIVE</u> BALANCE ACTIVITIES HE WILL BE DOING THROUGHOUT THE NEXT THREE STAGES.

Keep in mind that doing the passive balance program is a prerequisite for preparing your child for the active balance program explained in the next chapter.

In the end, these passive activities may become Dad's responsibility. Your baby may become too big and heavy for Mom to comfortably (and above all, *safely*) do the activities. Your baby will regret the day he becomes too big for you. He would just as soon continue doing these activities for the next several years!

STAGE IV
DAILY CHECKLIST FOR MOTHER

1. The Mobility Program

____ **Frequency:** Twenty to thirty opportunities to walk each day—a step or two at a time. The number of sessions will decrease until he is on his feet most of the day.

____ **Intensity:** Encourage him to gradually build up his walking distance toward nonstop goals.

____ **Duration:** From a few seconds to get his balance at the beginning and take those first few steps, to longer and longer sessions with a total duration of at least two hours a day.

____ **GOAL:** TO REACH FORTY FEET OF NONSTOP WALKING AND A TOTAL OF TWO HUNDRED YARDS IN A DAY.

Mother's comments: My child reached the goal of two hundred yards of nonstop walking in a day at age _____ .

2. The Manual Program

____ **Frequency:** Ten sessions a day of brachiating and five sessions of hanging.

____ **Intensity:** Varying amounts of weight-bearing, ranging from none in the beginning when you supported him, through a gradual increase to total independence.

____ **Duration:** Do this a little *less* than the length of time your child would *like* to do it, perhaps twenty to thirty seconds each session.

____ **GOAL:** YOUR BABY ENJOYS BRACHIATING WITH YOUR SUPPORT, MOVING DOWN THE FULL LENGTH OF THE LADDER.

Mother's comments: My child was able to brachiate the full length of the ladder (with some support) at age _____ .

3. The Balance Program

____ **Frequency:** Ten passive balance activities, each done twice a day, for a total of twenty sessions daily.

____ **Intensity:** This will be determined by the speed at which you move, spin and put your child through these activities. After you've been doing them for four months, gradually increase your speed of spinning and swinging.

____ **Duration:** One minute for each session; a total of twenty minutes a day.

____ **GOAL:** TO BE READY FOR THE ACTIVE BALANCE ACTIVITIES YOUR CHILD WILL DO BY HIMSELF IN THE NEXT THREE STAGES.

Mother's comments: _____

_____ .

The Institutes' Mobility Development Scale

BRAIN STAGE		TIME FRAME	MOBILITY
VII	SOPHISTI-CATED CORTEX	Superior 36 Mon. / Average 72 Mon. / Slow 144 Mon.	Using a leg in a skilled role which is consistent with the dominant hemisphere *Sophisticated human expression*
VI	PRIMITIVE CORTEX	Superior 18 Mon. / Average 36 Mon. / Slow 72 Mon.	Walking and running in complete cross pattern *Primitive human expression*
V	EARLY CORTEX	Superior 9 Mon. / Average 18 Mon. / Slow 36 Mon.	Walking with arms freed from the primary balance role *Early human expression*
IV	INITIAL CORTEX	Superior 6 Mon. / Average 12 Mon. / Slow 24 Mon.	Walking with arms used in a primary balance role most frequently at or above shoulder height *Initial human expression*
III	MIDBRAIN	Superior 3.5 Mon. / Average 7 Mon. / Slow 14 Mon.	Creeping on hands and knees, culminating in cross pattern creeping *Meaningful response*
II	PONS	Superior 1 Mon. / Average 2.5 Mon. / Slow 5 Mon.	Crawling in the prone position culminating in cross pattern crawling *Vital response*
I	MEDULLA and CORD	Superior Birth to .5 / Average Birth to 1.0 / Slow Birth to 2.0	Movement of arms and legs without bodily movement *Reflex response*

GLENN DOMAN
and
The Staff
of
The Institutes

THE INSTITUTES FOR THE ACHIEVEMENT OF HUMAN POTENTIAL
8801 STENTON AVENUE
WYNDMOOR, PA 19038

13
MULTIPLYING YOUR BABY'S PHYSICAL INTELLIGENCE

STAGE V, THE EARLY CORTEX

Mobility Competence

CLASS: Tiny Child.

BRAIN STAGE: The Early Cortex.

PROFILE COLOR: Blue.

FUNCTION: Walking with arms freed from the primary balance role.

AVERAGE AGE: This function is present in an average tiny child by eighteen months of age.

DESCRIPTION: The tiny child is now an established, if still less than perfect, walker. Where he formerly needed to hold his arms up in order to balance himself (as does the high-wire performer), the tiny child can now free his arms from the need to balance and carry them below his shoulders. He can now use his hands and arms to carry objects with him when he walks. He no longer needs to walk with his feet as widespread as he did initially but he still maintains a fairly wide base when he walks, which reminds one faintly of the wide-base gait of a sailor who has just come off a long cruise on a small ship. The sailor walks with a wide base and has need to do so because the *surface* upon which he has been walking is often plunging, rolling and unsteady. A tiny child does so because while the *surface* upon which he walks is steady, *he* is still unsteady and unskilled as a walker. Both child and sailor solve the problem in the same way, which is to walk with their feet planted widely apart.

PURPOSE:	When the emerging human no longer found it necessary to hold his arms above his shoulders in order to balance himself, he became the first creature in the long history of the world to free his hands from their role in locomotion and thus to use them for other purposes.
	The real significance of walking at Stage V is not actually that he *can* use his arms to carry things, although it is true that he can. Rather, *the true significance of walking at Stage V is that, having acquired good enough balance to walk without using his arms to balance himself, he can now use them to propel himself forward with piston-like strokes of his arms.*
	Now that he has become more skilled and experienced in walking, he will begin to walk faster, lean a bit further forward, and begin to use his arms slightly, ever so slightly, to pull himself forward.

As your tiny child begins to use his arms in this increasingly skilled way, that is, to pull himself forward, he will acquire a certain rather busy and determined look as he sails more and more swiftly across the room. As his arms come more into the bent-elbow-with-hands-forward position he will more and more remind you of a very aggressive salesman beginning his first calls of the day with his determined look and forward stride.

Why not?

No ambitious businessman ever sallied forth more determinedly, or more joyously, than does he.

THE MOBILITY COMPETENCE PROGRAM—STAGE V: THE INGREDIENTS FOR SUCCESS

The ideal environment provides unlimited opportunity for your tiny child to walk on all terrains with increased frequency, intensity and duration. Walk with him as often as possible. Give him the added opportunity to walk on varied *surfaces:* bare floors, linoleum floors, lightly carpeted and heavily carpeted floors when he's indoors, and grass, sand, cement, asphalt, leaves and snow when you're outdoors together. He needs to learn how to cope with each of them, so gradually give him the opportunity to conquer any and all surfaces.

Here's something that's vital to consider at this point:

There is a tendency for adults (usually because they're pressed for time) not to permit their small children to handle real physical problem-solving situations on their own. Dads especially, often transport their kids over and around any obstacle in their walking offspring's paths.

The typical scene begins with Dad walking across the street, holding onto little Jack's hand. As they approach the curb on the other side, Jack spies it and is preparing to lift his foot at the exact right moment, so he can step up on to it. For some time he has been wanting to see if he can do this for himself.

Suddenly (and without prior notice) the hand that Daddy is holding is pulled upward. There is a jerk on his entire arm. He is airborne! His landing is perfect, soft and on two feet. The curb is gone. The opportunity to climb his first mountain has been denied; his first mountain-climbing mission has been aborted.

As he is hustled down the adjoining sidewalk, Jack turns and looks behind him at the curb, still unconquered. Maybe another day, he thinks. . . . Let him have the opportunity to conquer different terrains.

What the More Skillful Walker Should Wear

Because your baby will still fall down occasionally, it's a good idea to put long-sleeved shirts and long pants on him to protect him while he's learning to be more skillful.

As you and he are preparing for him to walk on the varied terrains we are going to be discussing, you will want to think about having footwear for him that is appropriate to the individual terrain.

For the smooth, flat one, he'll need good quality running shoes. For the hill terrain and the "wilderness" terrain, your tiny child should wear high-topped kids' work boots, tied tightly for the most secure support.

Start When You Both Have Lots of Energy

As always, enthusiasm and affection rank first in motivating your tiny child.

In order that both you and your tiny child have the correct attitude, make sure you choose the time of day that your tiny child has enough energy. This is important for you, too, if you are going to remain a positive coach!

Use your imagination as you walk together so your walk is as enjoyable and productive as possible; throw balls and walk after them; walk with dogs or other kids; walk for an objective—to see the ducks, go to the store, and so on.

Make your daily walks an adventure, an exploration that your tiny child looks forward to every day.

Beginning to Walk Up and Down Stairs

Indoors, your tiny child should now have carefully monitored opportunity to tackle the stairs—both going up and going down. Watch him carefully, because he is still far from safe.

On the grounds of The Institutes is a beautiful old building with a long, elegant, curving stairway that leads to staff apartments.

This grand old stairway keeps the staff very fit and has provided a challenging environment for our children. As a creeper, Shea Hagy would be placed at the bottom of the stairs and encouraged to creep up. This activity, one we started advocating at Stage III for your child, put Shea into a position where his body was approximately 45 degrees from the steps, *thus working toward being in an upright position.*

This kind of "obstacle" creeping played a big part in providing the vestibular and respiratory experience necessary to make Shea an early walker.

As a walker, though, when Shea was faced with climbing a stairway, he *refused* to creep up. He was determined to walk up instead. At first, he held onto the vertical slats of the bannister. (Mom was always there to ensure safety.) The eventual challenge was to get up the stairs without holding onto anything. This opportunity continued to challenge Shea's balance and respiration, and proved a valuable aid to enhancing his mobility—as it has with many, many of our children.

Ideally, you will want to spend at least fifteen minutes daily working on this activity with your tiny child. One parent must always be *right there* with the child.

Walking on Three Different Terrains

We have observed children for decades as they develop at this stage. We have studied thousands of records their parents have carefully maintained of the total time and distance their children have walked. Our search has taught us that the totality of the experience necessary to develop this level can be concentrated into three terrains which are of the utmost importance.

Terrain One: Easy, Flat and Smooth

In an environment that is easy, flat and smooth, such as a running track or a parking lot, your child has no obstacles of any sort to negotiate. The surface should be smooth so he will not need to pick his feet up very high. This terrain is important. The higher he must lift his foot, the more likely he is to lose his balance. This terrain affords him the opportunity to walk for longer and longer distances without interruption. Additionally, it is in this environment that speed can increase. Because of the absence of any interference, your tiny child will be most successful on this terrain in attempting to walk quickly.

Terrain Two: A Smooth Hill

Smooth, paved roads that run uphill, a long driveway that undulates or a shopping mall with ramps between floors (often used by the mothers of The Evan Thomas Institute) provide an environment that will challenge your child's balance, causing him to lean forward as he goes uphill and backward as he goes downhill. To negotiate successfully on all terrains, your child must develop an ability to change his center of gravity in relation to the pitch of the terrain he is traversing.

This environment, particularly on the downhill, will help develop the speed of walking. As your tiny child's balance improves, his speed will increase considerably.

The pitch of the slopes should be increased gradually (as much as is possible in the area you live in). Your tiny child's balance and respiration will continue to develop as he learns to navigate steeper and steeper grades.

Your tiny child should now have carefully monitored opportunity to tackle the stairs — both going up and down. Watch him carefully, because he is still far from safe.

Margeaux Jackson, shown here at nine months old (creeping since five months of age), creeps upstairs.

Terrain Three: Rugged Wilderness

Completely opposite of the easy, smooth, flat surfaces of Terrain One, this is characterized by woods, plowed fields, pastures of tall grass and sand dunes. Here, you wish your child to be faced with obstacles that he can barely negotiate.

Start with a terrain that requires your tiny child to stop first, and then cautiously navigate. If you begin with a terrain that causes your child to fall every few feet, you have found a terrain that is too difficult. This is true of both the hilly terrain and the rugged one. When beginning, don't put your child in a situation where he is not or cannot be successful. Begin with gentle grades and few obstacles and gradually increase the "ruggedness" as your child's walking improves.

If you begin with a terrain that does happen to make your child fall every few feet, then you will *know* you have found one that is too difficult. Start over again with one that is not so difficult and when your child is successful in traversing that terrain, *then* progress to more difficult ones.

Do not encourage your child to run on this terrain. Continuous nonstop walking or hiking while negotiating rougher and rougher terrain is the objective here. In navigating himself through this challenging environment, your child will fight to maintain his balance while shifting his center of gravity from side to side and backward and forward. He will also need to be very visually aware of where he is placing his feet.

The result of this type of walking is that the vestibular areas of your tiny child's brain will grow, and thus his balance will be better and better.

Beginning to Walk on the Three Terrains

First, give your tiny child the opportunity to walk on a variety of easy indoor and outdoor surfaces. Simultaneously work on climbing stairs. (Kids love to do this, and adore the challenge.) When these are mastered, go on to the next step.

Second, begin to walk on the three terrains we have just detailed.

Begin with Terrain One—proceed in this way:
1. Start by walking for short periods of time.
2. Work up to the goal of being able to walk for thirty minutes nonstop on this terrain.
3. Now measure the distance covered during your thirty-minute walk. Walk the standard distance, but gradually pick up the pace, so *more distance* is covered in *less time.*

Continue to walk in Terrain One and now add Terrain Two. Master Terrain Two with the same three steps you used for Terrain One.

When both smooth and hilly terrains are conquered, drop the smooth (Terrain One) and add the rugged terrain (Terrain Three).

If you only have thirty minutes available each day for walking, do the first environment until it is conquered, and then proceed to the others in turn.

When Terrain Three is going well, then walk on each of the terrains for twenty minutes a day and work toward faster walking – cover greater distances in the same twenty-minute period. Total walking time a day is still one hour.

Frequency: Between one and three walking sessions a day, depending upon the combination of terrains you're working on.

Intensity: This is determined by the speed and distance your tiny child walks. Obviously, increasing speed directly affects how soon your tiny child will graduate from this level to become a runner.

Duration: Each session should be between twenty and thirty minutes in duration. Again, this is dependent upon what combinations of terrains you are using.

THE GOAL TO WORK TOWARD IS FOR YOUR TINY CHILD TO BE ABLE TO WALK (ON TERRAIN ONE) ONE-HALF MILE NONSTOP IN EIGHTEEN MINUTES.

Conclusions

When your tiny child is walking as fast as one-half mile nonstop in eighteen minutes, his balance and coordination will be such that (especially when walking downhill) he will occasionally find it necessary to walk so fast that he will have to do two things in order not to fall forward on his face.

In order to maintain his balance to the bottom of the hill he is descending, he will be forced to:

1. Move his arms and legs in an exaggerated but beautiful cross-pattern.

2. Break into a trot.

It is precisely this for which we are striving!

So now your baby is a confirmed walker. He walks well now, easily and confidently. In walking down hills, he will begin to be able to negotiate some reasonably steep ones. In descending them, he will have to walk in a cross-pattern and he will find it necessary to trot.

Mighty good thing that he does. Not only does this keep him from falling on his face but, a lot more importantly, it means that he has just trotted into a higher level of brain function.

Running in cross-pattern is a function of the primitive cortex, and he has just joyfully placed himself under its control.

If your child is twelve months old when he first runs in cross-pattern, his mobility intelligence is 300. If eighteen months, 200. If he is thirty-six months old the first time he runs in cross pattern (however shakily or briefly), he has a mobility intelligence of 100.

The chart that follows gives his exact mobility intelligence at these ages, and any other ages, as well.

However old he is, great excitement and great ability lie in this new function; he has an even firmer grasp on future full-fledged citizenship at the top level of the human cortex.

Mobility Intelligence
LEAVING STAGE V, THE EARLY CORTEX
ENTERING STAGE VI, THE PRIMITIVE CORTEX

AGE (in months)	MOBILITY INTELLIGENCE	OUR ADVICE
Nine	400	World's record?
Twelve	300	You are doing
Eighteen	200	a superb job!
Twenty-four	150	
Thirty	120	Keep up the splendid job you are doing!
Thirty-six	100	He is exactly average.
Forty-two	85	Give him a lot more
Forty-eight	75	opportunity.
Fifty-four	66	Give your child immediate
Sixty	60	and extraordinary
Sixty-six	54	opportunity to move, move, move.
Seventy-two	50	If your child is below 50 in mobility intelligence, you should waste no time in seeking professional help.

*As your child begins to use his arms in an increasingly-skilled
way (to pull himself forward), he will acquire a certain rather busy
and determined look as he sails more and more swiftly across the
room. No ambitious businessman ever sallied forth more
determinedly, or more joyously, than does he.*

Fourteen-month-old Marlowe Doman walks and carries a
box of tissues simultaneously. At this stage Marlowe had
walked over one mile a day and over one quarter of a
mile nonstop.

The Institutes' Manual Development Scale

BRAIN STAGE		TIME FRAME	MANUAL COMPETENCE
VII	SOPHISTI-CATED CORTEX	Superior 36 Mon. Average 72 Mon. Slow 144 Mon.	**Using a hand to write which is consistent with the dominant hemisphere** *Sophisticated human expression*
VI	PRIMITIVE CORTEX	Superior 18 Mon. Average 36 Mon. Slow 72 Mon.	**Bimanual function with one hand in a skilled role** *Primitive human expression*
V	EARLY CORTEX	Superior 9 Mon. Average 18 Mon. Slow 36 Mon.	**Cortical opposition bilaterally and simultaneously** *Early human expression*
IV	INITIAL CORTEX	Superior 6 Mon. Average 12 Mon. Slow 24 Mon.	**Cortical opposition in either hand** *Initial human expression*
III	MIDBRAIN	Superior 3.5 Mon. Average 7 Mon. Slow 14 Mon.	**Prehensile grasp** *Meaningful response*
II	PONS	Superior 1 Mon. Average 2.5 Mon. Slow 5 Mon.	**Vital release** *Vital response*
I	MEDULLA and CORD	Superior Birth to .5 Average Birth to 1.0 Slow Birth to 2.0	**Grasp reflex** *Reflex response*

GLENN DOMAN
and
The Staff
of
The Institutes

THE INSTITUTES FOR THE ACHIEVEMENT OF HUMAN POTENTIAL
8801 STENTON AVENUE
WYNDMOOR, PA 19038

MULTIPLYING YOUR BABY'S PHYSICAL INTELLIGENCE

STAGE V, THE EARLY CORTEX

Manual Competence

CLASS:	Tiny Child.
BRAIN STAGE:	The Early Cortex.
PROFILE COLOR:	Blue.
FUNCTION:	Cortical opposition bilaterally and simultaneously.
AVERAGE AGE:	This function is present in an average tiny child by eighteen months of age.
DESCRIPTION:	The tiny child is now able to pick up two very small objects, one of them grasped between the thumb and forefinger of each hand, and to do it simultaneously. He isn't very skilled yet, but he can do it.
PURPOSE:	His unceasing curiosity will provide him endless drill in picking up anything and everything on which he can get his hands. The size, shape, texture and weight of objects he chooses to hoist and to heist will not be limited only to objects he is *capable* of picking up. He will also finger innumerable objects he is *incapable* of picking up and from these, too, will he be learning what his remarkable fingers and the brain that runs them are capable of doing.

What is the purpose of this? It is, of course, an end in itself, and he can, and will, use this ability to feed himself, and to investigate things unknown; but by so doing he is also preparing himself to handle and to manipulate different objects in different ways in each of his hands. It will be the basis for the fingers of one hand depressing the strings of a violin while the other hand holds the bow that caresses them the night he makes his debut at Lincoln Center (if that's the way the wind blows for this tiny child), or it might be the basis for the way he handles the high bar, doing giant swings in the routine that wins him his first "10" as a gymnast in the Olympics after the year 2000!

How quickly your tiny baby will move through this intriguing area of brain function (while at the same time exploiting the multiplicity of functions that use of the early cortex makes possible) will be an unadulterated result of how often he has the opportunity to use this splendid function in the greatest variety of ways.

We shall help him to move through quickly if we give him an environment made rich in opportunities to develop his bilateral manual competencies in his early cortex. Give him rich opportunity and genuine enthusiastic approval when he uses these manual abilities and we will give him extraordinary brain growth in the manual portions of his cortex and a very high manual intelligence.

THE MANUAL COMPETENCE PROGRAM—STAGE V: INGREDIENTS FOR SUCCESS

Now you need to give your child opportunity to improve his cortical opposition in each hand, both individually and simultaneously. In addition, your child now needs to learn to use two hands simultaneously with one hand in a skilled role.

At first, give him a large cardboard box with a relatively medium-sized object to be taken out of it; he'll love to do this.

Then, give him a large, empty box with several small objects to put in it.

He will enjoy both taking them out and putting them in.

As he continues to enjoy learning to do this, make the boxes you give him smaller and smaller, until you are offering a box about six inches square, with small objects to put in and take out.

When he is dealing with a small box, he will tend, more and more often, to hold the box with one hand while he uses the other to put things into and take them out of it.

Inextricably tied to human mobility and manual function is human intelligence.

Christopher Coventry, age 30 months. Photo by Sherman Hines.

When he actually *does* that for the first time, he is using both hands to perform a task, with one hand being used in a skilled role.

Let him take poker chips out of a wide-mouthed jar, and put them back in again.

Fill a small metal pitcher with marbles and let him "pour" the marbles into a wooden box.

When he's good enough, let him get nuts with one hand from a jar he's holding in the other.

When he's *very* good, let him pour water from one cup into another. The bath tub is the sensible place to learn that one.

In addition to this opportunity, at this stage of his developing manual competence your baby is on a direct course that will end in independent brachiation. All the "hard work" is done. It is just a matter of his gradually learning how it feels to swing his body and support his weight.

The Best-Dressed Brachiators Wear Overalls

We strongly recommend overalls as *the* best clothing for brachiating. They are loose-fitting, but securely attached to the child, and therefore afford you a firm, safe grip while he is brachiating. Pants of any length that have no pockets or belt loops (for you to grab onto) are *not* recommended.

Again, bulky or tight-fitting clothing restricts the free movement that is so necessary for proper brachiation. Bare feet or socks are still in order, so *you* don't get hit by hard shoes or sneakers while spotting your child, and so they don't weigh him down and impede his movement while he is brachiating.

"We Love Brachiation . . . "

If brachiation isn't fun, the chances are high you won't succeed in teaching your tiny child to do it.

Parents have been absolutely ingenious over the years in the variety and number of amusing games they've created to "spice up" the process of getting a kid brachiating. Here's one example that still makes us smile:

One night we went to visit the Caputos. When we arrived, Adriana, age three, promptly dragged us into her parents' bedroom, where her brachiation ladder was. There on the wall was a huge poster labeled "The Go Fish Brachiation Game." It portrayed a crayoned ocean with thirty fish tails sticking out of thirty pockets. Adriana grabbed a fish tail, which slipped easily out of its pocket.

On it was written, "Hang for thirty seconds."

Adriana jumped up on the ladder and hung on a rung swinging back and forth for what seemed about thirty seconds. She put the fish back in its pocket head up, and then yanked out another fish which said, "Brachiate one trip." With a delighted squeal, Adriana brachiated down the ladder and then put the fish head up.

The third fish she chose said, "Go to Daddy for a surprise." Having finally found the fish she was looking for, Adriana ran off to show Daddy. Not a single word had passed between us, but Adriana had clearly had a great time brachiating and had received her just reward!

Then, not too long ago, we visited the house of some friends who had been teaching their kids to brachiate. We asked Mom how things were going. She said, "Great!" Turns out her kids were *singing* and brachiating simultaneously.

Mom then began singing, to the tune of *Alouette:*

"Bra-chi-a-tion,
We love bra-chi-a-tion,
Bra-chi-a-tion's the game we love to play.
First we put the left arm out,
Then we put the right arm out –
Left arm out, right arm out, oh . . . "

Laughing, the kids ran over to the ladder and brachiated. Their very wise mom told us the kids told her they had heard "The Brachiation Song" on the radio, but it was being sung in some other language!

Use your imagination and the sky's the limit as to what fun you and your tiny child can have on your brachiation ladder!

At this point, it is most important to sustain your child's interest in brachiation, and to create a variety of ways in which he can develop this ability (with complete safety) any time he wishes to without having you help him.

The more opportunities your child has to *swing* and hang and brachiate, the faster he'll master these skills.

Here are some other ways to prepare your tiny child for brachiation:

1. *Trapeze.* Set up a trapeze so that your kid can easily grab the wooden dowel and swing back and forth, holding on. It should always be available so the kids can swing on it when they please. The trapeze can be in a doorway, attached to your brachiation ladder, or outside, hanging from a tree limb. Full instructions are included on page 254 in the Appendix.

   Kids love it. It prepares arms and hands beautifully for brachiation while simultaneously teaching them how it feels to swing.

2. *Dowel in a Doorway.* We can return to using the dowel in the doorway on which your baby learned to hang. Now he can use it to swing.

   Set the dowel at the exact height that makes it easy for him to grasp. Whenever your tiny child wants, he will be able to grasp the dowel, pick up his legs, and swing back and forth.

3. *Brachiation Ladder Over Bed.* By placing both the bed and the brachiation ladder lengthwise against a wall with the bed underneath the ladder, you can create a very enjoyable location. Advantages to this are pretty obvious: the kids find the location different and very amusing. They should be able to stand on the bed on tiptoes and grasp the rungs of the ladder and swing. They don't have to worry about falling (and thus are even *more* secure because the bed is soft underneath!). It's best, of course, to put the bed on the floor. Then your tiny kid can't fall off and hit a bedpost or slip off and hurt himself by falling to the floor.

4. *Swimming Pools.* Some families fortunate enough to have pools

have even put their brachiation ladders over the shallow end of their pool. If you keep the height of the ladder low, kids can brachiate easily, because water is buoying them up. Then, if you gradually raise the ladder a little more at a time, they become more and more responsible for their own weight. *Since the kids are in the pool, this requires an adult with them 100 percent of the time!*

Now You Need to Become an EXPERT Spotter

As your child wants to brachiate more often, it becomes crucial that you become an expert spotter. Here are some further tips on spotting your child successfully.

As has been mentioned previously, spotting means physically helping your child to be successful while simultaneously protecting him from falling or hurting himself.

If you choose to keep your ladder *low*, so that your tiny child's toes are only two inches or so off the ground, spotting will become less and less necessary, until it is not necessary at all.

WHEN THE LADDER IS RAISED SO THAT AN ADULT CAN FIT COMFORTABLY UNDERNEATH IT, SPOTTING BECOMES AN ABSOLUTE MUST, REGARDLESS OF YOUR CHILD'S AGE OR DEGREE OF INDEPENDENCE.

Points About Spotting

In front of or behind your child?

You can spot from behind your tiny child (you are facing his back) or in front of him (you are facing his face). Choose the position most comfortable for you and your child. Spotting from behind is advantageous because you're not in his way. Spotting from the front is advantageous because you're able to observe his face to make sure all is going well.

Have a firm hold on your child.

For the not-yet-quite-independent brachiator, having a firm grip on him is essential if you are to prevent him from falling.

The safest way of grasping him is to put each of your hands inside each of the pockets on his pants, and hold tight. If your tiny child is wearing a belt, you can grasp the belt on both sides of his body.

If your child is very light, you can hold him firmly at the waist.

Watch your child's hands.

Keep your eyes on your tiny child's hands. This way, if his hands start to slip, you'll know about it, and thus be able to support him more. You'll also be able to tell him when to let go and grab the next rung. He should be concentrating on looking at the rung he is about to grasp.

Brachiate in a cross-pattern.

Smooth brachiation is done in a cross-pattern. This means that both hands are never on the same rung. Your child should be encouraged *always* to grasp the next unoccupied rung.

Swinging.

Swinging is perhaps the single most important part of the technique of brachiating. Observe a strong male trying to brachiate for the first time. He "muscles" his way down the ladder. He does so by *pulling his entire body up* with one arm so as to be able to reach the next rung. This is a difficult and cumbersome task. Experienced kids, however, brachiate like the experts, the gibbons, initiating a back and forth swinging action of their bodies, the way a pendulum moves. Once initiated, the action continues as one progresses from rung to rung. The movement is graceful. *Most important, it is much easier.* It is easier because the body weight carries the body forward so that the next rung is easily reached. Much less strength is required.

There are many ways to begin to teach swinging to your tiny child; indeed, we started telling you about them at Stage IV. Providing you have let him hang from a single dowel, or a trapeze, he can learn to swing grasping one dowel. This is a good means of preparing him for swinging on the ladder.

The most common method, and actually a *requirement* of correct spotting, is for you to swing your kid while spotting him. This is best accomplished in the following fashion (*This description is based upon your facing your child. If you choose to stand behind your child, reverse the instructions so that pulling motions become pushing ones.*):

Grasp your child securely by his pockets. One of his hands should be on the forward rung (let's say the left one in this case). The right hand will occupy the rung behind the left hand.

Pushing with both your arms, push him away from you to commence the swinging motion.

The most critical moment of brachiating is when one hand comes off a rung to reach for the next one. At this point your child is hanging by one hand. Now he needs your support! Just pick him up enough so he doesn't lose his grasp with the hand still holding on to the rung.

When your child's free hand has grabbed the next rung, you can let up again on the support. When the following hand comes off, repeat this process. The more you perform this act for your child, the more expert both you and he will become. You will "feel" the amount of support your child needs. You'll know just how much lift he needs to be successful. Don't give him any more. In fact, you will want to gradually decrease the amount of support you give him. Decrease it consistently, but gradually, until one day he brachiates down the ladder with spotting, but with no support from you, without realizing it!

The accompanying series of photographs shows a mom appropriately spotting her son, who's brachiating from rung to rung.

Over the years, parents have been absolutely ingenious in the variety and number of amusing games they've created to "spice up" the process of getting a kid brachiating — and keeping him at it!

The "best-dressed" brachiators wear overalls so moms who are "spotting" them can get a firm grip through their pockets or belt loops!

The more opportu to swing and han faster he'll maste

Marlowe Doman, age two years three months, begins brachiating with his left hand on the forward rung (helped by his Professional Mother, Rosalind Doman, Associate Director of The Institute for the Achievement of Physical Excellence, and

Rosalind helps Marlowe swing forward.

Marlowe swings f right hand one rung Rosalind, lifting with helps Marlowe's bo

es your child has
d brachiate, the
em.

It is most important to sustain your child's interest in brachiation, and to create a variety of ways in which he can develop this ability any time he wishes to.

Use your imagination and the sky's the limit as to what fun you and your tiny child can have on your brachiation ladder!

rd and places his
front of his left.
r left hand, then

Completing his forward swing, Marlowe is now starting to swing backward.

Rosalind uses her hands to push Marlowe back and then initiate the forward swing.

Conclusions

Now your tiny child's a real pro at picking up even the smallest objects, and he does so almost without effort, in either hand or in both of them at once.

Just about now he'll become interested in, and begin to learn about, containers and the things they contain.

Buckets, boxes, jars and bowls will begin to fascinate him. At first he'll be content to take things out of containers and put things into them. This will lead inevitably to putting things (such as blocks) into containers (such as cardboard boxes) for the purpose of taking them someplace else, all at the same time.

He is beginning to play around with using two hands simultaneously, with one in a more skilled role.

He will tend more and more often to hold the box in one hand and to take objects out with the other. When he begins to do this, he has crossed the border from the early cortex into the primitive cortex. He is raising himself by his bootstraps (with a major assist from you) to higher and higher levels of brain function.

When your tiny child does any of a dozen different acts that require him to use one hand in a skilled role and the other in a more assistive role, color him indigo and promote him to the primitive cortex, because that is precisely where he is.

If he is thirty-six months old, give him a manual intelligence of 100. He is exactly average in this respect. If he is older or younger, find his *exact* manual intelligence on the chart that follows. Of course, you are remembering in each of these cases that these levels of intelligence presuppose you have been teaching your baby since birth and following the text of this book very carefully.

However young or old he is, he is now operating out of his primitive cortex in manual areas and that's a very high level for a tiny child!

Frequency:	Fifteen times a day for brachiating. Multiple opportunities for your child to pick up objects, put them into boxes (and remove them), and to learn to pour.
Intensity:	Use only as much support as your tiny child still needs for success.
Duration:	The length of time it takes for your child to complete one trip down the brachiation ladder.
GOAL:	TO BRACHIATE FIFTEEN TIMES A DAY WITH YOUR CHILD SUPPORTING 75 PERCENT OF HIS OWN WEIGHT, TAKING ONE RUNG INDEPENDENTLY, AND TO USE HIS HANDS TO PICK UP OBJECTS SIMULTANEOUSLY.

Manual Intelligence
LEAVING STAGE V, THE EARLY CORTEX
ENTERING STAGE VI, THE PRIMITIVE CORTEX

AGE (in months)	MANUAL INTELLIGENCE	OUR ADVICE
Nine	400	World's record?
Twelve	300	You're doing
Eighteen	200	a superb job!
Twenty-four	150	
Thirty	120	Keep up the splendid job you are doing!
Thirty-six	100	He is exactly average.
Forty-two	85	Give him more opportunity
Forty-eight	75	to move.
Fifty-four	66	Give your child immediate
Sixty	60	and extraordinary
Sixty-six	54	opportunity to develop his manual competence.
Seventy-two	50	If your child is below 50 in manual intelligence, you should waste no time in seeking professional help.

THE ACTIVE BALANCE PROGRAM
FOR WALKING BABIES TO GYMNASTS

Prerequisites

If you started the program late, at least two or preferably four months on the passive balance program are a prerequisite for the active balance program. The vestibular mechanism, like the other parts of the brain, grows by use. The passive balance program gets the vestibular mechanism "into shape" (matured) for the active balance program. Without the passive program, these active techniques would be difficult for a tiny child. With the passive program already accomplished, the active techniques are a logical next step in the balance game. Perhaps the passive activities may be relegated to the position of special awards for deeds well done. As the active program expands, gradually reduce the passive program.

How It Works

The active balance program is so named because *all the activities are done by the child himself.* With the passive balance program, the parent does all the work and the baby passively "soaks up" all the information. The roles are now reversed; the kid does all the work and the parent becomes the coach and cheerleader simultaneously.

The Ingredients For Success

Your tiny child is already in loose-fitting overalls with a polo or T-shirt and is quite comfortable moving about in them, since he wears them for so many of his physical activities with you. His feet should be bare; he can move them better that way (especially over his head) and his shoes won't hurt him in any way or restrict his movements if he's not wearing them!

The following safety procedures must be observed at all times. (It is also wise to teach your tiny child these precautions.)

Before beginning an activity, always check the environment to see if the conditions are acceptable.

Indoors: Is the floor surface okay? Make sure it isn't too slippery, and that no objects are underfoot, or furniture in the way. Do not use an area other people may walk through unexpectedly.

Outdoors: Are the ground conditions safe, the weather conditions comfortable, and is the area free of other people who might inadvertently get in the way?

Show your child the activity he is about to do.

If your child sees you enjoying an activity, he will know what he is expected to do—and he will expect the activity to be enjoyable.

Be a coach for your child.

Coach? Yes, you—it's an extremely important role for a parent. Assume this role, because initially the child must be assisted physically with the activities until he becomes totally independent. Then, too, the coach is the person responsible for supervising and assisting with the program and making sure all safety precautions are observed by your tiny child. He is "in training" for far more advanced balance activities. You, as a coach, need to develop along with your tiny child. After graduation from the active balance program, your child will be ready for gymnastics and similar sports, such as figure-skating, diving and ballet.

At The Institutes, we believe gymnastics to be the highest level of balance activity. The gymnast is able to keep himself oriented in all positions in space. Furthermore, he is able to maintain this orientation in spite of split-second tumbles and turns. As the coach, each parent plays the all-important role of physically helping the child learn the feel of the activities he is doing. By coaching a child through the active balance program, both parent and child will be ready for gymnastics, or similar sports.

Be a cheerleader for your child.

Now that your tiny child does the activities, you can also become his cheerleader. Encourage, praise, and exult in your tiny child's doing activities that the average adult struggles through. This positive feedback lets your child know that his parents remain a vital part of the process of his becoming physically superb.

The Active Balance Program Activities
1. Rolling

Your child has been preparing for independent rolling repeatedly since you first assisted him in rolling over as part of his newborn balance program. Then all the rotational activities you did during the passive program continued the preparation. Once your child, regardless of his age, can roll over tummy to back, back to tummy, he is ready to pursue independent rolling.

All that is necessary is that he continues to roll over more and more times successively.

Follow these steps:

1. Once your child can roll over independently, kneel down by his side. With both hands, roll him on his side, then help him to roll over away from you, "kneewalk" after him, continuing the process several times. Now move to his other side and help him roll back to his original position.

2. When your child can do several rolls by himself, then lie down parallel to him, and roll in unison with him. Roll several times in one direction and then roll back to your original position. (This is important to maintain both clockwise and counterclockwise balance input.)

3. Gradually increase the number of rolls you both can do without stopping. If space is limited, you simply continue to roll back and forth over the same area.

Frequency:	Begin with many brief sessions, such as one roll ten times. As nonstop rolling develops, frequency can gradually be diminished to four sessions, five yards rolling nonstop in each direction.
Intensity:	Once independent rolling is well established, encourage (gradually increasing) faster and faster rolling.
Duration:	This will increase as your tiny child's nonstop rolling ability

increases. Always stop before he wants to stop. The minimum total daily duration should be five minutes.

2. Forward Rolls

Your tiny child has also been in training for independent forward rolls. The vertical rocking (head down) activity has prepared him to orient himself when his feet are over his head. Rotational activities have adapted his vestibular mechanism to intensive spinning activities.

As soon as your child walks for transport and can carry objects easily while walking, he is ready for forward rolls. If you've been setting a frequent example, you'll find your little sixteen-month-old child bent over with his head on the ground, looking through his legs and trying to push himself over. However, even before this, you can teach the somersaulting experience to your baby.

As early as six months, even though he is not walking yet, gently put your baby's head down on a soft mat, keeping his head tucked under with one hand and holding his hips with the other and rolling him over, ever so gently. Doing this ten to fifteen times a day will teach your baby's brain what it feels like to roll over (turn) on that axis.

As your baby becomes a walker, you continue this process of teaching somersaults. By now, he can put his head and hands down on the floor by himself, or can get himself into this position from the quadruped position. Now all he needs is some help getting over.

You can give a light push with one hand on his bottom as you tuck his head under with your other hand so that he rolls over.

Make sure your baby learns to tuck in his head, so he rolls with his chin on his chest. As he learns to do this, you no longer need to help him there, but merely need to give him a push over.

There are two ways to help him get the "feel" of doing a forward roll without any assistance: 1) Have your child do the forward roll, down a five or ten degree incline on a mat, or 2) outside, down a slight hill. Gravity will help pull his body over his head.

Teach your child to walk his feet toward his hands after he has put the top of his head on the floor. This action will eventually push his hips over his head, his balance will be off-center in a forward direction, and he will tumble over.

Continuing these approaches (and setting a constant example) will help your tiny child do forward rolls independently by sixteen months of age, maybe sooner. He will delight in tumbling around the house.

Frequency:	Begin with one assisted forward roll ten times a day. Once your tiny child can do a forward roll independently, increase the frequency of forward rolls to one independent roll fifteen times a day.
Intensity:	Begin slowly, and gradually increase to your child's level of enjoyment. Once independent forward rolling is well established, gradually encourage faster and faster forward rolling.

Teach your child to walk his feet toward his hands after he has put the top of his head on the floor. This action will eventually push his hips over his head, his balance will be off-center in a forward direction, and he will tumble over.

Marlowe Doman, age 15 months, walks into a forward roll. As soon as *your* child walks for transport and can carry objects easily while walking, he is ready for forward rolls.

Duration: This will increase as your child's nonstop forward rolling ability increases. Always stop before he wants to stop. The minimum total daily duration should be five minutes.

3. Walking the Balance Beam

Your child's entire balance program since birth has been designed to bring about superb balance and agility. This, in combination with your tiny child's rapid development of walking, has been preparing him for the balance beam.

Time and again we're surprised by moms telling us how babies who have been walking for only a few months love to try walking on a balance beam. The reason is that walking babies love a challenge. For this reason, it is wise to have your baby's balance beam ready early. (Marlowe Doman indicated a desire to walk it at twelve months of age.) You must also be careful to make sure the beam is situated in a safe place, because once on, your tiny baby won't want to stay *off* it!

Follow this step-by-step procedure gradually, to arrive at independent balance beam walking.

Feet should always be bare. Even socks can't begin to provide the traction and grip of the skin.

1.   On your floor, put down a strip of tape four inches wide and eight feet long. Play a game where you and your child walk the length of the tape without "falling off."

2.   Place a $2'' \times 4''$ eight-foot-long piece of wood with the four-inch-wide part lying flat on a carpeted floor. You now have a four-inch-wide, eight-foot balance beam*. You and your tiny child walk the length of it. Try not to hold his hands, as you want his brain to develop so he can walk the beam independently. Remember, by holding on, you cause your tiny child to rely on you for balance. Of course, watch him carefully and help him when necessary. You may wish to put the beam parallel to the wall, and within a few inches of it; that way he can use the wall to help himself.

Let him balance himself. One foot of walking by himself is better than 100 feet with your help.

3.   Make your own $4'' \times 4''$ eight-foot-long balance beam as discussed in the Appendix of this book (see page 255). You and your tiny child walk the length of it, as before; assist him as little as possible.

Frequency: Begin with walking one trip down the tape or beam, ten times a day.

Intensity: The intensity is regulated by the transition from tape to higher and higher beams. Of course, once independence is achieved, encourage faster and faster walking.

---

*Oddly enough, this is only 3½ inches wide by lumber industry standards, but still sufficiently wide for your baby's feet! By the way, if your beam feels rough to you when you bring it home from the lumber yard, take a few minutes to sand it down first, before baby's tender bare feet attempt to walk it.

Duration: As long as one trip takes. Always stop before your child wants to stop. Total daily duration should be a minimum of five minutes.

Total Duration: The entire active balance program entails doing three different activities, five minutes each, for a total of fifteen minutes.

THE GOAL HERE IS TO READY YOUR CHILD FOR EVEN MORE SOPHISTICATED ACTIVITIES SUCH AS GYMNASTICS, WHILE YOU RELINQUISH YOUR ACTIVE ROLE IN PROVIDING HIM VESTIBULAR INFORMATION AND TAKE ON THE ROLES OF COACH AND CHEERLEADER, AND HE BEGINS DOING THESE NEW ACTIVITIES FOR HIMSELF.

STAGE V
DAILY CHECKLIST FOR MOTHER

1. The Mobility Program

_____ **Frequency:** Between one and three walking sessions a day, depending upon the combinations of terrains your child is walking on.

_____ **Intensity:** Encourage your child to increase the speed and distance he walks, steadily going farther and faster.

_____ **Duration:** Twenty to thirty minute sessions of walking daily on each terrain successively, or on a combination of terrains.

_____ **GOAL:** FOR YOUR TINY CHILD TO BE ABLE TO WALK ONE-HALF MILE NONSTOP (ON AN EASY, SMOOTH, FLAT TERRAIN) IN EIGHTEEN MINUTES.

Mother's comments: My tiny child walked one-half mile nonstop in eighteen minutes at age _____ .

2. The Manual Program

_____ **Frequency:** Fifteen times a day of brachiating and lots of opportunities for various manual activities like picking up objects, putting them into and removing them from boxes, and learning to pour.

_____ **Intensity:** As much support as your tiny child still needs for success.

_____ **Duration:** The time it takes to brachiate one trip down the ladder.

_____ **GOAL:** TO BRACHIATE FIFTEEN TIMES A DAY WITH YOUR TINY CHILD SUPPORTING 75 PERCENT OF HIS OWN WEIGHT, AND NOW TAKING ONE RUNG INDEPENDENTLY. TO USE BOTH HIS HANDS TO PICK UP OBJECTS SIMULTANEOUSLY

Mother's comments: My child was able to accomplish bilateral and simultaneous cortical opposition in both hands at age

_____ .

3. The Active Balance Program

_____ **Frequency:** Many brief sessions of rolling, forward rolls and trips down the tape or balance beam, each one of three activities, ten times a day.

_____ **Intensity:** Once independence is achieved, encourage faster and faster rolls and trips down the beam.

_____ **Duration:** Three different activities (rolls, forward rolls and balance beam) five minutes each, a total of fifteen minutes daily.

_____ **GOAL:** TO READY YOUR CHILD FOR EVEN MORE SOPHISTICATED ACTIVITIES LIKE GYMNASTICS; INSTEAD OF YOU GIVING YOUR CHILD VESTIBULAR INFORMATION BY DOING THE PASSIVE ACTIVITIES FOR HIM, NOW HE'S READY TO DO THE ACTIVE ONES BY HIMSELF, WITH YOUR COACHING.

Mother's comments: _____

_____ .

AMF

You'll find every baby and kid within a hundred yards gravitating in your direction whenever they hear you're about to start your balance program -so be ready for the crowds!

Adriana Caputo, four years old.
Photo by Sherman Hines.

The Institutes' Mobility Development Scale

GLENN DOMAN
and
The Staff
of
The Institutes

BRAIN STAGE		TIME FRAME	MOBILITY
VII	SOPHISTI-CATED CORTEX	Superior 36 Mon. / Average 72 Mon. / Slow 144 Mon.	Using a leg in a skilled role which is consistent with the dominant hemisphere *Sophisticated human expression*
VI	PRIMITIVE CORTEX	Superior 18 Mon. / Average 36 Mon. / Slow 72 Mon.	Walking and running in complete cross pattern *Primitive human expression*
V	EARLY CORTEX	Superior 9 Mon. / Average 18 Mon. / Slow 36 Mon.	Walking with arms freed from the primary balance role *Early human expression*
IV	INITIAL CORTEX	Superior 6 Mon. / Average 12 Mon. / Slow 24 Mon.	Walking with arms used in a primary balance role most frequently at or above shoulder height *Initial human expression*
III	MIDBRAIN	Superior 3.5 Mon. / Average 7 Mon. / Slow 14 Mon.	Creeping on hands and knees, culminating in cross pattern creeping *Meaningful response*
II	PONS	Superior 1 Mon. / Average 2.5 Mon. / Slow 5 Mon.	Crawling in the prone position culminating in cross pattern crawling *Vital response*
I	MEDULLA and CORD	Superior Birth to .5 / Average Birth to 1.0 / Slow Birth to 2.0	Movement of arms and legs without bodily movement *Reflex response*

THE INSTITUTES FOR
THE ACHIEVEMENT OF
HUMAN POTENTIAL
8801 STENTON AVENUE
WYNDMOOR, PA 19038

14

MULTIPLYING YOUR BABY'S PHYSICAL INTELLIGENCE

STAGE VI, THE PRIMITIVE CORTEX

Mobility Competence

CLASS: Little Child.
BRAIN STAGE: The Primitive Cortex.
PROFILE COLOR: Indigo.
FUNCTION: Walking and running in complete cross-pattern.
AVERAGE AGE: This function is present in an average child by thirty-six months of age.
DESCRIPTION: Now the little child has become a skilled walker and rarely falls down, except when experimenting beyond his mobility abilities. He can now walk with good balance and is able to run in cross-pattern, but is a novice in doing so.

Two significant higher abilities have been added:

One, he now uses his arms to move himself forward, moving them with a forward and backward swing, rather like pistons. The faster the little child moves, the more piston-like does the use of his arms become, and the more clear and exaggerated is this movement. This piston-like movement is seen very clearly in a photograph of an athlete who is sprinting with one arm thrown fully forward (as if pulling himself forward, which, in fact, he is doing) and the opposite arm thrust totally behind him as if he is mightily pushing himself forward (which, in fact, he is doing). The little child is doing it as a rank amateur, a total beginner, and as he progresses through this primitive but exclusively human area of the brain into which he has newly come, he will do it better and better.

Two, he now adds another ability, which is that of cross-pattern running (right arm and left leg forward, left arm and right leg back, followed by reversing this pattern) and by so doing becomes entirely and exclusively human. Now he has left even the other anthropoids behind, and for good.

While the great apes can, so to speak, "ape" the human condition by getting onto their hind legs for brief distances and even, upon occasion, carrying things without leaning on their knuckles, they cannot do what our little child does now, because what he does is to walk and run in cross-pattern, a function unique to human beings and one that is a product of the unique human cortex.

PURPOSE: To move more swiftly and surely.

In his never-ending search for more efficient mobility, the little child begins to accelerate his walk. He leans his body forward, and lifts his feet higher off the ground, alternating his arms and legs in a cross-pattern.

Now as our little child moves, he moves his right arm and left leg simultaneously while he steps off with his right leg. He then moves his left arm and right leg forward, while he steps off with his left leg. The faster he moves, the more exaggerated this cross-pattern movement becomes.

If we could freeze his motion, as in the freeze-frame action of a motion picture, we would see that he has one leg completely extended behind him, thrusting into the ground with all his strength to push him forward, while the arm on his opposite side is stretched far ahead to pull him forward. Simultaneously, we see the other leg free of the ground and leaping forward while the opposite arm is thrust far behind as if it is thrusting him forward (which, of course, as we have said, it is).

The more skilled the little child becomes in cross-pattern walking and cross-pattern running, the bigger the variety of other skilled human mobility functions he can perform.

At this stage, your little child will soon become a confirmed runner, preferring that activity to walking since he loves to experience the sheer exhilaration of the fast motion. The feeling of speed, the wind blowing past the body, and the sensation of momentary flight that occurs as a leg pushes off the ground to thrust the body forward all add up to an unparalleled experience for your child. It is such joy that invariably, when young children run, they are laughing, smiling or squealing with glee. They love it!

Now the stage is set for developing your little child's running ability. Why?

Because running grows the cortex. It is a function of the human cortex. If the little child does not have a developed human cortex, he can't run as a means of transportation. Since running is a function of the cortex, running stimulates the cortex. It is as much a developmental stage as crawling, creeping or walking. To deny a child the opportunity to run is to deny him the opportunity to complete the development and organization of his brain.

And, because running will enhance the efficiency of your child's respiratory system. It will improve the regularity of breathing. This will occur as the result of running long distances nonstop. Also, it will improve the depth of his breathing. As a result of running over all terrains, your child's breathing will become more adaptable.

Anyone who has ever attempted to run up a flight of stairs or run to catch a train, or run because of fear, knows three facts:

1. Your breathing rate changes.
2. You breathe more heavily and deeply.
3. The longer you run, the more obviously regular your breathing becomes.

It is also clear that breathing is intimately tied to function. No matter what function we engage in, there is an optimal and often unique pattern of breathing for maximum efficiency.

When we sleep, we breathe differently from the way we do when we eat, which in turn is different from the breathing we use when we talk or sing or walk or run or climb or ski—and so on.

If our breathing cannot adapt, cannot get deeper and more regular when we need it to, we will not be able to perform a desired function.

The better you breathe, the better you function.

You know that when you decided to get back into shape and decided to start running again, it wasn't your legs that gave out the first day you went out to run a mile. It was your breathing. You were out of breath. Your breathing could not keep up with your function. You had to stop, because in making a choice between being able to breathe and finishing that mile, you chose breathing—the only choice you could make.

But you were determined to get back into shape, so each day you went out on the track and tried to go a bit farther than the previous day. Gradually, over a period of weeks, your respiration improved.

As a result, you could run farther. You felt great; you had more energy! And then you thought, wouldn't this be a good thing for my kids? Wouldn't they function better if they ran?

The answer is, yes. Of course.

Running grows the cortex.

Running enhances the efficiency of your child's respiratory system.

Now we know *why*, let's find out *how*.

THE MOBILITY COMPETENCE PROGRAM—STAGE VI: INGREDIENTS FOR SUCCESS

Now that your child is a good, mature walker and a beginning runner, he will spend most of his time transporting himself by trying to run. It's more of a challenge—and more fun. As he develops his run, his walk will become even more fluid, since running is an exaggerated form of walking. Because of this, you want to encourage longer and longer periods of running.

As you are building up distance, stay on a flat, smooth running surface. Your child's respiration will mature. The only exception to this rule of flat running is that in order to make running easier initially, we propose providing your child with the opportunity to run downhill. This is explained in the running schedule that follows.

A soft running surface is essential, in addition to wearing good-quality running shoes. Hard concrete and macadam surfaces do not "give," and can be hard on the legs.

Packed dirt, short grass, packed gravel, hard-packed sand or a running track are all surfaces that give a little. On them, you and your child will enjoy comfortable running.

At The Institutes, we have thirty children and thirty adults who run *daily!* They cover distances ranging from two miles to twenty-six miles nonstop. We have followed the rules about using flat, smooth surfaces that give, and wearing good running shoes over the years, and have had few problems. Hard surfaces help provoke injuries and muscle aches and incorrect running shoes, or old ones, can also provoke aches and pains.

What the Well-Dressed Runner Should Wear

Shoes are the most important aspect of dress for running. As we've said, *your child must have good quality running shoes that fit him well.*

This is important, because good running shoes are made to absorb the shock imposed on the ankles and feet while running. Nike and New Balance make good running shoes for tiny children. Do not spare a penny on purchasing the best-quality shoes you can find. Any top-quality sporting goods supplier or running shoe store can steer you in the right direction. If the shoes wear out (which they will), or your child outgrows them (which he will), you must buy new ones.

Your child must have light, loose-fitting, but proper clothing.

This is an essential point, to keep running easy for your little child, and thus to maintain that positive attitude he holds toward running.

In warm weather, shorts and a T-shirt are clearly in order, but for those of us who contend with the cold weather too each year, warmer clothing is also necessary.

Notice we said *warmer*, not bulkier.

Cumbersome, bulky sweaters and coats are annoying when running, because they impede the movements of your child's arms and upper body—yours, too, because you'll be running with him. This kind of garb will weigh you down and dampen anyone's enthusiasm. We don't want it to dampen your child's *or* yours—not the slightest bit.

It is such joy that invariably when young children run,
they are laughing, smiling or squealing with glee — they
love it!

Christopher Coventry,
Twenty-four months old.

It's easy to overdress when going out to run in the cold weather, but once you've started running, your body can warm up to the point where you're too hot. Then, if you've put on a bulky coat and feel forced to remove it, you've set yourself up for a chill!

If *layers* of clothing are worn, clothes can be removed one layer at a time, until comfort is achieved.

Put layers of light clothing on your little child (and on you!). Build layers of warmth from underneath. Start with a layer of long underwear (two, if necessary), shorts, a turtleneck shirt, a sweatshirt, a watchcap, and gloves. Heavy, good quality, thick cotton or finer wool socks will keep your feet warm. Since your feet are getting the most action during the run, this is all that's necessary. Just remember to come indoors right away after the run, especially if your child's shoes, or yours, are wet.

Of course, if the temperature outside is such that it *alone* will make running unpleasant, an indoor track or shopping mall (early in the morning, or at dinnertime, when few people are around) makes a good alternative.

Do keep in mind that *walking* in snow can provide a good respiratory challenge. If conditions do not permit running, an hour or so of climbing back up a hill after sledding down, or just plain hiking to enjoy the scenery will allow a good respiratory workout, and lots of good times together as a bonus!

Common Sense Will Tell You Lots of Things

Common sense will tell you lots of things. Listen to it. Don't ask for trouble by running on slippery, icy surfaces, or at locations where potholes or similar dangers exist. Never run if your child is tired, hungry or thirsty. Take care of these basics before running with a rest, a nap, a light meal or snack, or a drink. Running helps provide an appetite, so have a snack ready for when you're finished, too.

Never push your child to run, either emotionally or physically. Never attempt to pull him or hold his hand while you are running together. Only positive means of encouragement will create success. If your child refuses to run, accept this. (It will be temporary.)

Let your child sit in the stands and watch you run. You set the example. Eventually he won't be able to resist hopping down and joining you. Kids go through phases, so don't be surprised if your little child does decide to sit out running for a while. As in setting an example by brachiating for your child, do the same thing here—set a joyous example.

Your little child doesn't give a hoot about his brain development, nor about his physical fitness; what he does care about is being with you. He *enjoys* life with you!

Try to be careful not to discourage your child by talking about your own problems. Sometimes kids are doing just great and we say something thoughtless that fouls things up: Mom and kid are running and Mom says, "Gosh, it's *freezing* out here." In some cases, this never occurred to her kid, but he'll be cold in no time.

Dad is running with his son: "Ouch, that old knee injury is acting up!" Like father, like son, the child will be groaning sooner or later.

You've Got to Set the Pace

The primary reason for running *with* your child is to establish a pace. When we first began running with the children of The Evan Thomas Institute, they were incredibly enthusiastic about the idea.

We took them to the track, lined them up and said, "Ready, set, go!"

They burst off the starting line like thoroughbreds out of the starting gate, galloped down the track at top speed—and were completely exhausted after a hundred yards.

They collapsed, panting, on the track.

They had no idea about pacing themselves.

At first, you set the pace. Stay a step ahead of your child. As he becomes able to traverse longer and longer distances, let him become the leader during the run. Run side by side at times. Games like "Run on My Shadow" (in which your child has to stay on top of your shadow while running) help to establish a pace that will last for longer distances. In the absence of a sunny day, "Follow the Leader" will do!

Run Outdoors and in the Same Location Regularly

When Tegan Hagy was two years old and out with Dad to run for the first time, they went to a beautiful part of Fairmount Park, near the outskirts of Philadelphia, to get started.

The park has a long, wide, flat bridle path that stretches for five miles alongside a creek, surrounded by woods. There are no motor vehicles permitted, so it is a safe place. Only hikers, joggers, cyclists and an occasional horseback rider frequent the trail. This was the perfect place to begin a running program.

As Tegan and her dad started off on their one-mile walk-run, they went about five yards before Tegan stopped to pick up a pretty rock from the ground. This delayed them a bit, while they examined it. Then they went on and about ten yards later had to stop again to examine a bug.

This "stop-start" procedure continued for the full mile. Tegan learned a lot about the woods but did not extend herself physically at all. Her dad questioned whether he had chosen a good spot to begin.

Each day they walked one mile and spent a lot of time examining the environment and a little time running. Every twig, leaf, stone, bug, and piece of litter was scrutinized. Eventually, however, Tegan began spending less time looking at the ground, and more time looking ahead to where they were going.

They would race between telephone poles about a hundred yards apart; Dad would run ahead and she would follow, diving into his arms for a big hug. Her running distance increased until she could run to the first bridge and back—her first mile of nonstop running. Tegan stopped being distracted by her environment as soon as she learned about it.

Had her dad's reaction to her picking things up and wanting to know about them been "Put that down! Get over here!" it would have been a very long time before she got over the phase of wanting to discover this new environment, and she would not have had a positive attitude toward running.

In starting out to run with your child, respect his desire to learn about his environment. Every stop he makes to examine something is a chance for you to teach—but always come back to the task at hand. Finish the run! Sooner or later, the environment will become commonplace.

As long as weather conditions permit, running should be done outdoors. Running in the house is as confining to a two-*year*-old as being in a playpen is to a two-*month*-old. The next best thing to being outdoors is that indoor running track we've told you about. Failing that, running at the shopping mall (when shoppers are few) can be a good alternative.

Structure the Running Program

In preparation, you've already established *where* you will run every day. You've worked out your child's running outfit, complete with nice, bright, new running shoes. You have also worked out the time of day that is best.

Now, all you have to say is, "Okay, Jason, today we are going to run around this track four times." Jason has run three-and-a-half laps already, so he is pretty sure he can run four.

Or, you might say, "We are going to run to the third telephone pole today, Christopher. We ran to the second one last week. Do you think we can do it? Good. Okay, let's go!"

In short, the more familiar your little child is with his environment and your desire, the better he'll perform.

1. *Tell* your little child how far you will run, before you run.
2. *Show* him how far you will run, before you run.

Keep the Running Enjoyable

Sometimes, running for longer periods becomes boring to the little child, and even if he *can* continue, he just doesn't want to. In this case, you need to be a bit ingenious.

Frank Caputo, one of our staff members, and three-year-old daughter Adriana would go out for two- to three-mile runs and also work in a little dancing.

We often suggest making an activity as *easy* as possible for kids. Sometimes kids like things tougher.

When Adriana began to run at longer and longer distances, Frank would take along a battery-run tape recorder that played Adriana's favorite song at the time, "Do The Hokey-Pokey." To maintain Adriana's interest for longer distances, he'd flip on the tape.

Adriana would trot and break into her version of the "right foot in, right foot out . . . " of the dance. It was difficult, but she loved it! We find parents' imaginations unceasingly creative—and absolutely vital to making activities as enjoyable as possible.

You realize, of course, that running with your little child is the best incentive for getting into shape yourself. *We have a lot of Evan Thomas Institute moms and dads who look just great and who don't have to do aerobic dancing!*

From Trotting, to Running Several Miles

Ahead we have outlined a program for taking your little child from just a few feet of trotting to running several miles. Obviously, this is not a process that occurs overnight. It may take two years or more to build up to miles of running. The entire process occurs gradually, step by step, with your child's enjoyment, and yours as well, as the top priority.

Your little child will grow, change, develop and mature in so many ways during this process. For you parents, the challenge will be to design the program properly, depending upon what your child needs at any given moment. Don't be afraid to change gears when necessary.

Because of the extended period of time required for a little child to run longer and longer distances, the *frequency, intensity* and *duration* of the running program are constantly evolving as your little child develops.

As with any new motor function you may pursue with your child, always begin with high frequency, low intensity and brief duration.

Running sessions should be brief at first, only ten to fifteen seconds each, and spread out into as many opportunities a day as it is possible to offer.

Eventually, all three components—frequency, intensity and duration—should take this form:

Frequency: One running session a day, or every other day.
Intensity: Running as fast as possible.
Duration: Thirty minutes of nonstop running.

The following pages tell you how to help your little child make the transition from running very brief distances to running miles. A tiny child as young as eighteen months can begin this time process.

Phase One

1. Building up running on a downhill slope.

As in the previous chapter, choose for the downhill walking environment a gentle slope that you know will allow your child to build up running speed while still keeping his balance.

Initially, all you need is a slope twenty to thirty feet long. Make clear start and finish lines on the ground. Then you and your little child run down from the start to the finish line, hug and kiss, do some balance swings, and walk back up.

Start with ten frequencies of this, and build up to twenty or fifty, done within the twenty-minute period.

As your little child's speed increases, you'll find him running past the finish line! Then it's time to lengthen the distance of your sprints by ten feet. Continue to add distance as his speed increases.

First Goal: Build up to twenty yards of running downhill.

Continue to add as much distance as is possible in relation to where you live, and the number of hills in your area.

Even if you cannot find long, smooth-surfaced hills, continue to increase the distance between start and finish lines. If the start of the downhill run begins on an incline, and then levels off after your little child gets beyond the end of the slope, the momentum he has built up on the downgrade will carry him for some distance before he starts to slow down.

Even if you live in Kansas and can find no *real* hills, any downward slope can be useful in helping your little child learn what it feels like to accelerate. If your child is running down the grade from the barn entrance, that will do.

Once your little child has conquered running downhill, you're ready to transition him gradually to running on the flat.

2. *Building up running on a flat surface.*

On a smooth, flat terrain, as described in the preceding chapter, take your child out for a one-mile walk and encourage as many brief trots or runs as possible. Start with running twenty feet ten times throughout a one-mile session, walking in between runs.

Gradually increase running distances to thirty feet, and do those thirty feet twenty times per mile. At that point, continue to increase the distance of running (and begin to decrease the frequency) within each one-mile session.

Follow these routines three times a week and *gradually increase the distance daily to make the gradient of increase as gradual as possible.*

Schedule

Each session, run according to this schedule:

Week 1   – 30 feet, twenty times
Week 3   – 40 feet, fifteen times
Week 6   – 50 feet, twelve times
Week 9   – 60 feet, ten times
Week 12 – 75 feet, eight times
Week 15 – 100 feet, six times
Week 18 – 125 feet, four times
Week 21 – 200 feet, three times
Week 24 – 300 feet, two times

How do you encourage trotting? It's easy. It is simply a matter of arousing your child's desire to accelerate.

This translates into "Let's have some fun." Chasing, throwing or kicking a ball while you walk are usually high on the kids' list of preferred activities.

Second Goal: The second objective is for your little child to run 100 yards nonstop.

By now your little child will use running as a means of transportation. Now, in glee, or in determination to get somewhere, he will break into a run spontaneously, to reach a destination.

With this new ability, it is now possible to develop your child's breathing, and thus his general function, *beyond that* of the *average* child.

Congratulations!

Phase Two

3. *Running one hundred yards to three miles.*

In order to begin this stage of a running program, your little child should be able to run 100 yards nonstop. If all is going well, he should be starting this stage at eighteen months of age.

Our goal will be to achieve three miles of running nonstop.

We frequently see four-year-olds who can run three miles nonstop.

Obviously, this is a long, long-term goal.

The time it takes to reach this goal will depend on one thing: how much opportunity you give your child to run at longer and longer distances.

How often should you run with your tiny child? Four days a week as a minimum—running each day is even better.

How do you build up to three miles?

Slowly and gradually, using short, frequent running sessions initially, and then gradually building up duration as your little child becomes a better runner.

Here's a schedule of steps to follow for building up to one mile of nonstop running:

Schedule

1. Your little child should walk one mile a day and, within that mile, run 100 yards four times (4 × 100 yards of running).
2. You should *gradually* increase to 150 yards of running four times in his one-mile walk (4 × 150 yards of running).
3. You should *gradually* increase to four sessions of 200 yards of running during his one-mile walk (4 × 200 yards of running).
4. You should blend your child's running sessions until he runs 400 yards nonstop twice during his one-mile walk (2 × 400 yards of running).
5. You should combine his two sessions until he runs 800 yards (almost one-half mile) nonstop within the one mile (1 × 800 yards of running).
6. You should run 800 yards and gradually increase this distance by twenty yards a day, walking the rest of the mile (run 820 yards and walk 940 yards, and so on).
7. Gradually increase the running distance while decreasing the walking distance until your child runs one mile nonstop.

CONGRATULATIONS! HAVE A CELEBRATION!
YOUR LITTLE CHILD RUNS ONE MILE NONSTOP.

From this point on, it's easy to build up to three miles.

The hard part is over. Simply build up the nonstop distance that your child runs, *gradually* but regularly.

A very gentle gradient would be to add at least 250 yards to your child's total daily nonstop distance. Not all at one time, but gradually, over the course of a month. In fourteen months' time, then, your child will be running three miles nonstop on a regular basis.

Increase your total nonstop running very gradually, and in consideration of your child's age. If your two-year-old can run a mile, then an increase of 100 to 200 yards per month to his total nonstop running distance would be excellent. If your child is three years old and has just accomplished a mile nonstop, then an addition of 300 yards per month would be appropriate.

By the way, if your little child is already beyond Step 1 or 2 or 3 on the schedule you have just read, plug him in where he belongs. If he can run 200 yards nonstop, start with that distance.

On paper, it looks easy to build up to three miles. However, a nice neat schedule does not always go exactly as you planned it. Do allow for other factors that can influence when you achieve your goals as you begin this running program. But remember: you have in your grasp right now the *most important* factor that will lead to success.

That is—your little kid loves to run.

Kids think running is a means of transportation. We adults spend our time chasing them down to convince them this is not true. Fortunately, we don't always succeed. To a kid, the feeling of wind blowing through the hair, and being airborne for that split second, is totally exhilarating.

Many of our kids in The Evan Thomas Institute run three miles nonstop by the time they are four years old. Once you and your child have built up to three miles of nonstop running, stay at that distance and work at reducing the time it takes to run that three miles until he can run three miles in thirty-six minutes.

The goal for our five-year-olds in the first grade of The International School is to run three miles in thirty-six minutes.

By the time your little child is four years old, he will be physically superb, not as compared to four-year-olds, but as compared to *adults*. Few adults, let alone four-year-olds, can run three miles nonstop.

Third Goal: *The goal at this level is for your child to run three miles nonstop.*

Now that he has developed good, regular breathing through distance running, you can begin sprints.

Running develops efficient respiration and thus creates better brain function.

Improve your kid's respiration by teaching him how to sprint and run long distances!

Sprinting: Start the sprints only after your child can run three miles nonstop.

There is generally little difference between a sprint run and a jog in a beginning runner, but once your child has developed good, regular breathing with distance running, a real sprint is possible.

A sprint, of course, is running at the fastest possible speed. Start with sprints of twenty yards, ten times a day.

Gradually increase the distance until your child can sprint sixty yards, ten times a day. (The sprints are done in addition to the three-mile run.)

Cross Country: You can now move from three miles of running on flat, even terrain, to cross-country running on its up-and-down, hilly terrain. This difference in the terrain being traveled creates a variance in breathing. This type of running creates adaptable breathing.

Conclusions

Your little child is now not only physically excellent compared to other four-year-olds, but he is also excellent compared to the vast majority of all of the five billion adults who inhabit the planet.

The chances are excellent that he will by now, and without conscious effort on your part or his, have established laterality.

He should, by now, be right-sided—which is to say, he will be right-eyed, right-eared, right-handed and right-legged, as is the case with about 80 percent of us—or he will be left-eyed, left-eared, left-handed and left-legged, as is the case with the other 20 percent or so of us. This, as we shall see, is due to control of these functions by the opposite side of the brain.

When he walks and runs in cross-pattern, and has established single-sidedness (as is demonstrated by kicking a ball with the leg on the same side of the body as the hand he uses to throw the ball), he is now operating at the highest brain level the world has ever known. He is operating from the sophisticated cortex.

If your child is two years old when he establishes sidedness and walks and runs in cross-pattern, his mobility intelligence is 300. If he is three years old, 200. If he is six years old, 100. If he's seven already, give him a good deal more opportunity than he's had.

At whatever age, he has entered into the highest level of human function. From here on in, the sky's the limit!

Mobility Intelligence
LEAVING STAGE VI, THE PRIMITIVE CORTEX
ENTERING STAGE VII, THE SOPHISTICATED CORTEX

AGE (in years)	MOBILITY INTELLIGENCE	OUR ADVICE
One and a half	400	World's record?
Two	300	You're doing
Three	200	a superb job!
Four	150	
Five	120	Keep up the splendid job you are doing!
Six	100	He is exactly average
Seven	85	Give him more opportunity
Eight	75	to move.
Nine	66	Give your child immediate
Ten	60	and extraordinary
Eleven	54	opportunity to move, move, move.
Twelve	50	If your child is below 50 in mobility intelligence, you should waste no time in seeking professional help.

If mobility plays such a basic role in our lives, and in our culture, why have we not paid more attention to it? This is not a situation in which there are any villains. We simply haven't known.

The McCartys: Heather, four-and-one half; Paul, eighteen months; and Mom! Photo by Sherman Hines.

The Institutes' Manual Development Scale

GLENN DOMAN and The Staff of The Institutes

BRAIN STAGE		TIME FRAME	MANUAL COMPETENCE
VII	SOPHISTI-CATED CORTEX	Superior 36 Mon. / Average 72 Mon. / Slow 144 Mon.	**Using a hand to write which is consistent with the dominant hemisphere** *Sophisticated human expression*
VI	PRIMITIVE CORTEX	Superior 18 Mon. / Average 36 Mon. / Slow 72 Mon.	**Bimanual function with one hand in a skilled role** *Primitive human expression*
V	EARLY CORTEX	Superior 9 Mon. / Average 18 Mon. / Slow 36 Mon.	**Cortical opposition bilaterally and simultaneously** *Early human expression*
IV	INITIAL CORTEX	Superior 6 Mon. / Average 12 Mon. / Slow 24 Mon.	**Cortical opposition in either hand** *Initial human expression*
III	MIDBRAIN	Superior 3.5 Mon. / Average 7 Mon. / Slow 14 Mon.	**Prehensile grasp** *Meaningful response*
II	PONS	Superior 1 Mon. / Average 2.5 Mon. / Slow 5 Mon.	**Vital release** *Vital response*
I	MEDULLA and CORD	Superior Birth to .5 / Average Birth to 1.0 / Slow Birth to 2.0	**Grasp reflex** *Reflex response*

THE INSTITUTES FOR THE ACHIEVEMENT OF HUMAN POTENTIAL
8801 STENTON AVENUE
WYNDMOOR, PA 19038

MULTIPLYING YOUR BABY'S PHYSICAL INTELLIGENCE

STAGE VI, THE PRIMITIVE CORTEX

Manual Competence

CLASS: Little Child.

BRAIN STAGE: The Primitive Cortex.

PROFILE COLOR: Indigo.

FUNCTION: Bimanual function, with one hand in a skilled role.

AVERAGE AGE: This function is present in an average little child by thirty-six months of age.

DESCRIPTION: Pouring water from a pitcher held in a skilled hand into a glass held upright in the unskilled is a clear example of "bimanual function with one hand in a skilled role." And, writing with one hand on a paper held by the other is an even clearer and higher function.

However, these examples are much too highly skilled for a little child who has just entered the indigo areas of function that are controlled by the primitive cortex; as this area of the brain develops, so, too, will his manual abilities.

PURPOSE: To set the stage for greater manual skill.

At each of the earlier stages of manual competence, your little child has been refining his ability to pick up objects in both his hands and release them. Now he has the ability to use both hands together, with one of them assisting the other. Although one hand may be used more than the other, both hands are almost equally skillful.

Now one hand will begin to emerge as the more skillful of the two. This will be the hand that pours the milk from the pitcher while the other hand holds the glass.

Now your baby begins to take objects apart, and to put them back together again. He will use the same hand more and more consistently to perform the more skilled role. If it is his right hand, we will call him right-handed. If it is the left hand, we will call him left-handed.

Now he gains and fine-tunes the bimanual abilities that may one day lead to performing the intricate neurosurgical procedures necessary in the operating room to save a life—or to the skills needed to build a beautiful piece of furniture that becomes a family's prized heirloom.

How shall we make sure our little child will be good enough?

THE MANUAL COMPETENCE PROGRAM—STAGE VI: INGREDIENTS FOR SUCCESS

At the previous stages of manual function, your child learned to brachiate and began to strive for independent brachiation. As this ability develops, your child will begin to use his hands for more skilled bimanual tasks.

What the Well-Dressed INDEPENDENT Brachiator Should Wear

As long as your child needs some help from you to brachiate, he should continue to wear overalls. Once he is independent, however, he can wear any clothing that is comfortable and somewhat loose.

Now shoes do not become a big factor, so sneakers are fine; heavy shoes should still be avoided—at least until he is a very strong brachiator.

Everyone Does It, Every Day

Brachiation must be a family affair. Everyone does it, and they do it for *fun!* If this attitude does not prevail in your house, the chances of your child achieving independent brachiation are next to nil.

This point cannot be stressed enough and therefore, we say it again:

The single most important factor in succeeding with your child in brachiation is that brachiation must be a way of life for the family and for your child.

EVERYONE DOES IT, EVERY DAY, WITH JOY!

THE GOAL, OF COURSE, IS FOR YOUR CHILD TO BRACHIATE TOTALLY INDEPENDENTLY. ONCE THIS IS ACCOMPLISHED, THE OBJECTIVE IS FOR HIM TO DO SO AT LEAST FIFTEEN TIMES A DAY.

Sometimes moms comment that their kids can brachiate very well, but that after many months they still require support or help in swinging.

For the full range of benefits from brachiation to be achieved, it is absolutely necessary that your tiny child becomes totally independent.

When kids do not reach the final step of independent brachiation, the reason for this difficulty is almost always LACK OF FREQUENCY. The child is probably getting only enough opportunity and frequency of brachiation to maintain the same level of competence. To go on to independence, he needs more opportunity (more trips a day) to establish the security and confidence he needs to become totally independent.

We almost always recommend that our mothers *double* the total number of daily trips when kids are at this point. By doubling his opportunity, your tiny child will rapidly achieve independence. This additional time will be well spent. The alternative is many more months of constant spotting and attention needed to bring about independence.

Frequency: Thirty sessions a day of brachiating the length of your ladder.

Intensity: You give *zero* support and only help to *swing* his body, *if needed*.

Duration: One trip of the ladder at a time. Once your tiny child is totally independent and *insists* on doing the ladder alone (which he will), you can teach him to turn at the end of the ladder and brachiate back the way he came, a round trip.

Here are some other points that may give your child the boost he needs to become a totally independent brachiator.

How High Should the Brachiation Ladder Be?

Mother's height?

If you make the height of the ladder one or two inches higher than your head, the advantage is that you can carefully and comfortably spot your child as he brachiates. The disadvantage is that the height is *so* high that your child should never be permitted on the ladder without your being right there touching him; thus the frequency of brachiation is limited to your time.

Kid's height?

Adjust the ladder to a height that your tiny child can climb up to from a three-inch-high box and grasp the rung. As a result, as he brachiates, his toes will just clear the floor. If he falls off, he won't hurt himself any more than he would if he fell while walking. He can brachiate whenever he pleases; he is secure. However, it's more difficult for you to spot him at this level.

Our recommendation.

The ideal situation would be to keep the ladder at Mom's height until such time as your child is almost totally independent. When this occurs, drop the ladder to the kid's height we talked about before, so that he can confidently conquer the last stages before independence.

Angle the ladder.

Some moms have found it helpful to put the ladder on a slightly descending angle. Brachiating "downhill" is easier, because gravity helps supply the forward-swinging momentum necessary to reach the next rung, and he doesn't have to stretch as high or as far to grab it. This will help him in the final stage of achieving independence.

Tiptoe height.

If you think you've tried everything with little success, you may want to consider dropping the ladder so that your tiny child can *just* reach the rungs by himself. He can "brachiate" on his tip toes. Of course, this is not truly brachiation, but kids can do it independently and frequently. If your child has not been feeling successful, this can help him gain confidence.

Every couple of weeks, remember to raise the ladder a fraction (1 centimeter if possible). This can be accomplished if the space between adjustments is 1 centimeter. To minimize the increase, raise only one end at a time. Kids grow quickly, and it is advantageous to keep them stretching for the rungs as much as possible.

On pillows.

If your tiny kid improves with the tiptoe technique, you can embellish it by raising the ladder still higher, and placing pillows in a stepping-stone pattern directly under the rungs. The rungs should be high enough that they can be reached only by standing on tiptoes on the pillows. To get to the next pillow, the child has a brief moment of independent swing.

These techniques are to add to your battery of options to keep your child's interest until he is an independent brachiator. Only you can decide what is best for you and your tiny child.

One thing is certain, though: once your tiny child can brachiate by himself, you won't be able to stop him!

Some Variations on a Theme

Here are some variations on brachiation that are enjoyable and challenging for the child who's already brachiating independently.

Skipping Rungs.

Kids should be encouraged to skip rungs once they are brachiating independently.

By this, we mean they grasp only every second rung as they continue down the length of the ladder.

Skipping rungs makes brachiation *easier*. The benefits of brachiation to your child's physical development are *enhanced*.

The reason that it is easier for your child to brachiate this way is because he needs to grasp only half the number of rungs. With less stress placed on his hands, they retain their strength for a longer period. Also, the swing becomes exaggerated, making forward body motion quicker: therefore he swings closer to the rung he is reaching for.

Skipping rungs enhances the benefits of brachiation because the chest expands even more with the increased swing and the extended reach for each rung.

Because the number of dowels to be grasped is decreased by 50 percent (or more, depending on how many rungs he skips), he can brachiate for longer distances nonstop. This increases all the beneficial effects of brachiation.

Brachiating Backwards.

When kids are accomplished at skipping rungs, they're ready for backward brachiation. When your child mounts the ladder, simply have him face away from it. All that he needs to do to be able to brachiate backward is to learn how to swing his body backward so he can grasp the rung behind him.

Backward brachiation improves the convergence of vision because kids *must* tilt their heads backward in order to see the next rung.

Sideways Brachiation.

The next challenge once your child's had the fun of learning to brachiate backward is to learn how to brachiate *sideways*.

It is not easy to swing the body from side to side so this activity is more difficult. It also requires changing the position of your child's hands. No longer can both palms face forward. The leading hand must grip the bar with the palm turned toward the child's head, or away from the direction in which he is brachiating.

The hand "behind" remains facing forward, as with the usual forward method of brachiating.

Your child must always keep his hands on different rungs—this is important! There is a tendency to grasp the same rung with both hands.

This is more difficult to do, and it also makes it much more difficult to swing.

So, teach your kid to move sideways by encouraging him to have his hands always placed one or two rungs apart. The same hand should always be in the lead while the trailing hand moves from two rungs behind to one rung behind. Then the leading hand moves to two rungs ahead, and so on.

Twisting.

This is the *crème de la crème* of brachiating activities.

It involves turning the body around as one brachiates forward. Figure it out and practice it yourself prior to teaching it to your child.

It is difficult, because the position of the hands is different.

Begin by grasping the first two rungs of the ladder with both palms facing each other.

Your body is in the same position as it was for sideways brachiating.

If your right hand is forward, you *must* twist *counterclockwise*.

If your left hand is forward, you *must* twist *clockwise*.

The reason is that your wrists can't rotate the other way (you'll hurt your wrists if you do the opposite) so do it correctly and ensure that your child also follows this rule.

If you begin with the left hand forward, let go with your right hand and rotate *clockwise*.

<u>Sideways Brachiation</u>:

        Once your child's learned to brachiate backwards, he should
           have the fun of learning to brachiate <u>sideways</u>. The palms of his

Twisting:
Begin by grasping two rungs of the
ladder with both hands facing each
other. Your child's body is in the san
position as it was for sideways
brachiation. Palms facing each othe
he rotates to the next rung.

Palms facing away from each other,
he rotates to the rung after that, then
palms facing each other... and so on,
for "twisting."

Grasp the next rung with your right hand; now you must *reverse* your hand grip. You must grasp the next rung with your right palm *facing away*.

The trick can be reduced to: palms facing each other, rotate to next rung, palms facing away, rotate to next rung, palms facing each other, and so on.

It will take time for your kid to figure it out, but once he's watched you, and once he does it himself, he'll really enjoy twisting!

Developing More Bimanual Abilities

As your child becomes a more accomplished brachiator, his hand function becomes more sophisticated. He now takes a strong interest in bimanual activities, which in most kids means "taking things apart." Kids would *like* to put things they've disassembled back together (and indeed, they try), but the fact is that almost everything comes apart easier than it goes back together. With your help, however, your child can learn to do constructive bimanual activities.

Start with a simple bimanual activity and break it down into its individual steps. Let's take, as an example, pouring from a pitcher held in one hand into a glass held in the other. The hand holding the pitcher is the hand in the skilled role.

The steps are:
1. Picking the pitcher up and holding it in an upright position.
2. Picking an empty glass up with the other hand.
3. Tilting the pitcher and pouring juice from it into the glass.
4. Putting the pitcher back on the table.
5. Putting the filled glass on the table.

You guarantee your child's easy success with this task if you get a small pitcher and a glass that is a size your child can easily hold, and begin with a small amount of his favorite juice in the pitcher. Now there can be an end product to the activity—a drink of his favorite juice!

The first few times you introduce this activity, you would be wise to hold your hand over his so you can guide his hands through the activity.

You can do a variety of manual activities together in this manner:
1. Pulling the top off a pen and putting it back on.
2. Unscrewing the top from a jar, and screwing it back on.
3. Unbuttoning a *large* button through a large buttonhole, and buttoning it.
4. Buttering bread.
5. Washing dishes.

The list is long, and you will come up with many activities that will be fun for both of you.

One important point to keep in mind is that there should be an end product for each activity; otherwise you will create the same situation as is created with a toy—your little child will be bored as soon as he has mastered it.

The chances are good that at the time an average mom has finally decided she must put the family's prized possessions away for safekeeping, you can begin to bring some of yours out. By now you should be able to show something to your child, tell him about it, let him hold it, then put it on the shelf without being in constant fear for its safety.

THE GOAL AT THIS POINT IS FOR YOUR CHILD TO ACCOMPLISH BIMANUAL FUNCTION, WITH ONE HAND CONSISTENTLY IN A SKILLED ROLE.

Conclusions

So now your child has been doing manual functions for years instead of months and, having been given a superb environment for the development of manual competence, his hands may well be as strong and supple as those of a paratrooper, and he may be able to brachiate farther than his ranger brother. If he has had opportunity to do so, he may already have begun to play the violin, write and paint. (See *How to Multiply Your Baby's Intelligence*, Doubleday & Company.)

If he has actually begun to write, and if the hand he uses to do so is consistent with the leg he uses to kick a ball, and the eye he uses to look through a telescope (or keyhole) is on the same side of his body as that hand, and that leg, you may color him violet and know that he is functioning at the very highest brain level this ancient world has ever known. He is using his sophisticated cortex.

He need *not* be brachiating to achieve credit. Brachiating is a bonus for being physically splendid.

If your child is two years old when he is doing these wonderful bimanual things, he has a manual intelligence of 300; if he's six years old, he has a manual intelligence of 100. Even if you did not start with him from birth, if he is more than seven years old and cannot do these things, there is reasonable cause for concern.

He has, however old he may be, entered into the supreme level of the brain, the exclusively human sophisticated cortex, which he will continue to "sophisticate" all his life.

Manual Intelligence LEAVING STAGE VI, THE PRIMITIVE CORTEX ENTERING STAGE VII, THE SOPHISTICATED CORTEX		
AGE (in years)	**MANUAL INTELLIGENCE**	**OUR ADVICE**
One and a half	400	World's record?
Two	300	You're doing
Three	200	a superb job!
Four	150	
Five	120	Keep up the splendid job you are doing!
Six	100	He is exactly average.
Seven	85	Give him more opportunity
Eight	75	to move.
Nine	66	Give your child immediate
Ten	60	and extraordinary
Eleven	53	opportunity to develop his manual competence.
Twelve	50	If your child is below 50 in manual intelligence, you should waste no time in seeking professional help.

THE ACTIVE BALANCE PROGRAM
FOR SKILLED WALKERS TO GYMNASTS

You have already introduced your tiny child to the active balance program. Now he is ready for a more sophisticated program.

The active balance activities listed ahead comprise a myriad of activities that place the brain and body in every conceivable position in space and in relation to gravity. Those listed are common activities but, of course, many, many more activities and vestibular techniques exist.

Don't hesitate to add any balance-related activity that you and your child might enjoy. Some of the techniques have already been mentioned in detail previously in this book—walking, holding objects, negotiating stairs, walking rough terrain—these serve the dual purpose of developing mobility and balance simultaneously.

Begin by choosing the activities that appeal to you and your child.

Frequency: Choose from the list ahead any ten activities you wish to start with. Do each one at least once a day.

Intensity: First, work at helping your child become independent at the chosen activities. Once independence is achieved, encourage faster and faster accomplishment of the activity, within the bounds of safety and enjoyment.

Remember, intensity remains vital to the growth of the vestibular mechanism. The more quickly the activity is attempted, the more rapidly the balance mechanism adapts to the complexity of spatial and gravitational change.

This adaptive process develops better brain function, which keeps the body balanced and oriented in space.

Duration: Do each of the ten chosen activities for at least one minute each.

Total daily duration should be ten minutes *minimum*.

Active Balance Activities
1. Walking, while holding objects
2. Rolling
3. Forward somersaults
4. Backward somersaults
5. Seesawing
6. Walking on rough terrain
7. Negotiating steps
8. Walking on varying heights and levels, such as on walls
9. Climbing (ladders, rope ladders, walls, trees)
10. Jumping down
11. Broad jump
12. High jump
13. Hopping
14. Jumping rope

15. Balance beam
16. Handstands
17. Sit-ups
18. Squat thrusts (squat all the way down, then jump up)
19. Pirouetting (spinning the body around and around, as a ballerina does)
20. Directional walking (forward, backward, sideways)
21. Swinging
22. Stepping stones
23. Rope swing
24. Hiking
25. Running over and under a series of objects set at various heights off the ground
26. Brachiation activities (forward, backward, sideways and twisting)
27. Sliding board
28. Jogging or running on a rebounder (be mighty careful on this and 29)
29. Jumping on two feet, and hopping on one foot on a rebounder
30. Push-ups, touching-toes exercises

THE FUNDAMENTAL ACTIVE BALANCE PROGRAM

We will now embark upon a dual course. One objective is to virtually complete the process of developing the balance areas of the brain. Then, when your tiny child has mastered the specifics of the active balance program, he will be capable of pursuing *any* balance-related activity. The range of activities is limitless—and totally up to you and your child's discretion.

Our preferences are for gymnastics and ballet, because those graceful and beautiful activities are superb in every way in and of themselves *and* they also provide constant balance stimulation at the highest level known to man.

In short, they continue to develop the brain.

However, if figure skating, diving, surfing, skiing, skating, pole vaulting, judo and/or aikido suits your fancy, and your child's, he will be well prepared for them.

The second course provided for by this program is that your child is being specifically prepared to pursue the initial gymnastics program described in detail in The Institutes' publications on mobility.

The passive and active balance programs are the ideal preparation for any gynmastic program.

TECHNIQUES

1. Rolling on side and forward rolling (somersaults)
   These continue to improve your child's ability to roll and forward-roll, by increasing the speed and nonstop duration of rolling and forward rolling. *Maintain the same frequency*, as established earlier, of four sessions of rolling and forward rolling daily. Increase *intensity* by encouraging your child to roll more quickly, with duration gradually building from five yards of nonstop rolling to twenty-five yards nonstop.
   Do the same with forward rolls: for each session, encourage your child to

do more and more forward rolls in a row—one roll followed by another, and another, and another, and so on. . . .

When your child is doing many forward rolls in succession, measure the distance. Build this distance up to a total of twenty-five yards nonstop.

Eventually, your child will show signs of being able to forward roll and land on his feet, not his bottom.

This is the beginning of true tumbling.

You can speed up the process by having your child forward roll down a gentle slope. The increased speed created by rolling downhill will help him to get his feet underneath him.

Provide your child with five minutes a day each of opportunity for rolling and forward rolling.

2. The Balance Beam

    To sophisticate your child's ability on the beam, proceed with these steps.

    Step 1: Once your tiny child has mastered walking the length of the beam totally independently, then begin having him walk backward the length of the beam. At first, he may look back over his shoulder, but encourage him to keep his head facing forward.

    Step 2: Once your child is able to walk the beam forward *and* backward without falling off, he graduates to an elevated beam. Raise the beam by constructing a box 6 inches high by 11 inches square, as shown in Appendix I, page 255. As your child becomes increasingly more successful at walking the balance beam, increase the height by adding one more box. Do not use more than two boxes in height.

    As you add the more advanced activities, *gradually increase the frequency to twenty-five trips a day down the balance beam.* The intensity of the activity will be determined by how fast he walks both forward and backward, as well as by the height of the beam. The duration continues to be the time it takes to walk one trip of the beam. Spend a minimum of five minutes for the balance beam.

3. Backward Rolls

    Once your tiny child has mastered many forward rolls in succession, it is wise to begin teaching him how to do backward rolls. Help him to roll backward on a mat, carpet or grass. Remember the importance of teaching him how it feels to do a new activity. As you learned with forward rolls, if he rolls backward down a slope, he will know how it feels to have his body and legs roll over his head. Teach him how, as he rolls backward, to place his hands, palms down, on the carpet or grass, with his fingers just touching his shoulders.

    Give your child one opportunity to roll backward, with help, ten times a day, at first. This may take as much as five minutes in duration. Work towards twenty-five yards nonstop. Work towards twenty-five yards nonstop backward rolling.

4.   Climbing and Jumping
     Kids love climbing up and down ladders, rope ladders, knotted ropes
     and trees. Climbing up objects, climbing across them, and climbing down
     provides excellent vestibular opportunity. Jumping over obstacles,
     broadjumping, and jumping down likewise provide opportunity. It is
     difficult to *prevent* children from doing these activities, so it is wise to
     teach your tiny child how to do them safely. Aid and abet him by pro-
     viding exciting environments for climbing and jumping, under your
     supervision.
     Total daily duration should be a minimum of five minutes.

Total Program Duration
     By combining the ten minutes of vestibular techniques with the twenty-
five minutes total of all the fundamental active balance activities, the total
duration of the program amounts to thirty-five minutes.
     Having mastered the fundamental active balance activities as well as
some of the other active balance techniques you have devised, your child is
well prepared to launch into the exhilarating world of gymnastics.

     YOU HAVE MET YOUR COMBINED GOAL. YOUR HARD
WORK, LOVE AND ENTHUSIASM HAVE MADE HIM A NATURAL
FOR ANY SOPHISTICATED BALANCE ACTIVITIES.

STAGE VI
DAILY CHECKLIST FOR MOTHER

1. The Mobility Program

____ **Frequency:** Four days a week minimum (every day is better); one running session a day, or every other day.

____ **Intensity:** Running as fast as possible, but at a steady pace, gradually increasing distance as the child's running speed increases.

____ **Duration:** From brief, ten- to fifteen-second sessions to thirty-six minutes of nonstop running.

____ **GOAL(S):** FOR YOUR CHILD TO:
1) BUILD UP TO TWENTY YARDS OF RUNNING DOWNHILL.
2) RUN 100 YARDS NONSTOP.
3) ACHIEVE AROUND THREE MILES OF RUNNING NONSTOP.

Mother's comments: My child accomplished these goals at
1) age _____ , 2) age _____ , 3) age _____ .

2. The Manual Program

____ **Frequency:** Thirty sessions a day of brachiating the length of your ladder.

____ **Intensity:** Your child supports all his weight independently; you give *zero* support, and help only to swing his body if needed.

____ **Duration:** One trip of the ladder at a time; gradually build up as your child wishes; once he is totally independent, teach him to turn and make a round trip.

____ **GOAL:** TO BRACHIATE ONE HUNDRED PERCENT INDEPENDENTLY, AND TO ACCOMPLISH BIMANUAL FUNCTION, WITH ONE HAND CONSISTENTLY IN A SKILLED ROLE.

Mother's comments: My child brachiated the length of the brachiation ladder totally independently at age_____ , and showed consistent use of one hand in a skilled role at age _____ .

3. The Balance Program

____ **Frequency:** Ten sessions of the active balance activities and many sessions of the Fundamental Active Balance Techniques each day.

____ **Intensity:** Once independence is achieved, encourage faster and faster accomplishment (within the bounds of safety and enjoyment).

____ **Duration:** Ten minutes for the active balance activities and twenty minutes for the fundamental active balance techniques.

____ **GOAL:** TO PREPARE YOUR CHILD COMPLETELY, THOROUGHLY AND SAFELY FOR ANY AND ALL SOPHISTICATED BALANCE ACTIVITIES HE MAY WISH TO PURSUE.

Mother's comments: _____

_____ .

From here on in, the sky's the limit.....

The International School kids aboard their raft, RA III.

The Institutes' Mobility Development Scale

GLENN DOMAN
and
The Staff
of
The Institutes

BRAIN STAGE		TIME FRAME	MOBILITY
VII	SOPHISTI-CATED CORTEX	Superior 36 Mon. / Average 72 Mon. / Slow 144 Mon.	Using a leg in a skilled role which is consistent with the dominant hemisphere *Sophisticated human expression*
VI	PRIMITIVE CORTEX	Superior 18 Mon. / Average 36 Mon. / Slow 72 Mon.	Walking and running in complete cross pattern *Primitive human expression*
V	EARLY CORTEX	Superior 9 Mon. / Average 18 Mon. / Slow 36 Mon.	Walking with arms freed from the primary balance role *Early human expression*
IV	INITIAL CORTEX	Superior 6 Mon. / Average 12 Mon. / Slow 24 Mon.	Walking with arms used in a primary balance role most frequently at or above shoulder height *Initial human expression*
III	MIDBRAIN	Superior 3.5 Mon. / Average 7 Mon. / Slow 14 Mon.	Creeping on hands and knees, culminating in cross pattern creeping *Meaningful response*
II	PONS	Superior 1 Mon. / Average 2.5 Mon. / Slow 5 Mon.	Crawling in the prone position culminating in cross pattern crawling *Vital response*
I	MEDULLA and CORD	Superior Birth to .5 / Average Birth to 1.0 / Slow Birth to 2.0	Movement of arms and legs without bodily movement *Reflex response*

THE INSTITUTES FOR THE ACHIEVEMENT OF HUMAN POTENTIAL
8801 STENTON AVENUE
WYNDMOOR, PA 19038

15

MULTIPLYING YOUR BABY'S PHYSICAL INTELLIGENCE

STAGE VII, THE SOPHISTICATED CORTEX

Mobility Competence

CLASS: Child.

BRAIN STAGE: The Sophisticated Cortex.

PROFILE COLOR: Violet.

FUNCTION: Using a leg in a skilled role which is consistent with the dominant (and opposite) hemisphere.

AVERAGE AGE: This function is present in an average child by seventy-two months of age.

DESCRIPTION: Almost forty years ago that genius, Temple Fay, described the process of mature walking as "a symphony of movement." It is precisely that. It is a miracle of human function, exceeded in its glory only by the miracle of human speech.

To this beautiful miracle the child falls heir at an average age of six years. He now walks, runs and jumps using a distinct cross-pattern. A perfect example of jumping in cross-pattern is the Olympic star clearing the high hurdles. Now our child is able to do these things. He is neither sprinter nor hurdler, but he *is* a cross-patterner.

To round him off as a human being, we will now add the final characteristic of child brain development. He will by now have sidedness. The left half of the brain controls the right side of the body and the right side of the brain controls the left side of the body.

PURPOSE:	Providing you have been doing the activities described in this book up to now, your child will have already established splendid sidedness. Every time he has reached for a spoon, pencil, or scissors and *used* the implement, *his* brain has made a decision as to which side of the body will be used. This process of the brain determining sidedness is a brain organization process. It is brought about by activities that aid in general brain organization such as the bilateral functions of crawling, creeping, walking and running and through opportunity to use a side of the body in a skilled role. The more opportunity he has for all these activities, the faster your child will establish his sidedness and the firmer will be the base of neurological organization upon which his finished laterality (sidedness) rests.
	What is important here is *not* whether one is right-sided or left-sided, but rather, if one is intended, at conception, to be right-sided, that one be entirely right-sided, and that if one is intended to be left-sided, that one be entirely left-sided.

While stepping up a very high step he will stand on his leg of "sidedness" in order to balance skillfully on it while advancing the less-skilled leg.

In any event, you may congratulate yourself.

You have brought your newborn to a truly unique human condition in mobility. Your child can go wherever he wants to go and be whatever he wants to be. *You* deserve to be congratulated!

THE MOBILITY COMPETENCE PROGRAM—STAGE VII: INGREDIENTS FOR SUCCESS

Providing you've followed the programs in this book, enjoying your child's development, he will by now have clearly established whether he is left- or right-footed.

All of our kids in The Evan Thomas Institute reach Stage VII by the age of three or earlier. Many moms comment that even from the age of a year or less they had strong indications as to whether their child would be right- or left-sided. Other mothers comment that they were constantly confused: they were certain their child was left-sided, only to find him going through a period that convinced them equally that the child was right-sided. However, finally, as the child reached Stage VII, he had clearly established his sidedness.

Your child's journey through the Mobility Stages can be a superb one — an expedition to truly high adventure. Rejoice in his mobility.

Already an independent brachiator and having developed splendid sidedness by two years ten months, Shea Hagy has reached the highest level of mobility development, accomplishing this in *less* than half the time it takes the average child.

Your Child: Right-Sided or Left-Sided?

In the event you believe your child has reached Stage VII in all ways *but* you still aren't sure whether he is clearly left- or right-footed, then the path is simple:

1. All you need to do is provide your child with the opportunity to kick balls, hop on one foot, jump over hurdles, walk on a balance beam, and do gymnastic activities such as a cartwheel where the activity is "led" with a particular foot.

   The more the frequency, intensity and duration of the opportunity, the more quickly your child will be completely left- or right-sided.

2. *In this process, it is vital that you do not influence your child's choice of sidedness.* Only *his* brain, from within, can determine the correct sidedness.

   Sometimes we can unconsciously affect sidedness. For example, instead of kicking a ball *between* a child's legs, we kick it toward his right foot and thus, to some degree, influence which side he uses.

   We must be careful to present him with objects directed to the *midline* of his body.

Teaching Your Child ANY Physical Activity

Now is the time your child can pursue *any* physical activity. Physically and neurologically, he is ready to begin to learn anything. To be a great coach for him, *you* must have two qualities:

1. You must know your student very well; *and*
2. You must know your sport very well.

As far as number one goes, is there anyone even close to being in the same league with you?

You've taken your child from the womb and immobility to Stage VII! You know when he can do better and just needs some confidence-building.

You know when he's pushing himself too hard, and you need to slow him down a little. In terms of knowing your student, you're the best coach in the world!

As far as number two goes, you may well have no expertise in sports, athletics, or physical activity. But this is where the discovery and the excitement begin! Now you and your child together can explore the exhilaration of human mobility. Follow these steps:

1. Decide what physical activity you wish to pursue. Choose something *you've* always wanted to do.

   Let's say you choose gymnastics.

2. Go out and buy books about how to learn gymnastics. There are a hundred and one books out there about learning any activity— archery to yachting. Read up on gymnastics; get a feel for it.

3. Using the techniques described in *How to Teach Your Baby to Read* and *How to Give Your Baby Encyclopedic Knowledge* (Doubleday & Company, Inc., and The Better Baby Press), teach your child the words of gymnastics. Using Bits of Intelligence, teach him the various gymnastic positions and equipment. Make a

homemade book in which your child stars in a gymnastic exposition. Now you've whetted his appetite!

4. Keep your eye on the TV schedules to see when gym meets are being televised and watch them together. Don't hold back your enthusiasm or inhibit your cries of admiration for the beauty you see.

5. Go to a gymnastic meet. Get in the front row. This will *triple* your child's excitement and anticipation. After the meet, rub shoulders with some gymnasts. Get your questions answered.

6. Write out your program. Write a schedule saying exactly when you plan to introduce each activity. Make goals as to when you plan to achieve a certain level.

7. Start to do some of the activities yourself. Get a few steps ahead of your child.

8. Now begin the activities with your kid. Keep frequency *high*, keep intensity *low*, keep duration *very low*. Always stop before your child wants to stop. Design each session so your child *always* succeeds and *never* fails.

9. Try to keep up with your kid. He'll rapidly outstrip you. You will always be struggling to present him with new activities; enjoy the discovery together!

10. Eventually you will probably have to seek outside help (when you have accomplished everything you can with your child and gymnastics). If you go out to look for a coach, be sure to handpick the one who you believe will be most sensitive to your child's needs and development. If your coach is wise, she'll be bowled over by what you've accomplished and will see you as the best ally she ever had; if she isn't, she'll scoff at what you've attempted. If she scoffs, run, don't walk, to the nearest exit.

Be careful, no matter what happens, that competition is neither stressed nor placed above personal development. You don't need pressure and competition to displace the love of mobility you have so delicately and dedicatedly created.

Conclusions

Where are we now?

By giving your child extraordinary opportunity in the ideal environment, you have speeded his growth from one brain stage to the next. He has grown in strength and agility. His sophisticated balance activities have supplied his brain with advanced vestibular stimulation. Running has developed his respiration so that he can handle any physical situation readily. His brain has a splendid supply of oxygen and the adaptability to stand him in very good stead in any emergency situation or illness he may encounter.

Now the stage is set. The real fun lies just ahead, because your child has the coordination, the balance, and now, the respiration he needs to launch into the highest echelons of human movement.

Now your child has all the basic ingredients needed to undertake the most sophisticated forms of physical activity performed by human beings.

He is now, in terms of mobility, a complete human being. He has the base required to perform any physical task that human beings can perform.

He is now firmly ensconced in the territory of the sophisticated cortex. He is there to stay. He has all of his sixth year of life to put the finishing touches on it.

The only question now is, what will he do with it?

Will he be an average adult, with average human function? Perhaps.

Will he be a graceful, strong, highly capable human being who enjoys his own body with splendid potential for health and pleasure? Perhaps.

Will he be a superb athlete who runs, skis, swims, rides, and jumps, and who, in the pure joy of doing so, reaps medals of gold and brings honor to his nation? Perhaps.

What will determine which of these things will be the outcome?

Well, if you have simply gotten him across that border, at whatever age, so that he walks, runs and jumps in cross-pattern, and is consistently right- or left-sided, you've given him what he needs to be *any* of those things, if he is determined enough.

The younger you brought your child across the border to walking, jumping and running in cross-pattern and to being consistently right- or left-sided, then the easier it will be for him to be any of the things he wishes to be—with your help.

Remember, if you got him there at less than thirty-six months of age, he has a mobility intelligence of more than 200; if at exactly thirty-six months, exactly 200; at seventy-two months, 100.

If the last is the case, is the jig up for him in a mobility sense?

Of course not.

You can continue to build on the rock-solid foundation of superb breathing, balance and coordination you've developed in your child!

We believe human mobility and physical excellence to be a beautiful process of nature, a process whereby a tiny, immobile infant learns to adapt to his environment and pull himself up to higher levels of mobility <u>and</u> higher levels of brain function.

However, if you ask the <u>world</u> what <u>it</u> believes physical excellence to be, you will get a very different answer – one that involves bristling muscles, the powerful athlete, the great competitor.

At The Institutes, we are not too thrilled by what we call "games". Games like baseball, football and basketball are all contrivances of man. Maybe a hundred years ago, no one had ever heard of them – and who knows, maybe a hundred years hence, no one will have heard of them, either? One of the major problems of these games is that they pit man against man in a simulation of war.

We think there's more than enough of that going around today. We don't have to run around simulating it!

Is this to say that we are <u>opposed</u> to competition?

We are opposed to any brand of competition that dictates that I must score more points than you, I must overcome you – or prove that I am somehow superior to you.

The chances are good that if you are today a little flabby, overweight, or simply avoid physical activity, you were probably assigned to one of the "losing" teams as a kid. What a great sadness that so many of us, because of past competitive situations, have been turned off to the sheer exhilaration of human mobility and experiencing all of our lovely planet and its beautiful terrains.

We do teach our children here at The Institutes what we believe to be a <u>higher</u> brand of competition, one that goes like this: "If I want to reach some new higher level of mobility, one that I have never yet attained, only <u>I</u> can be the obstacle. If I overcome myself and achieve my goal, then I have won." In short, we teach the children <u>self</u>-competition.

We believe that if there is ever going to be a higher level of mobility, a Level XVIII, a higher, more sophisticated level of brain function, it will come about based on our ability as human beings to adapt better to our environment, and environments <u>other</u> than our earth's surface.

We advocate for our children those physical activities that are essentially extensions of basic mobility: activities such as ballet, gymnastics and figure skating are examples of human mobility made into an art form while other activities like swimming, climbing, skiing, hiking and even sailing and horseback riding are ways we human beings have devised to explore our planet. These activities pit us against our environment; they encourage us to better ourselves; they have been around for a long time and are destined to remain with us for a long time to come. They can be done by one person alone, or by a team of people. When accomplished together as a team, the team is working <u>together</u> – not to defeat another group of people – but to get happily and safely through the activity.

The Institutes' Manual Development Scale

BRAIN STAGE		TIME FRAME	MANUAL COMPETENCE
VII	SOPHISTI-CATED CORTEX	Superior 36 Mon. / Average 72 Mon. / Slow 144 Mon.	**Using a hand to write which is consistent with the dominant hemisphere** *Sophisticated human expression*
VI	PRIMITIVE CORTEX	Superior 18 Mon. / Average 36 Mon. / Slow 72 Mon.	**Bimanual function with one hand in a skilled role** *Primitive human expression*
V	EARLY CORTEX	Superior 9 Mon. / Average 18 Mon. / Slow 36 Mon.	**Cortical opposition bilaterally and simultaneously** *Early human expression*
IV	INITIAL CORTEX	Superior 6 Mon. / Average 12 Mon. / Slow 24 Mon.	**Cortical opposition in either hand** *Initial human expression*
III	MIDBRAIN	Superior 3.5 Mon. / Average 7 Mon. / Slow 14 Mon.	**Prehensile grasp** *Meaningful response*
II	PONS	Superior 1 Mon. / Average 2.5 Mon. / Slow 5 Mon.	**Vital release** *Vital response*
I	MEDULLA and CORD	Superior Birth to .5 / Average Birth to 1.0 / Slow Birth to 2.0	**Grasp reflex** *Reflex response*

GLENN DOMAN
and
The Staff
of
The Institutes

THE INSTITUTES FOR THE ACHIEVEMENT OF HUMAN POTENTIAL
8801 STENTON AVENUE
WYNDMOOR, PA 19038

MULTIPLYING YOUR BABY'S PHYSICAL INTELLIGENCE

STAGE VII, THE SOPHISTICATED CORTEX

Manual Competence

CLASS:	Child.
BRAIN STAGE:	The Sophisticated Cortex.
PROFILE COLOR:	Violet.
FUNCTION:	Using a hand to write (and to perform other skilled roles) that is consistent with the dominant hemisphere.
AVERAGE AGE:	This function is present in an average child by seventy-two months of age.
DESCRIPTION:	At this stage, the child has become quite skilled in bimanual function. The bimanual skill he has developed by such acts as creeping and brachiating he may now continue to perfect. They will give him the opportunity to be very skilled in gymnastics, ballet, swimming, skiing and other activities that require bimanual skill.

These things, however, are only the beginning. Now he begins to use the hand on the skilled side of his body along with the eye on the skilled side of his body to perform certain highly skilled and one-sided functions such as shooting at a target with a bow and arrow (during which he holds the bow with the *unskilled* hand while he holds the feathered end of the arrow with the *skilled* hand while sighting along the arrow with his skilled eye).

So also does he throw a javelin at a target using his skilled *hand* (whether right or left) while sighting along the shaft with his *eye* on the same skilled side of the body.

PURPOSE:

So does he throw a ball with his skilled hand on the skilled side of the body.

Most important of all, he now begins to write using the hand of "sidedness" to hold the pen or pencil. The purpose of the function of handedness is to complete your child's unique humanness by successful use of his uniquely human sophisticated cortex. Exactly as was the case in "leggedness" in mobility, it will not matter whether he is right-handed or left-handed. What matters is that if he is right-*handed* that he will also be right-*legged*, right-*eyed* and right-*eared* (which is to say, as we have before, entirely *left*-brained, which controls sidedness on the right side of the body). It is precisely this characteristic that gives us our unique human abilities of reading, writing and speech.

Writing

Writing is of such importance to us human beings and to child development that it requires a book of its own. However, the key and most important aspects of the physical act of writing are actually detailed in this book.

At The Institutes, it is *common* for our two-year-olds to write *words*; it is *common* for our three-year-olds to write short sentences. Why?

In order to be able to write, there are two vital requirements on the part of the brain. First, manually, the child must be able to *control* the tip of the pen so as to write legibly. What the control consists of is excellent cortical opposition. Having developed his manual ability and having accomplished independent brachiation, your child will have the control he needs to write.

The second brain requirement is to be able to see what the pen is doing. This requires excellent convergence of vision. Convergence of vision is created as a baby creeps. Providing your child had enough opportunity to creep, he should now have the ability to *see* the fine detail of his pen moving on paper.

These two abilities are what permit our tiny children to write at such an early age.

Conclusions

Now you have set the stage for all of your child's life.

He's developed the bimanual skill and strength that are the base of doing push-ups, giant swings on the horizontal bar, or aerials, or setting world records in brachiation, if any of those things are what you and he want for him.

He's developed the sidedness skills required as the base for pitching baseballs, throwing football passes, aiming a bow and arrow, standing on one hand, or whatever else you and he want to do.

He's also developed the single-sided "brainedness" that will permit him to use a paintbrush skillfully enough to paint a painting, perhaps a great one, or permit him to hold a pen to design a cathedral or an aircraft.

Most of all, he's got the base he'll need to take pen in hand to write a grocery list, a note to his mother, a poem, or perhaps, a document even more beautiful and more earth-shaking than the Declaration of Independence. Who is to say?

In all events, you've got him there. He has crossed the line into the operation of the sophisticated cortex. He's got the rest of his sixth year of life to be firmly in this area and beyond that, the rest of his *life* to perfect all the functions of his sophisticated cortex.

Not only has he reached the *highest* level of the brain, Stage VII, the sophisticated cortex, but turned right or left in that cortex to become right-sided or left-sided.

If you started him on purpose a little or a lot earlier than most other kids who make this superb journey almost entirely by accident, then he is now a little or a lot more physically superb, and that, it seems to us, is precisely what you set out to do!

Kids are what tomorrow is made of.

Glenn Doman and the kids of The International School, The Evan Thomas Institute. Photo by Sherman Hines.

LAND OF HOPE AND GLORY
BIG KIDS

Extraordinary, extremely capable, charming and beguiling little kids grow routinely into extraordinary, extremely capable, charming and beguiling big kids—and kids, without exception, are what tomorrow is made of.

People of my generation, living and dead, were raised during the Great Depression and we fought the Big War to which there seemed at the time no alternative (looking back I still see no alternative given the situation that existed).

Every infantryman who fought the Big War, *really* fought it, is a confirmed pacifist. Who in his right mind doesn't want peace?

But we are honestly divided on how to make that happen. Some good honest and sincere human beings believe it can be achieved only with big armies and big arms. Some good, honest and sincere people believe that it can be achieved only by peace at any price. Some good, honest and sincere people believe that some point between those extremes is the only way.

My generation managed to survive both the Depression *and* the Big War with some degree of credit to ourselves.

But if you have read the papers lately or listened to the TV news, the fact that the world is still considerably less than perfect may have crossed your mind.

We all want peace and a good world, even the you-know-who's.

The problem is not that we don't all want peace and a better world, the problem is that we just aren't bright enough or perhaps even good enough and certainly not secure enough to bring it about.

It isn't the secure and capable people in the world who cause the problems, it is the insecure and incapable people in the world who do.

Extraordinary, extremely capable, charming and beguiling big kids, virtually without exception, grow into extremely capable, charming and beguiling adults, and mighty secure ones who don't find it necessary to beat up on other people or groups of people to prove who they are.

They *know* who they are.

They are tomorrow.

Perhaps we grown-ups of the present day will have our best chance of survival and even prospering if we can do two things.

First, to hang on and do our damnedest not to destroy ourselves for another decade or two, by whatever means seem to work.

Second, to raise individually, but simultaneously, a new breed of kids, who are extraordinary, extremely capable, charming and beguiling, who are secure because they know who they are, Renaissance kids, kids for all seasons.

Then, in due course, we could turn the world over to them. We're going to in any event.

Every time that I'm fortunate enough to have one of those super days, the days when I get to watch the kids in The Evan Thomas Institute do their stuff, I look in their faces and I see tomorrow written there. I see a land even brighter than the spectrum lands of red, orange, yellow, green, blue, indigo and violet through which they have traveled so joyously and elegantly.

I see a land even brighter than the rainbow sweaters they wear.

I see on their faces a Land of Hope and Glory.

Enough of tomorrow, glorious as it promises to be.

Back to today and back to physical superbness for a final look.

What will your child be in terms of physical intelligence?

The most important thing of all is how he will *feel* about physical excellence.

If you simply gave him the opportunity to do so he may simply enjoy his physical prowess and that's a fine reward indeed.

If, on the other hand, you gave him that greatest treasure, which is a *love of movement*, he has a treasure indeed.

If, through all the days you have spent together, he has felt your own joy and pleasure at his physical accomplishments and if you have taught him to look forward with pleasure and eager anticipation to your sessions together then you will have taught him to love physical excellence itself.

We have learned, over all the long years, that the greatest single gift a teacher may give a child is a love of the subject.

We have learned that if a teacher truly loves a child and gives that child a love of the subject then nothing more is necessary.

A child who truly loves the subject will make it his business to learn all there is to know about the subject he loves.

On the other hand, if the world's leading authority on a subject does *not* succeed in giving a child a love of the subject all the teaching in the world will not suffice to make the child an expert.

If you have given your child superb opportunity in physical splendidness, which is to say a perfect environment in which to develop that ability *and*, in addition, the love of moving superbly, there will be no stopping him.

Does it mean, then, that we believe that every child should have as his goal winning a gold medal in the Olympics?

Not a bit.

We don't believe that *any* child should have such a goal.

We believe that every child should love physical grace, strength and agility.

If his love of movement happens to have as one of its *consequences* winning a gold medal in the Olympics, well that's nice. Not dreadfully important, but nice.

For such a child, does being physically superb mean sacrificing the right to be president of the United States, or a superb engineer, or the Pope, or a great musician, or a great artist?

Not on your life.

Quite to the contrary, it will enhance his or her chance of becoming any or all of these things.

Now being the senior author of this book and the chairman of the board of The Institutes, and having lived nose to nose with more than fifteen thousand kids and thirty thousand mothers and dads and all of that, I'd like to close with a personal word of advice to *you*, the parent who's had the patience and the determination to read this book.

What should you actually *do?* Here are the courses open to you.

If you've managed to finish this book but have done so with a growing sense of apprehension (of any kind), you should close the book and run, do not walk, to the nearest exit.

If you've read it with some degree of pleasure and if you feel comfortable working with your baby or little kid ten minutes a day doing physical things, then *do* it ten minutes a day and don't let *anybody*, especially us, talk you into eleven minutes. What that means is that you will do it *well* ten minutes a day and both you and your baby will have a fine time and he'll be a lot better off than if you didn't do it at all.

If you've read this book with a large degree of pleasure and you feel comfortable doing it an hour a day then *do* it an hour a day and don't let *anybody*, especially us, talk you into doing it sixty-one minutes a day. That means you'll both enjoy yourselves for the whole hour and he'll have a real chance for physical excellence.

If you've read this book with real joy and if you're hooked on physical excellence, then do *all* the things this book proposes. It means that you and your baby will have an absolutely elegant time and he will be physically superb with a whole and magnificent physical future for the taking.

If you've read this book with mounting excitement and new dreams for your child's future and you can't wait to get started because you think that your child is the greatest thing that ever happened, then *you* are a Professional Parent. There are, you may be surprised to know, a multitude of you. You may wish to be a fulltime Professional Parent and to teach your baby how to read, have encyclopedic knowledge, do math, and multiply his intelligence as well as making him physically superb and a superb gymnast.

If you can't wait to work with him all day every day, then *go to it* and don't let anybody, especially us, talk you into doing one minute *less* than full time.

If you'd like to know how to do those intellectual things as well as the physical things, drop me a line and I'll tell you how to go about them.

Why shouldn't I?

First, it's my job, and second, I'll feel a lot more hopeful about tomorrow with one more Renaissance kid growing up to be an adult for all seasons. And safer, too.

"We thank them all ...."

ACKNOWLEDGMENTS

Our journey across the rugged and (astonishingly) uncharted terrain that taught *us* to teach *parents* to teach their *babies* has been a long and sometimes exhausting one—yet full of the most exhilarating, exciting and rewarding days of our lives. We wouldn't have missed *any* of them for the world, but they could not have existed were it not for some of the most inspiring individual human beings (and groups of *very* human beings) the world has ever known.

We wish first to acknowledge the billions of children who have so faithfully traveled the ancient road that this book so carefully details.

The vast majority of those children have followed it happily, instinctually —and without the foggiest notion of the profound effect it would have on every phase of their lives.

For all of them, the journey began at birth—and for most of them it ended between six and seven years of age, causing them to be referred to as "normal" children. For reasons that have already become apparent, we refer to them as "average" children because average they certainly are—if by "average" we mean typical, common, ordinary kids.

For a minority of them (about one in twenty), the trip is not happy and instinctual but heroic and harrowing, and ranges from difficult to simply impossible. These are the brain-injured children who, given the opportunity, fight with endless determination and unique courage to conquer the seven stages of mobility and manual development that average children achieve so joyfully and blithely.

To the ten thousand or more children *we* have known intimately (for whom following this ancient road requires conduct far above and beyond the call of duty) and to the twenty thousand superb parents whose love for them and devotion to doing all in their power to see they finish that ancient path triumphantly (and for whom we have had the privilege of describing, illuminating and detailing every inch of that pathway), we pay our profound respect, and offer our unrestricted appreciation for all *we* have learned in the process of being their teachers and guides.

The process of achieving by heroic effort for those children what is accomplished so instinctually by average children is the responsibility of the black-jacketed group of physically superb and highly intelligent young members of our Institutes for the Achievement of Physical Excellence staff. Their years of day-and-night work with those parents and kids perfected the *how-to-do-it* techniques that had been pioneered by the senior staff members almost a half century earlier. They also, for the first time in history, *quantified* what must be done in each of the stages of mobility to stimulate the brain growth necessary to move to the next highest stage of brain development and mobility. They gave us the time required to write this book by doing *our* work, adding untold hours of time to their own already herculean schedule. They are Rosalind Klein Doman, Lidwina Van Dyk, Fred Hill, Matthew Newell, Susan Cameron, Yael Joseph, Kim Norris and Thomas Culhane.

The students of The School for Human Development have taught us every day since 1974, time and time again, what physical excellence really is. These young brain-injured men and women have set world records in every area of human development—running in national marathons and hiking the entire 2050-mile Appalachian Trail as a "through hike." We thank them for causing us to open our eyes even wider, learning more and more from them and developing an ever-increasing and deeper respect for each one of them.

These young adults and the little brain-injured children who began completely paralyzed have made it as clear as clear can be that virtually anyone can be physically excellent.

In addition to the billions of average children who have followed the ancient pathway from immobility at birth to walking, running and jumping in cross-pattern at six years of age, and the millions of brain-injured children who have done so with incredible difficulty, there is another group of children who have covered that ancient pathway superbly—*and in one-half the time of the average child.*

This group is very tiny indeed, both in size and in number. Each child who is a part of it began as an ordinary child both genetically and environmentally. They were completely "ungifted" in any sense at all except in the extraordinary gift of having parents who combined a special love for their babies with the very special knowledge this book contains. So, most obviously, we are indebted to *the superb children and parents and staff of The Institutes' Evan Thomas Institute.* Their names and eager faces shine throughout this book, in photographs and illustrations and text, and because of them there are dozens of impressive stories to relate about what these kids can do in their first year of life through to their superb gymnastic achievements at age eight.

Without the following extraordinary individuals, there would either have been no book—or it would have appeared in the final decade of this century. We thank them all:

Janet Joy Doman, Director of The Institutes for the Achievement of Human Potential, who believed so steadfastly that our knowledge would make a highly powerful difference in the lives of children and parents that she insisted Douglas and Bruce begin writing it while gently bullying her father,

Glenn Doman, into authoring the chapters that explain *why* it is of paramount importance to all children.

Ralph Pelligra, M.D., Chief Medical Officer of NASA–Ames Research Center, California; *Edward B. LeWinn, M.D.*, Director of The Institutes' Research Institute, who completed his life's work before he could see the final version of this book which was, like all our work, of such profound interest to him; and *Dr. Roselise Wilkinson*, Medical Director of The Institutes—together and separately they advised, exhorted and inspired us to write it for families everywhere.

Dick Norton, Director of The Edward LeWinn Institute, who encouraged us relentlessly and urges us daily to continue pursuing active as well as passive respiratory programs for *all* our kids.

Sherman Hines, "Photographer Laureate" of The Institutes, whose camera captures beauty in most anything and everything—and always in the children.

David Kerper, who took so many of the photos in the book, and who has always been so responsive to our needs, because he cares about the children as well.

Roz and *Chuck Mansfield*, who drop other projects at the ringing of their phone, to create covers, illustrations and charts for so many of our projects, and most especially for this book.

Mary Ellen Cooper and *Bob Derr*—they undertook the highly skilled, creative and always "dangerous" job of producing and publishing this book.

Lee Pattinson, Margaret Melcher and *Donald Barnhouse*, who at one stage of production or another did the *sometimes* "dangerous" job of helping with the editing.

Cathy Ruhling, Gloria Rittenhouse, Martha Clement, David and *Pam Coventry* and *Linda Pollack-Johnson*, who did the just plain hard work of typing, endless retyping and keeping the manuscript in order, while *Beth Granger* and *Marian Necker* took care of countless details.

Most important, we thank our own wonderful families, who not only *forgave* the trespasses this book caused, but encouraged us to make them, believing as they do that what this book can do for the children of the world is worth the price they so willingly paid.

Glenn Doman

Douglas Doman

Bruce Hagy

Water is yet another rich environment your baby can positively thrive in!

Rosalind and Marlowe Doman (24 months). Carol and Benjamin Newell (14 months). Photo by David Kerper.

APPENDIX I

ADDITIONAL INFORMATION FOR PARENTS ABOUT SWIMMING

Swimming is a basic, very important, human function that goes hand in hand with every step of child development discussed in this book. Providing your child is developing his swimming ability, his ability to do *every* program will be enhanced.

Your child will crawl better, sooner, if he is also swimming.

He will swim better, sooner, if he is crawling on the floor.

Swimming benefits mobility; mobility benefits swimming. This fact extends through each stage of brain development. Your child will be a more advanced gymnast if your child swims.

Swimming is important to mobility and brain development because it rapidly develops respiration.

"Water babies," those babies who learn to swim at birth, have more highly developed respiratory systems than nonswimming babies. This respiratory ability aids in stamina and endurance activities such as running and walking.

Enhanced respiration develops language quickly as well.

All of these benefits of swimming are in addition to the fact that "water babies" *thrive* in the water, and on swimming.

They adore it.

Every year, here at The Institutes, children come from around the world with the *most profound of brain injuries, because they nearly drowned.*

Seeing one of these children is more than enough evidence to convince anyone that all children should learn to be competent swimmers at the earliest possible age.

Why *shouldn't* newborns be splendid swimmers? They have been swimming for nine months. Indeed, the primary problem the baby meets at birth is taking his first breath of *air*, from which he must *now* get the oxygen his brain so desperately needs.

Several Institutes' babies have actually been born under water. The mothers found the warm water to be a much more comfortable way to give birth and the baby was born into the warm fluid environment in which he had already existed for nine months.

Although swimming from birth on is an extremely important adjunct to physical development (but is not vital to physical splendidness), and since swimming deserves a whole book of its own, the staff is presently engaged in writing a state-of-the-art book called *How To Teach Your Baby To Swim*.

For parents of infants who wish to teach them to swim at the same time they are using this book and teaching their babies to be physically superb, there are several reasonably adequate books already available that they should be able to obtain from local libraries or bookstores, or parents who wish to do so may write to The Institutes to obtain copies of two booklets on swimming that we use with our Institutes' families and children.

As we have said, but will say again in closing, swimming is a basic human function that goes hand in hand with *every* step of child brain development discussed in this book.

All of the babies on The Institutes' physical programs swim. Here, Paul McCarty, at six months, swims to his mother's waiting arms.

Providing your child is developing his swimming ability, every program contained herein will be greatly enhanced. Your child will crawl better, sooner, will have a more highly developed respiratory system to aid him in walking and running—and will develop his language skills even more quickly.

Best of all, water is yet another rich environment your baby can positively thrive in, and swimming can add another dimension to the great joy in learning to be physically superb your child is bound to feel!

ON THIS AND THE FOLLOWING PAGES OF APPENDIX I, YOU WILL FIND COMPLETE INSTRUCTIONS FOR:

THE CRAWLING TRACK

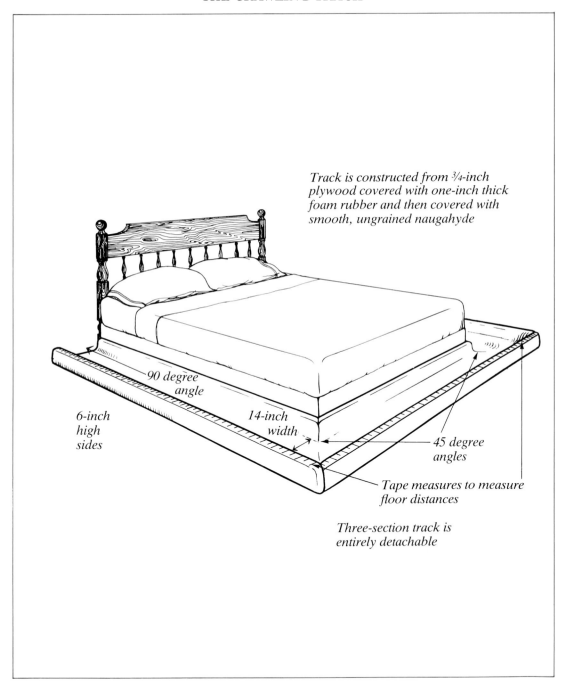

Track is constructed from ¾-inch plywood covered with one-inch thick foam rubber and then covered with smooth, ungrained naugahyde

90 degree angle

6-inch high sides

14-inch width

45 degree angles

Tape measures to measure floor distances

Three-section track is entirely detachable

EQUIPMENT YOU CAN BUILD AND MAKE FOR YOUR BABY

EACH OF THE THREE SECTIONS SHOWN IS COMPLETELY DETACHABLE:

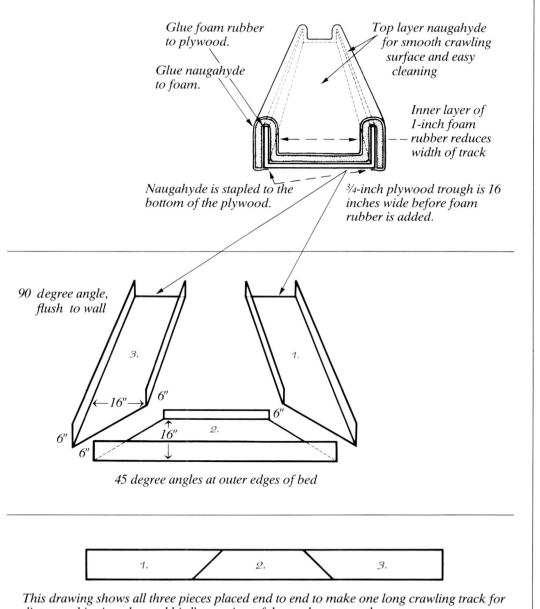

Glue foam rubber to plywood.

Glue naugahyde to foam.

Top layer naugahyde for smooth crawling surface and easy cleaning

Inner layer of 1-inch foam rubber reduces width of track

Naugahyde is stapled to the bottom of the plywood.

¾-inch plywood trough is 16 inches wide before foam rubber is added.

90 degree angle, flush to wall

3.

1.

←16"→   6"

6"

6"

6"

16"

2.

45 degree angles at outer edges of bed

1.   2.   3.

This drawing shows all three pieces placed end to end to make one long crawling track for distance; this gives the total bird's eye view of the tracks put together

HOW TO MAKE A NECK COLLAR FOR YOUR BABY

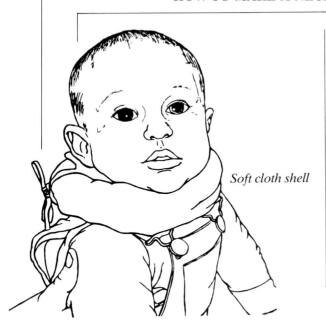

Soft cloth shell

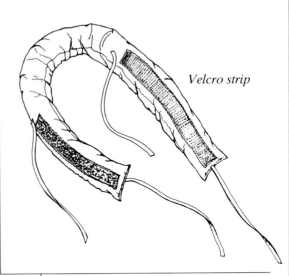

Velcro strip

In all the activities we recommend you do with your baby, your baby's safety is our prime concern. It's important to be particularly careful of babies' necks, so neck collars are definitely in order, especially for every single one of the passive balance activities at Stage III.

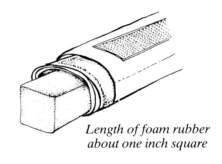

Length of foam rubber about one inch square

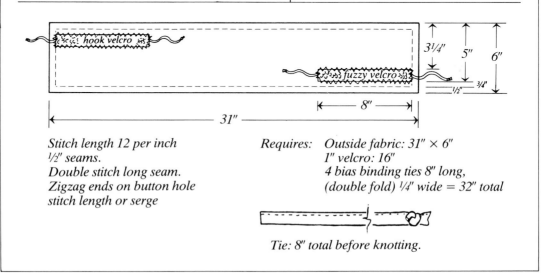

Stitch length 12 per inch
½" seams.
Double stitch long seam.
Zigzag ends on button hole stitch length or serge

Requires: *Outside fabric: 31" × 6"*
1" velcro: 16"
4 bias binding ties 8" long,
(double fold) ¼" wide = 32" total

Tie: 8" total before knotting.

THE DOWEL TRAVERSING A DOORWAY

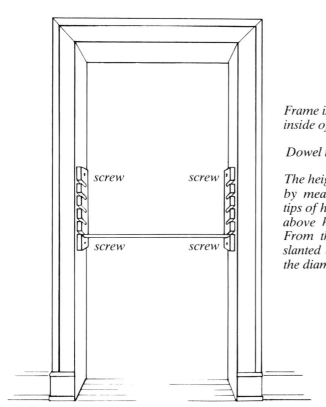

Frame is screwed into inside of door frame.

Dowel is seated in slots or notches.

The height of the first notch is determined by measuring from the child's toes to the tips of his fingers (with arms held straight above his head) and adding 2 inches. From this notch upward, the notches are slanted downward and are 1/8" larger than the diameter of the dowel.

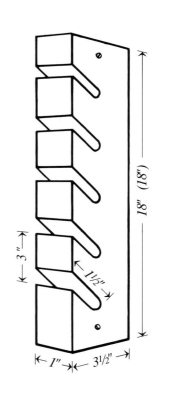

The bar across the doorway should serve you well. You will use it until your child becomes an independent brachiator. Even after he brachiates, he will enjoy playing on it.

A TRAPEZE

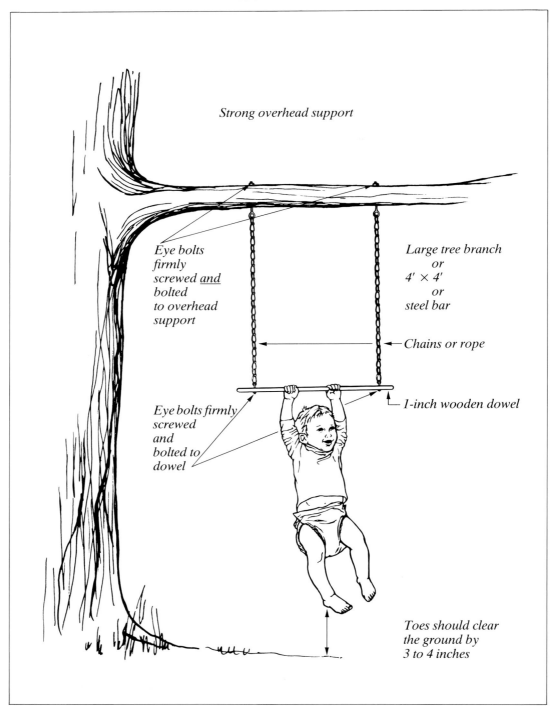

Strong overhead support

Eye bolts
firmly
screwed *and*
bolted
to overhead
support

Large tree branch
or
4' × 4'
or
steel bar

Chains or rope

Eye bolts firmly
screwed
and
bolted to
dowel

1-inch wooden dowel

Toes should clear
the ground by
3 to 4 inches

HOW TO MAKE A BALANCE BEAM

Step 1

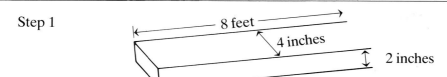

Start off with a piece of wood 2-inches by 4-inches by 8 feet. Lay this on the floor with the 4-inch side down.

Step 2

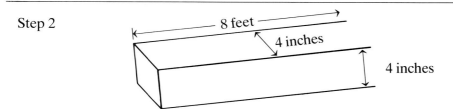

When your child walks across the full length of the beam consistently without falling off, begin to use a piece of wood 4-inches by 4-inches by 8-feet

Step 3

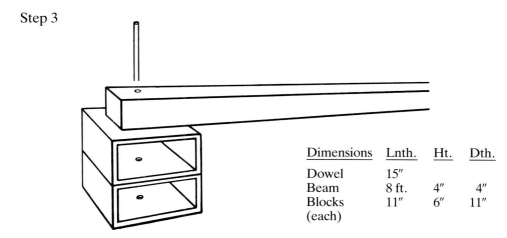

Dimensions	Lnth.	Ht.	Dth.
Dowel	15″		
Beam	8 ft.	4″	4″
Blocks (each)	11″	6″	11″

Once your child is able to walk this beam consistently without falling off, he graduates to an elevated beam. Raise the beam by constructing a box 6 inches high by 11 inches square, as shown in the diagram. As your child becomes increasingly more successful at walking the balance beam, increase the height by adding one more box. Do not use more than two boxes.

NOTE: Birch or maple beams are the most desirable woods for a balance beam. They may be covered with a smooth ungrained naugahyde to prevent your child from getting splinters and to provide him with a good surface for traction.

BUILDING A BRACHIATION LADDER

The brachiation ladder is constructed by first making its major parts, then assembling the whole for a sturdy ladder that can be used by either babies or adults.

Oak is recommended for the rungs, because of its strength. For the rest of the brachiation ladder, fir is recommended, because of the absence of knots.

The first parts to build are the two vertical post assemblies.

The third part is the ladder itself.

The final step is to assemble the parts.

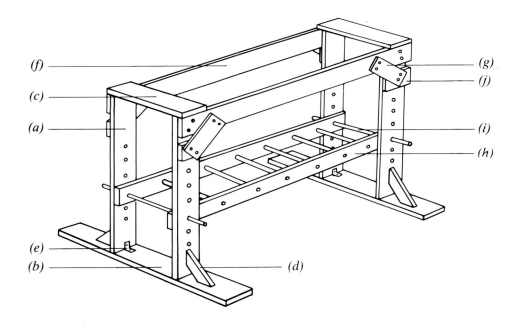

Vertical Post Assemblies (two required)

Materials: Four 2″ × 6″ × 7½′ sides (a)

Two 2″ × 6″ × 5′ bottom plate (b)

Two 2″ × 6″ × 21″ top plate (c)

Four 2″ × 4″ × 29″ braces (d)

Eight ¼″ × 3″ lag bolts

Eight 1″ wide 4″ leg, angle irons with clearance holes (e)

Thirty-two No. 12 ½″ screws for angle irons

Assembly instructions

Drill ¾″ clearance holes in sides (a), starting 28 inches from floor, and spaced every 2 inches up sides (29 holes).

Nail sides (a) to bottom plate (b), maintaining 18 inches between sides (inside dimension).

Nail top plate (c) to sides.

Set braces (d) in place (after cutting to proper angle) and nail to both side pieces and bottom plate.

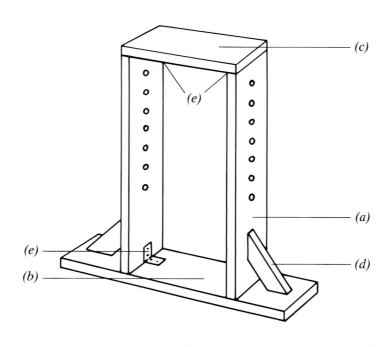

Drill ¼″ clearance holes through side pieces and bottom plate for screwing lag bolts through sides and bottom plate into braces. Countersink holes to make bolt heads flush with surfaces.

Insert lag bolts. Mount angle irons as shown, with two screws per leg.

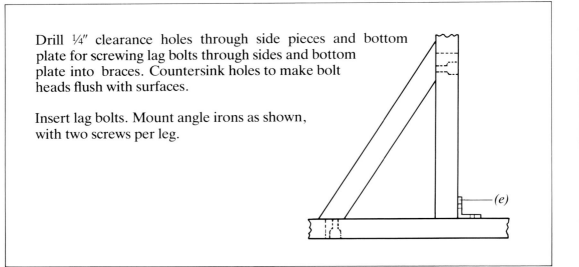

Horizontal Top Rail Assembly (two required)
Material: Two 2″ × 6″ × 10′ rails (f)
Four 2″ × 6″ × 22″ braces (g)
Eight ¼″ × 4″ round-head bolts
Eight 4″ nuts
Eight washers

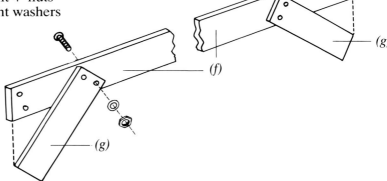

To assemble:

Drill ¼″ clearance holes at each end of the rail for bolts, as shown in the diagram.

Hole locations should be clear of angle irons mounted from top plate (c) to sides (a).

Loosely mount braces to rail with bolts and nuts with washers. Head of bolts should be towards inside of ladder; washers and nuts on outside. Tightening will take place at final assembly stage.

Ladder Assembly (one required)

Materials: Two 2″ × 4″ × 10′ sides (h)
Nineteen 1″ diameter hardwood rungs*, 18″ long (i)
Thirty-eight finishing nails

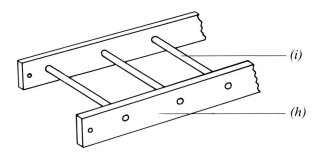

(i)

(h)

To assemble:

Drill ¾″ clearance holes, 3 inches from both ends of each side.

Drill 1″ clearance holes, same diameter as rungs, 6 inches from ends and then every 3 to 12 inches thereafter, according to child's size.

Put rungs in holes and secure with finishing nails and wood glue, if desired.

Final Assembly

Materials: Two vertical post assemblies
Two horizontal top rail assemblies
One ladder assembly
Eight ¼″ round-head bolts, 4″ long
Eight ¼″ round-head bolts, 6″ long
Sixteen ¼″ nuts
Sixteen washers
Two 2″ × 6″ × 6″ spacers (j)
Two ¾″ diameter dowels, 30″ long (k)

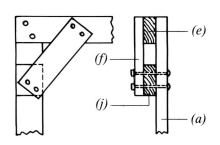

(e)

(f)

(j)

(a)

* NOTE: Diameter of rungs and spacing between them depend on child's size. Suggest:

6 – 18 months	18 – 36 months	36 months and older
½″ rungs 4″ spacing	¾″ rungs 6″ spacing	1″ rungs 12″ spacing

Construction:

Place vertical post assemblies 10 feet apart.

Place horizontal rails at top and mark hole locations for drilling corresponding holes in vertical sides.

Dril ¼″ clearance holes in side.

Mount rails to vertical post assemblies with 4″ bolts, nuts and washers.

Clamp 2″ × 6″ × 6″ spacers in position.

Drill ¼″ clearance holes through vertical sides, rail brace and spacer.

Bolt rail braces to sides with 6″ bolts, nuts and washers, with head of bolt towards inside of ladder.

Tighten *all* hardware securely.

In mounting of rails and braces to vertical sides, if any holes in the vertical sides are covered, drill through so the dowel can be put in place.

Place ladder at desired height and hold in place with dowels at both ends.

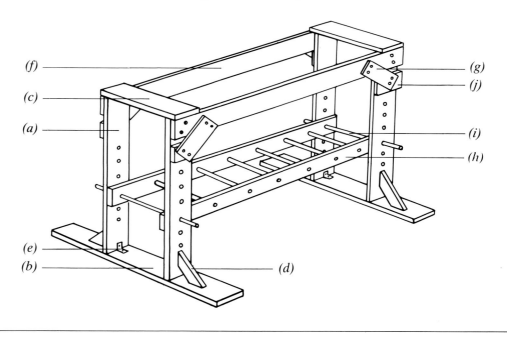

Dimensions and Adjustments for children of different ages:			
	6 – 18 Months	18 – 36 Months	36 Months and up
Dowel size	½ inch	¾ inch	1 inch
Ladder width	18 inches	18 inches	18 inches
Ladder length	10 feet	10 – 15 feet	15 – 18 feet
Space between rungs (center to center)	4 inches	6 inches	12 inches
Ladder height	Walking height of baby OR mother's height	Mother's height	Add an extra 4 inches to the measurement of the brachiating child (from hands to toes)

VALENTINE AUDITORIUM & BETTER BABY STORE →

DRIVE CAREFULLY
CHILDREN
EVERYWHERE
8
MILES PER HOUR

"You may wish to teach your baby
how to read, have encyclopedic
knowledge, how to do math and to
multiply his intelligence in other ways
in addition to teaching him to be
physically superb.

If you'd like to know how to do these
intellectualy things as well as the
physical, drop me a line and I'll tell
you how to go about them ...."
Glenn Doman

APPENDIX II

RELATED BOOKS, VIDEOS & KITS IN THE GENTLE REVOLUTION SERIES

HOW TO TEACH YOUR BABY TO READ
Glenn Doman and Janet Doman
Also available:
How To Teach Your Baby To Read™ Video
How To Teach Your Baby To Read™ Kits

HOW TO TEACH YOUR BABY MATH
Glenn Doman and Janet Doman
Also available:
How To Teach Your Baby Math™ Video
How To Teach Your Baby Math™ Kits

HOW TO GIVE YOUR BABY ENCYCLOPEDIC KNOWLEDGE
Glenn Doman, Janet Doman, and Susan Aisen
Also available:
How To Give Your Baby Encyclopedic Knowledge™ Video
How To Give Your Baby Encyclopedic Knowledge™ Kits

HOW TO MULTIPLY YOUR BABY'S INTELLIGENCE
Glenn Doman and Janet Doman
Also available:
How To Multiply Your Baby's Intelligence™ Kits

HOW TO TEACH YOUR BABY TO BE PHYSICALLY SUPERB
Glenn Doman, Douglas Doman, and Bruce Hagy
Also available:
How To Teach Your Baby To Be Physically Superb™ Video

WHAT TO DO ABOUT YOUR BRAIN-INJURED CHILD
Glenn Doman

HOW SMART IS YOUR BABY?
Glenn Doman and Janet Doman

CHILDREN'S BOOKS

ENOUGH, INIGO, ENOUGH (Ages 1 to 6)
written by Janet Doman, illustrated by Michael Armentrout

NOSE IS NOT TOES (Ages 1 to 3)
written by Glenn Doman, illustrated by Janet Doman

COURSES

Courses offered at The Institutes for the Achievement of Human Potential:

HOW TO MULTIPLY YOUR BABY'S INTELLIGENCE™ COURSE

WHAT TO DO ABOUT YOUR BRAIN-INJURED CHILD™ COURSE

For information regarding these courses, please contact:
The Institutes for the Achievement of Human Potential®
8801 Stenton Avenue
Wyndmoor, PA 19038 USA
www.iahp.org
PHONE: 215-233-2050
FAX: 215-233-9646
E-Mail: institutes@iahp.org

For information about these books and teaching materials, please contact:
The Gentle Revolution Press™
8801 Stenton Avenue
Wyndmoor, PA 19038 USA
www.gentlerevolution.com
PHONE: 215-233-2050, x2525
FAX: 215-233-3852
Toll-Free: 866-250-BABY
E-Mail: info@gentlerevolution.com

THE *HOW TO MULTIPLY YOUR BABY'S INTELLIGENCE™* COURSE

Eighty sessions of this world-famous Course for parents, presented over the past twenty years, have brought more than eight thousand parents to the Philadelphia campus of The Institutes for the Achievement of Human Potential to learn how to teach their children at home. Having read books by Glenn Doman or the Staff, or seeing them on TV, or reading about them in the newspapers (or, even more likely, having been recommended by a past participant), these parents come to learn the unique information available at The Institutes on how to teach babies and children under six to read, learn math, gain encyclopedic knowledge and physical excellence, and learn foreign languages and music. Flying in from all over the world, the French pediatrician-mom bumps elbows with a dad from NASA, while the waitress from West Virginia who mortgaged her house and sold her living room furniture to get to Philadelphia takes notes besides a burly bus driver from Manhattan's Queens who's tired of hearing about *other* people's kids succeeding!

For seven days straight, from early in the morning through early evening, the families and staff will participate in lectures, demonstration sessions, and question-and-answer periods. Foreign language translation will be supplied at some additional cost for those participants who require it, and the highly sophisticated learning environment of the Valentine Auditorium is more than equal to the task of supplying the finest translation.

All students attending every session of the Course receive certification at the Professional Parent Level of Human Development and are fully qualified to teach their *own* children all the exciting things they've learned throughout the week. They leave with a notebook full of extremely thorough outlines and materials on all points covered, their own copious notes, and enough confidence and happiness—and new friends with the same benefits in mind for their own children—to last a lifetime!

More information about the Course, including schedules, availability, and costs, may be obtained by calling the *How To Multiply Your Baby's Intelligence* Course Registrar at: (215) 233-2050, ex. 283, or by writing to the Registrar at: 8801 Stenton Avenue, Wyndmoor, PA 19038.

THE OFF-CAMPUS PROGRAM OF
THE EVAN THOMAS INSTITUTE

The Off-Campus Program of the Evan Thomas Institute was established in 1980 to aid parents who wish to build upon the knowledge gained during The Institutes *How To Multiply Your Baby's Intelligence* Course (presented for seven days each, a few times each year, drawing parents from around the world). The Program has served thousands of parents who have gained certification at the Professional Parent Level of Human Development through their Course attendance. As the program continually expands and develops, newly gained knowledge is passed on to the members in order to encourage, support, and enrich them as they teach their children.

The Program's specific goals are:
1. To answer parents' questions on a continuing basis.
2. To provide on-going instruction on teaching children at home.
3. To provide materials to assist in that teaching.
4. To provide graduate courses for senior families.

Members of the Off-Campus Program receive significant benefits throughout the year, including:

1. A specific reading program and physical program for each child.

2. The opportunity to telephone, fax, or write for advice on their child's programs, organization, or problems they may encounter.

3. Their choice of twelve sets of teaching materials, choosing from over 150 packets. These include booklets on swimming, music, nutrition, or gymnastics; lecture tapes from the Gentle Revolution Series; foreign language tapes and materials; and information and materials for creating Bit of Intelligence cards on a broad range of subjects such as mythology, Greek and Latin word roots, history, geography, and the sciences.

4. A year's subscription to *The IN-REPORT*, the quarterly journal of The Institutes for the Achievement of Human Potential.

5. The Institutes videos: *How To Teach Your Baby To Read, How To Teach Your Baby Math, How To Give Your Baby Encyclopedic Knowledge,* and *How To Teach Your Baby To Be Physically Superb.*

6. Preferential reservations for graduate courses and other future programs. In addition, local families often receive invitations to attend field days, concerts, and other special events at The Institutes.

Applications for the *How To Multiply Your Baby's Intelligence* Course and enrollment forms for the Off-Campus Program are available from the Registrar, 8801 Stenton Avenue, Wyndmoor, PA 19038. A parent's satisfactory completion of the Course is a prerequisite for enrollment in the Off-Campus Program.

is out and all that, is a new one. Now that the kids can read and thus increase their knowledge, perhaps beyond anybody's wildest dreams—what will they do with this old world and how tolerant will they be with us old parents, who by their standards may be nice—but perhaps not very bright?

It was said long ago, and said wisely, that the pen is mightier than the sword. We must, I think, accept the belief that knowledge leads to greater understanding and thus to greater good, while ignorance inevitably leads to evil.

Little children have begun to read and thus to increase their knowledge, and if this book leads to only one child reading sooner and better, then it will have been worth the effort. Who can say what another superior child will mean to the world? Who is to say what, in the end, will be the sum total of good for man as a result of this quiet ground swell which has already begun, this gentle revolution.

The Brain grows by use.

Heather McCarty, five years old.
Photo by Sherman Hines.

Glenn Dornan

ABOUT THE AUTHORS

Glenn Doman
Douglas Doman
Bruce Hagy

GLENN DOMAN is the Founder and present-day Chairman of Philadelphia's world-famous Institutes for the Achievement of Human Potential, to which parents from every continent have been finding their way for a third of a century. It is difficult to know if he and The Institutes are more famous for their originally controversial but now highly respected work with brain-injured children, or for their work in creating excellence in all children.

He has dealt intimately with more than 15,000 families over the last forty years and has strongly influenced the lives of millions of families through his best-selling books, which are presently published in seventeen languages.

How to Teach Your Baby to Read and What to Do About Your Brain-Injured Child are classic works in the fields of well children and of hurt children respectively.

Glenn Doman has lived with, studied or worked with children in more than 100 nations, ranging from the most civilized to the most primitive. He has conducted expeditions to study pre-Stone Age children in Brazil's Mato Grosso, Bushman children in the Kalahari Desert and Eskimo children in the Arctic, as well as journeys to see children in the world's most civilized major cities, from London to Tokyo and from Johannesburg to Moscow. He still does.

He has been decorated by many nations, often with their highest awards. It is ironic but not inconsistent with his character that his earliest decorations were for his role in warfare as a combat infantry officer while all of his decorations of the last thirty-five years have been for saving lives.

He was decorated by George VI with the British Military Cross for outstanding heroism in action during World War II. He received the Distinguished Service Cross from the United States for extraordinary heroism in combat, the Silver Star for gallantry against an armed enemy and the Bronze Star for heroism in close combat. He was decorated by the Grand Duchess Charlotte for services to the Duchy of Luxembourg during the Battle of the Bulge.

In contrast to those decorations for hand-to-hand combat, he was knighted by the Brazilian government in 1966 for his services to the children of the world, and received Brazil's highest decoration, the Knight Order of the Southern Cross. His services to children have also won him decorations from Britain, Ireland, Argentina, Peru and Japan. Other honors include the Raymond A. Dart Award of the United Steelworkers of America in 1971.

He continues to maintain a staggering schedule of search for new answers, teaching and writing.

DOUGLAS MAC DOMAN is the Vice-Director of The Institutes for the Achievement of Human Potential. He is the son of Katie Massingham Doman and Glenn Doman. He was raised on the campus of The Institutes and grew up with the well and hurt children of The Institutes.

As a child there, he spent his days climbing trees, hiking and running. He entered school at the age of six, physically at the same level as the rest of his class. Through his years of school, he was forced to take physical education classes, which involved honing the "competitive spirit." Later, he was required to play football. He grew to deplore physical activity of any sort. In 1971 he graduated from Chestnut Hill Academy in Chestnut Hill, Pennsylvania, overweight and soft.

He accompanied Institutes' research teams on three expeditions to study primitive peoples while he was still in his early teens. In 1965 he lived with and studied Navajo Indians in Arizona; in 1967 he went to the Arctic to study the Eskimos; and in 1969, he went to the Kalahari Desert, in Botswana, to live with and study the Bushmen.

As part of his undergraduate study at Bard College, Douglas joined the Experiment in International Living. For seven months he studied child development among the Guambiano Indians of Colombia, South America. Living in the mountains of the Sierra Nevada (at an elevation of eight thousand feet), Douglas spent his days working in the potato fields with the Indians and hiking many miles a day. He again experienced the pure joy of feeling physically excellent that he had lost in his youth.

In 1975, at the invitation of the Sony Corporation, he went to Japan to teach English to tiny Japanese children. After living in Japan, Douglas went to Melbourne, Australia, to work with Tim and Claire Timmermans, world authorities in the techniques of teaching parents to teach their babies to swim.

Douglas's early years working at The Institutes were spent creating The School for Human Development. This is The Institutes' school for brain-injured young adults. He worked closely with Bruce Hagy to create the world's first Human Development Course, a circuit utilizing physical activities that promote brain organization and development.

In 1977, under the direction of Glenn Doman, Douglas and Bruce continued this work specifically to accelerate the physical development of well babies and brain-injured children.

During the years 1977 to 1980, Douglas and Bruce and their staff of ten developmentalists made repeated breakthroughs in the field of children's physical development for both well babies and brain-injured children. The

Douglas with son, Marlowe.

Douglas Doman

Photos by Sherman Hines

most important of these breakthroughs include the quantification of children's physical development and working in collaboration with the National Aeronautics and Space Administration, Ames Research Center, on the design and creation of the Vehicle for Initial Crawling.

Douglas holds the Human Development Certificate at both the Developmentalist and Teaching levels. In 1978, he became the International Director responsible for Italy and continues to be responsible for The Institutes' operations and families in Italy. As a result, he is a much-requested lecturer in Italy and other countries.

The honors bestowed on him for his work with the children of the world include the Brazilian Gold Medal of Honor (1974), the British Star of Hope (1976), and the Leonardo da Vinci Medal of The Italian Institute (1979).

He is married to Rosalind Klein Doman, and both she and their first two children, Marlowe and Spencer, are the subject of many of the photographs and discussions throughout this book. They have two younger children, Morgan and Noah Glenn Doman.

BRUCE HAGY is the former Director of The Institute for the Achievement of Physical Excellence of The Institutes for the Achievement of Human Potential.

He spent his childhood years being involved in every kind of outdoor sport he could find. This led him to major in health and physical education at West Chester University in Pennsylvania, where he graduated in 1972. Bruce spent two years in the Peace Corps as a college and high school athletic director in the Philippines. During this period, he also served as regional consultant for athletics for the Bical Region.

He joined The Institutes staff in 1974. As Vice-Director of The School for Human Development, he assisted Douglas Doman in the creation of the world's first Human Development Course for brain-injured young adults.

In 1977, Bruce began to work in the Children's Center of The Institutes. Here, again, he assisted Douglas Doman in pioneering new methods of fixing the physical problems of brain-injured children. At the same time, Bruce introduced and developed the gymnastics program for well children of The Evan Thomas Institute.

As Director of The Institutes for the Achievement of Physical Excellence, Bruce was responsible for the physical development of over five hundred severely brain-injured children from around the world. Bruce holds certification as Human Developmentalist at the Developmentalist and Teaching levels. He has lectured on the subject of child brain development internationally.

His services to the children of the world have earned him awards and decorations of the Brazilian Gold Medal, British Star of Hope, the Raymundo Veras Award of Humanity and Science, and the Award of the International Forum for Neurological Organization, the Statuette with Pedestal.

Bruce is married to Chris Brennan Hagy and is the father of three children, Tegan, Shea, and Brennan, who are shown in photographs and drawings and mentioned throughout this book.

Bruce, with son Shea.

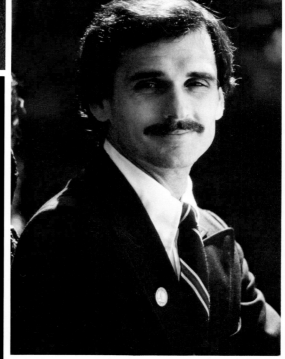

Bruce Hagy

Photos by Sherman Hines.

"... I'll feel a lot more hopeful about tomorrow with one more Renaissance kid growing up to be an *adult* for all seasons. And safer, too."
Glenn Doman

Cara Caputo, seven years old.
Photo by Sherman Hines.

BRAIN STAGE		TIME FRAME	VISUAL COMPETENCE	AUDITORY COMPETENCE	TACTILE COMPETENCE
VII	SOPHIS-TICATED CORTEX	Superior 36 Mon. Average 72 Mon. Slow 144 Mon.	**Reading with total understanding** *Sophisticated human understanding*	**Understanding of complete vocabulary and proper sentences** *Sophisticated human understanding*	**Tactile identifi-cation of objects** *Sophisticated human understanding*
VI	PRI-MITIVE CORTEX	Superior 18 Mon. Average 36 Mon. Slow 72 Mon.	**Identification of visual symbols and letters within experience** *Primitive human understanding*	**Understanding of 2000 words and simple sentences** *Primitive human understanding*	**Ability to determine charact-eristics of objects by tactile means** *Primitive human understanding*
V	EARLY CORTEX	Superior 9 Mon. Average 18 Mon. Slow 36 Mon.	**Differentiation of similar but unlike simple visual symbols** *Early human understanding*	**Understanding of 10 to 25 words and two word couplets** *Early human understanding*	**Tactile differen-tiation of similar but unlike objects** *Early human understanding*
IV	INITIAL CORTEX	Superior 6 Mon. Average 12 Mon. Slow 24 Mon.	**Convergence of vision resulting in simple depth perception** *Initial human understanding*	**Understanding of two words of speech** *Initial human understanding*	**Tactile under-standing of the third dimension in objects which appear to be flat** *Initial human understanding*
III	MID-BRAIN	Superior 3.5 Mon. Average 7 Mon. Slow 14 Mon.	**Appreciation of detail within a configuration** *Meaningful appreciation*	**Appreciation of meaningful sounds** *Meaningful appreciation*	**Appreciation of gnostic sensation** *Meaningful appreciation*
II	PONS	Superior 1 Mon. Average 2.5 Mon. Slow 5 Mon.	**Outline perception** *Vital perception*	**Vital response to threatening sounds** *Vital perception*	**Perception of vital sensation** *Vital perception*
I	MEDULLA and CORD	Superior Birth to .5 Average Birth to 1.0 Slow Birth to 2.0	**Light reflex** *Reflex reception*	**Startle reflex** *Reflex reception*	**Babinski reflex** *Reflex reception*